Law, Governance and Technology Series

Volume 61

The *Law, Governance and Technology Series* is intended to attract manuscripts arising from an interdisciplinary approach in law, artificial intelligence and information technologies. The idea is to bridge the gap between research in IT law and IT-applications for lawyers developing a unifying techno-legal perspective. The series will welcome proposals that have a fairly specific focus on problems or projects that will lead to innovative research charting the course for new interdisciplinary developments in law, legal theory, and law and society research as well as in computer technologies, artificial intelligence and cognitive sciences. In broad strokes, manuscripts for this series may be mainly located in the fields of the Internet law (data protection, intellectual property, Internet rights, etc.), Computational models of the legal contents and legal reasoning, Legal Information Retrieval, Electronic Data Discovery, Collaborative Tools (e.g. Online Dispute Resolution platforms), Metadata and XML Technologies (for Semantic Web Services), Technologies in Courtrooms and Judicial Offices (E-Court), Technologies for Governments and Administrations (E-Government), Legal Multimedia, and Legal Electronic Institutions (Multi-Agent Systems and Artificial Societies).

Gergely Gosztonyi

Censorship from Plato to Social Media

The Complexity of Social Media's Content Regulation and Moderation Practices

Springer

Gergely Gosztonyi
Faculty of Law
Eötvös Loránd University (ELTE)
Budapest, Hungary

ISSN 2352-1902 ISSN 2352-1910 (electronic)
Law, Governance and Technology Series
ISBN 978-3-031-46528-4 ISBN 978-3-031-46529-1 (eBook)
https://doi.org/10.1007/978-3-031-46529-1

This Springer imprint is published by the registered company Springer Nature Switzerland AG
The registered company address is: Gewerbestrasse 11, 6330 Cham, Switzerland

I dedicate this book

to ██████████,
to ██████████,

and to all the victims of censorship.

Acknowledgements

I am most grateful to some people without whom this book would have been much less fun to write. János Tamás Papp for his valuable editing, scientific inputs, and constructive feedback; Series Editors Pompeu Casanovas and Giovanni Sartor for accepting my book in the series; Publishing Editor Manuela Schwietzer for the excellent handling of the manuscript as well as to all anonymous peer reviewers for their helpful suggestions and insightful comments. And, of course, Professor Mihály T. Révész for being my mentor from the very beginning.

This book was supported by the János Bolyai Research Scholarship of the Hungarian Academy of Sciences and the ÚNKP-23-5 New National Excellence Program of the Ministry for Culture and Innovation from the source of the National Research, Development and Innovation Fund.

Contents

List of Abbreviations

ACHPR	African Commission on Human and Peoples' Rights
AI	Artificial Intelligence
AVMS	Audiovisual Media Services Directive
CGM	Consumer-Generated Media
CJEU	Court of Justice of the European Union
CMC	Computer-Mediated Communication
DMA	Digital Markets Act
DPI	Deep Packet Inspection
DSA	Digital Services Act
DST	Digital Services Tax
ECHR	European Convention on Human Rights
ECtHR	European Court of Human Rights
EU	European Union
FCC	Federal Communications Commission
FTC	Federal Trade Commission
GDPR	General Data Protection Regulation
ISP	Internet Service Provider
NAM	Notice and Action Mechanism
NN	Notice-and-Notice
NSD	Notice and Staydown
NTDS	Notice-and-Takedown System
OAS	Organization of American States
OSCE	Organization for Security and Co-operation in Europe
RSF	Reporters Sans Frontières (Reporters Without Borders)
RTBF	Right to be Forgotten
UGC	User-Generated Content
UN	United Nations
UNESCO	United Nations Educational, Scientific and Cultural Organization

UNHRC	United Nations Human Rights Council
VPN	Virtual Private Network
VR	Virtual Reality

Chapter 1
Introduction

An online newspaper article on the amendment of the Audiovisual Media Services Directive (AVMS) stated that "15 MEPs voted against ten on Wednesday morning to adopt a proposal that could in future oblige big online content sharing providers like YouTube and Facebook to filter the content we post on them automatically. The proposal protects copyright but risks censoring the internet if it's misapplied."[1] The backs of buffalo crawling out of the water have been censored on Iranian public television. In China, the protagonist in Disney's Winnie-the-Pooh movie has become a symbol of criticism of those in power. In Romania, police the confiscated the registration plate and driver's licence of a man who had bought a personalised number plate in Sweden that obscenely mocked the current ruling party in Bucharest. In Egypt, in September 2018, "Egyptian President Abdel-Fattah al-Sisi signed a law giving the authorities the right to block a user's account on social networking sites and to fine journalists for spreading content that is considered fake news"[2] It has also been reported in Hungary that "Megafon is fed up with Facebook censoring Trump's existence retrospectively",[3] and, in the context of the vaccination programme for the pandemic,[4] that "information to the public is incomplete, often wrong or misleading: there is total censorship".[5] However, the same was also raised after the withdrawal of US soldiers from Afghanistan, that "the Taliban say that they want to ensure internet access in Afghanistan, but they could face substantial technical and financial challenges to keep it running. Afghans say they fear more surveillance and censorship."[6] In mid-September 2022, the Iranian Guidance Patrol, the religious morality police of the government, arrested Mahsa Amini for

[1] Kugyela (2018).

[2] 24.hu (2019).

[3] 888.hu (2021).

[4] Cendic and Gosztonyi (2020), pp. 14–29.

[5] Király (2021).

[6] Tangen (2021).

G. Gosztonyi, *Censorship from Plato to Social Media*, Law, Governance and Technology Series 61, https://doi.org/10.1007/978-3-031-46529-1_1

improperly wearing the hijab, who fell into a coma at the police station and died. Later protests started and, among others, Mahsa Amini's home province of Kurdistan has been completely cut off from international internet access.

These are just brief examples from the late 2010s and early 2020s, but the list could be extended. Anyone can read about the methods of the Russian authorities, the practices of North Korea or the problems of Iran, South America or South Africa.[7] However, the above illustrate that all these issues, which branch off in many directions, are linked by one word: censorship. There are few more accessible accusations than that of censorship. It is also used in meaningful debates, often without merit or meaning. "Following Frederick Schauer, we can conclude that an overly broad use of the term censorship can render the concept's scope and thus devalue it."[8] Even so, a quick search on the Internet reveals how much the word censorship and the verb censor are present in our lives. The practice shows what Derek Jones argues in his almost 3000-page World Encyclopaedia of Censorship: it is not just prior approval of content that constitutes censorship, and the concept needs to be interpreted as broadly as possible to protect freedom of expression fully.[9]

The question is, therefore, where freedom of expression bows and to what wills and demands. In 2017, we saw the news that the Russian Ministry of Justice had put a ban on pictures of the head of the State's face with make-up, i.e. cartoons of Vladimir Putin with a kissy mouth, and that violators of this ban could even be brought to court on charges of terrorism (*sic!*). Moreover, according to the 2023 World Press Freedom Index,[10] there are a growing number of countries in the world where freedom of expression is being exercised under increasingly strict legal frameworks, or as the saying goes, more and more countries are darkening the world map.[11]

The Mapping Media Freedom project,[12] co-funded by the European Commission (EC), allows anyone to add to a virtual map newspaper articles and content that may be related to censorship anonymously. Between 2014 and 2023, 7507 submissions were made to the site.[13] Scanning through the submitted content, one gets the same feeling as in the cases above. As if there is no uniform treatment in the world of where the boundaries of what can be expressed lie. And nothing is surprising in this: the social, economic, political set-up and history of different continents and countries influences this as much as the socialisation, intrinsic values and current interpretative frameworks of individual people. As Jonathon Green put it in his massive,

[7] Mchangama and Alkiviadou (2021).

[8] Koltay (2014), p. 78.

[9] Jones (2015), p. xi.

[10] https://rsf.org/en/ranking.

[11] The reason for this is that the World Press Freedom Index uses colours ranging from light yellow to blood red and black to indicate countries' position in the survey: the darker the colour, the lower the country's ranking for that year.

[12] https://mappingmediafreedom.org/.

[13] There is a similar project called magma: https://magma.lavafeld.org/guide/.

almost 800-page encyclopaedia of censorship, co-authored with Nicolas J. Karolides: "Censorship is international, continuous and pervasive, but it is not a seamless monolith. Concerns that seem paramount to one nation are meaningless to another."[14]

Moreover, there is no uniform framework for censorship. Is it censorship to kill journalists? On the one hand, of course not, it is a much more severe crime, but on the other hand, Julian Petley argues that it is the most direct and simplest form of censorship.[15] It is in this context, that the European Centre for Press and Media Freedom's 2017 Mapping Media Freedom report[16] shows that six journalists were murdered in connection with their work. UNESCO's World Trends in Freedom of Expression and Media Development 2020/2021 report[17] further chiselled the picture with the data that, between 2016 and the end of 2020, 400 journalists were killed on the job.[18] The same question can be asked in a milder form: does physical abuse count as censorship? Is it censorship? What about court proceedings? The multitude of criminal and civil lawsuits? Withholding information of public interest? Are politicians being misinformed or not answering journalists' questions? Where do we draw the line between content regulation and censorship?

If we consider—and with good reason—all of the above as an attack on freedom of expression the European Centre for Freedom of the Press and Media has highlighted five countries in the world that deserve particular attention, with more than 60 incidents within their borders in 2017.[19] If you were to ask 100 people to guess these countries, they would most likely be China, Russia, Turkey, North Korea, Cuba, Egypt, Iran, Saudi Arabia, Venezuela and Argentina. Of course, the list could, unfortunately, go on and on. However, this is not the surprise of the entire list. The list looks like this: Russia, Turkey, Belarus, Ukraine and Spain. One country that is a member of the European Union (EU), one that borders EU, and three countries that are now referred to as illiberal.[20] Of course, it is almost impossible to draw up a complete list: we can be convinced that not all cases are known to the Western public when it comes to China, and the same can be said of the African and Gulf states. Moreover, if we examine trends, not just data, we can focus on several problematic issues, because he numbers are increasing year on year. Whichever of the above types of attack or influence against journalists we look at, we see a

[14]Green and Karolides (2005), p. xx.

[15]Petley (2009), pp. 17–32.

[16]EFJ – IPI – ECPMF (2018).

[17]UNESCO (2021), p. 17.

[18]It would be natural to see a decrease compared to recent years if the two figures were compared, but while Mapping Media Freedom only counted professional journalists, UNESCO also counted semi-professional and citizen journalists (such as bloggers), in line with the changing media environment.

[19]EFJ – IPI – ECPMF (2018), p. 17.

[20]Mudde (2018).

worrying rise in each, and this unease permeates the web of the world. It permeates political action and the news that reaches us; it permeates our lives.

And more and more people are feeling helpless and powerless in the face of this. That the world is run by algorithms, invisible Big Brothers, out-of-touch politicians, bank bosses and billionaire business people. And they are now even honest with the people.[21] And the helplessness, fear, and panic breed the wrong responses: closure in an open world, simplistic 'one-bit' responses, unnecessary and often forced domestic and international conflicts, blaming selected individuals or groups (usually minorities), increasing corruption, economic influence, self-censorship, loss of social trust in officialdom, the opening of the economic scissors, and many other factors. „Today, we face a democratic paradox. In many ways, we live in a golden age of freedom of expression, because never before has it been so easy to get an idea out into the open and reach as many people as possible. At the same time, it has never been so easy to restrict, filter and block speech, and the prevention of speech has never been concentrated in the hands of so few private actors."[22] Moreover, lack of information can kill honest social discourse. An information-deficient society is no longer a true democracy. and the same is valid on the other hand when communities are flooded with fake information, the *brave new world* of fake news. We are seeing a new level of info-communication warfare today.

In 2011, the international journalists' organisation Reporters Without Borders (RSF) launched an ironic campaign against censorship, entitled "censorship tells the wrong story."[23] The (original) pictures showed the world's—at the time—leading politicians in a completely innocuous, harmless and problem-free environment. But the modified pictures showed something else: among others, David Cameron 'showed his middle finger', Vladimir Putin 'touched himself' or Barack Obama 'sexualised' Hillary Clinton. The cheeky 'trick' was the use of censorship, And the photographs illustrate better than a thousand words why undue restrictions on speech are problematic.

This book aims to explain this broad and often unpredictable range of problems. It traces the history of censorship, analyses the types and forms of censorship and, of course, attempts to describe the state of censorship today, revealing the connections that may be overlooked in the chaos of the news race. The subject matter is mainly human rights-based, so issues of copyright and related rights, competition law, data protection and advertising law are deliberately not discussed.

Examining this historical experience may help us to understand how we have moved from the intense censorship of the seventeenth and eighteenth centuries to the twenty-first century, when political censorship as a concept is becoming almost meaningless and new types of (private) control mechanisms are emerging. How and why states have 'privatised' the issue of content control, and why we see a completely different set of points on the internet today. How this essentially free

---

[21] Gosztonyi (2023).

[22] Badouard (2020), pp. 11–12.

[23] https://designyoutrust.com/2011/07/censorship-tells-the-wrong-story/.

form of communication came—almost by definition—under legal regulation and where freedom was lost. Bruce Sterling put it in 1992: "Why do people want to be on the Internet?" One of the main reasons is simple freedom. The Internet is a rare example of a true, modern, functional anarchy. There is no 'Internet Inc.' There are no official censors, no bosses, no board of directors, no stockholders."[24] Today that is no longer true. Censorship, or, as many now prefer to call it, content regulation, is part of our everyday lives in one form or another. Censorship is a living historical present. To borrow Jonathon Green's words again, censorship "is an enormous, wide-ranging topic, far more complex than simply cutting the 'naughty bits' out of the movies, shutting down adult bookshops, or muzzling civil service whistle-blowers. It affects the quality of every life—aesthetically, emotionally, socially, and politically."[25]

References

24.hu (2019) Nagyon durva médiatörvényt vezet be Egyiptom (Egypt introduces a very harsh media law). 24.hu, 27 Sep. https://1.hu/kulfold/2018/09/02/egyiptom_net_cenzura/

888.hu (2021) A Megafon megelégelte, hogy a Facebook Trump létezését már visszamenőleg is cenzúrázza (Megafon is fed up that Facebook is already retroactively censoring Trump's existence). 888.hu, 1 Apr. https://2.hu/censored/a-megafon-meglegelte-hogy-a-facebook-trump-letezeset-mar-visszamenoleg-is-cenzurazza-4307090/

Badouard R (2020) Les nouvelles lois du web. Modération et censure (The new laws of the web. Moderation and censorship). Le Seuil, Paris

Cendic K, Gosztonyi G (2020) Freedom of expression in times of COVID-19: chilling effect in Hungary and Serbia. J Liberty Int Aff 6(3)

European Federation of Journalists (EFJ) – International Press Institute (IPI) – European Centre for Press and Media Freedom (ECPMF) (2018) Mapping Media Freedom annual report 2017. https://mappingmediafreedom.org/index.php/2018/03/16/mapping-media-freedom-annual-report-2017/

Gosztonyi G (2023) Being honest with people? The state of freedom of expression and censorship in Central and Eastern Europe during the COVID-19 pandemic. In: Gosztonyi G, Lazar E (eds) Media regulation during the covid-19 pandemic: a study from Central and Eastern Europe. Ethics International Press, Cambridge

Green J, Karolides NJ (2005) Encyclopedia on censorship. Facts on File, Inc, New York

Jones D (ed) (2015) Censorship. A world encyclopedia. Routledge, London

Király A (2021) A lakosság tájékoztatása hiányos, gyakran téves, vagy félrevezető, totális cenzúra van. Information to the public is incomplete, often wrong or misleading, there is total censorship. 444.hu, 16 March. https://444.hu/2021/03/16/a-lakossag-tajekoztatasa-hianyos-gyakran-teves-vagy-felrevezeto-totalis-cenzura-van

Koltay A (2014) A médiatartalmak közzététel előtti korlátozásának lehetőségei: engedélyezés, regisztráció, cenzúra, végzések (Pre-publication restrictions on media content: licensing, registration, censorship, injunctions). Iustum Aequum Salutare 10(1)

[24] Sterling (1993).

[25] Green and Karolides (2005), p. xxi.

Kugyela T (2018) Most gyilkolja meg az EU az internetet? (Is the EU now killing the internet?) index.hu, 20 June. https://index.hu/kulfold/eurologus/2018/06/20/eu_internet_jogdij_szabalyozas/
Mchangama J, Alkiviadou N (2021) Protecting the freedom of expression in an Era of "Platformization:" paving a road to censorship? In: Bayer J, Holznagel B, Korpisaari P, Woods L (eds) Perspectives on Platform Regulation. Concepts and Models of Social Media Governance Across the Globe. Nomos Verlagsgesellschaft mbH & Co, KG, Baden-Baden
Mudde C (2018) When illiberal forces win, the answer is more – not less – democracy. The Guardian, 6 June. https://www.theguardian.com/commentisfree/2018/jun/06/when-illiberal-forces-win-the-answer-is-more-not-less-democracy
Petley J (2009) Censorship. A beginner's guide. Oneworld Publications, Oxford
Sterling B (1993) A short history of the internet. Magaz Fant Sci Fict 84(2). https://www.internetsociety.org/internet/history-internet/short-history-of-the-internet/
Tangen Jr O (2021) Will the Taliban restrict internet access in Afghanistan? DW, 30 Aug. https://www.dw.com/en/will-the-taliban-restrict-internet-access-in-afghanistan/a-59029364
UNESCO (2021) World Trends in Freedom of Expression and Media Development. Global Report 2021/2022. UNESCO, Paris

Chapter 2
Content Management or Censorship?

The history of censorship may be as old as the history of communication. Although we do not have sources on this issue from prehistoric times, we can be sure that the ruling elites attempted to control expressing an opinion—even in the early stages of the development of society and the state—was by. Jonathon Green summarised this as follows: "Communication has always been subjected to control. The two phenomena are linked in mutual adversity and as communication has proliferated, so has censorship."[1]

The word censorship itself is derived from the Latin censura, meaning investigation. The Hungarian Etymological Dictionary says: "(This) in ancient Rome meant the office or dignity of the censor, the chief officer who carried out the quinquennial tax assessment, the census; the linguistic source of this is the verb censere ('to assess, estimate')."[2] The two censors, after compiling the tax lists, were also given the task of compiling the lists for the election of the Senate; for example, the quasi right to determine who was worthy of high office in the Empire. From there, it was only a small leap for the censors to become the chief guardians of the private and public life of Roman citizens; that is, they took upon themselves the responsibility of upholding the old Roman morals and values *(mos maiorum)*.[3] They also had special powers for this purpose, which, according to the sources, existed and functioned alongside the traditional judicial system, almost complementing it. It was the adoption of these measures, their supervision of morals and their action against those who violated them, that led to the modern interpretation of the word censorship and to its use, as it is still part of our language today.

[1] Green and Karolides (2005), p. xxviii.

[2] Tótfalusi (2001).

[3] Hegyi (2018), p. 125.

G. Gosztonyi, *Censorship from Plato to Social Media*, Law, Governance and Technology Series 61, https://doi.org/10.1007/978-3-031-46529-1_2

2.1 Typification of Censorship

It is generally accepted that freedom of expression is a fundamental human right. It is the cornerstone of democracy,[4] key to the protection of all human rights, and one of the basic conditions for its development and, as the European Court of Human Rights (ECtHR) has stated in several judgments, for the development of all human beings. [5] However, it should be noted that the centuries-long struggle for the fullest possible freedom of expression[6] has been in vain if censorship prevents the publication of certain opinions. There are countless definitions of what exactly censorship is, but there is no single, widely accepted definition. Sophia Rosenfeld states that "Censorship is not an easy topic to discuss at present. (. . .) There seems no longer to be any consensus about what censorship is."[7] In addition, censorship is difficult to study empirically because it often wants to go unnoticed.[8] However, typifying the possible means that fall under the concept of censorship may bring us closer to understanding the concept. The most important of the possible groupings are shown in the table below.

1. Categorisation by censorship **performer**	(a) Political, i.e. censorship by the state		
	(b) Economic or private censorship, i.e. censorship driven (primarily) by private economic interests		
	(c) Self-censorship, i.e. (mostly) by users		
2. Censorship by **institutional system**	(a) (Any kind of) State Censorship Authority		
	(b) With the participation of other state authorities		
	(c) Economic operator 'privatised' by the state		
3. Grouping by the **'width'** of censorship	(a) Censorship in the narrow sense of the term only considers arbitrary and prior authorisation procedures as censorship		
	(b) Censorship in the broad sense of the term has a broader scope of use		

(continued)

[4] Mendel (2010).

[5] *Engel and Others v The Netherlands* App nos 5100/71, 5101/71, 5102/71, 5354/72, 5370/72 (ECtHR, 8 June 1976) [41.]-[42.], [100.]; *Handyside v The United Kingdom* App no 5393/72 (ECtHR, 7 December 1976), [49.]; *Association Ekin v France* App no 39288/98 (ECtHR, 17 July 2001), [56.]; *Perna v Italy* App no 48898/99 (ECtHR, 6 May 2003), [39.].

[6] For a summary in the literature cf. Barendt (2007); Smith (2019); Garton Ash (2016); Sorabji (2021). In the arts cf. Bradbury (1991).

[7] Rosenfeld (2001), p. 117.

[8] Roberts (2018), p. 7.

4. Grouping by censorship **period**	(a) Prior censorship, where the publication is linked to the authorisation		
	(b) Ex-post censorship, when a decision is taken on the dissemination of what has been published/released	(i) Before the distribution starts	
		(ii) At the same time as the distribution starts	
5. Categorisation by the **impact of** censorship	(a) Direct from		
	(b) Indirect from		
6. Categorisation by **purpose of** censorship	(a) Censorship to prevent speech		
	(b) Censorship to prevent access to information		
7. Categorisation by **subject of** censorship	(a) Book censorship		
	(b) Press censorship		
	(c) Music censorship		
	(d) Film censorship		
	(e) Theatre censorship		
	(f) Video game censorship		
	(g) Comic book censorship		
	(h) Internet censorship		
	(i) Dress censorship (clothing, hairstyle etc.)		
8. Grouping by **frequency of** censorship	(a) Permanent		
	(b) Casual		
9. Categorisation by censorship **consequence**	(a) Remove content	i. Holding the author liable	(1) Legal (2) Physical
		ii. No liability of the author	
	(b) Destruction of content	i. Holding the author liable	(1) Legal (2) Physical
		ii. No liability of the author	

The grouping according to the 'width' of censorship (i.e. whether the concept is to be understood in a narrow or a broad sense) deserves special mention. There are arguments for both. In favour of a narrow interpretation is the formulation by Eric Barendt, who uses the term in a broad sense in his writings, that "the term 'censorship' is emptied of real meaning if it is applied to any social convention or practice which makes communication for some individuals more difficult."[9] On the same point, Matthew Bunn argues that many historians are afraid of over-expanding the term, as this would mean losing its original meaning. In arguing for a broader interpretation, he also argues for the introduction of a 'New Censorship Theory',[10]

[9] Barendt (2007), p. 151.

[10] For a summary of the theory see Freshwater (2004), pp. 225–246.

which would encompass "a growing share of practices and structures that shape the form and content of communication."[11] According to this, after the classical liberal definition of censorship and the Marxist concepts that questioned it, it should be acknowledged that by, the 2010s censorship, has become "a diffuse, ubiquitous phenomenon in which a host of actors (including impersonal, structural conditions) function as effective censors."[12] And while of course accepting that too broad a framework of interpretation can undermine the effectiveness of legal regulation, a broad use of censorship can also lead to a more complete protection of freedom of expression.

In the history of censorship, all of the above types existed, but the different groupings do not mean that there was no crossover between typifications. In the history of communication, prior censorship by the state has been the most common (and legally the most restrictive) form of censorship, and is therefore the most frequently and most commonly identified with the term censorship. However, Doris Lessig also points out the difficulty that "direct and unambiguous censorship, as part of state control, is easier to combat than the indirect results of it."[13] The main problems of censorship according to Eric Barendt are summarised below:

- the censor is suspicious—by virtue of his or her position—of the content that is presented;
- conflicting fundamental rights should be decided by a court, not a censor;
- it would also be up to the courts to impose sanctions in the event of a breach of fundamental rights;
- covert operation;
- lack of defences;
- the lack of predictability and standards, meaning. arbitrary decisions.[14]

However, the various content restrictions[15] include both legal and illegal cases.[16] Of course, while removing illegal content (terrorism, child pornography, hate speech, etc.) is in the intrinsic interest of a well-functioning society, removing or preventing access to legal content can be problematic. Thus, it can be argued that censorship may include "actions that a public or private governing entity takes on a selective basis to delete expressive content or to prevent speakers from engaging in further expression. 'Censorship' therefore encompasses certain laudable policies

[11] Bunn (2015), p. 26.

[12] Ibid., p. 27.

[13] Lessig (2015), p. vii.

[14] Barendt (2007), pp. 122–123.

[15] Of course, this does not include restrictions on the internet where there is human error or a natural problem. This was the case in 2008 when two cables in the Mediterranean Sea were accidentally damaged, which then caused an almost total internet blackout in 14 countries for a longer or shorter period. Zetter (2008). Larger countries usually have two main cables to ensure internet access, but this is not always possible for smaller, developing countries. Bateman (2022).

[16] Riordan (2016), pp. 463–473.

(such as removing non-consensual pornography), as well as policies that may be viewed as politically oppressive."[17]

The diversity behind the definitions is palpable, so perhaps Charles Oppenheim and Victoria Smith captured the issue best when they wrote that "the general sentiment behind most definitions is that something is withheld from access by another."[18]

2.1.1 *Political Censorship*[19]

In the public's mind, the most common association with censorship is surely a snooty, fat, balding bureaucrat, using scissors and black ink to cut out unsupported content from newspapers in a small room. However, as Benett and Naim have collected, there are now many more ways for states to restrict or interfere with free speech.[20] The two authors put the measures into a four-tier matrix, according to which there are direct and indirect, and visible and stealthy tools. They also point out that these are not only used by non-democratic governments, but that "stealth censorship appeals to authoritarian governments that want to appear like democracies – or at least not like old-style dictatorships."[21] It is not easy to decide, however, whether a tendentious distribution of subsidies and grants[22] or a paper shortage, of which we have seen many examples in history, constitutes censorship. Their matrix is therefore nothing other than a broad interpretation of the concept of censorship: any instrument in the hands of politicians that stands in the way of freedom of expression is considered censorship.

2.1.2 *Economic Censorship or Private Governance of Speech*

In this second group, it is not the state that decides the fate of the content to be (or to be) published, but a private company driven by private interests. Obviously, it is impossible to make general statements on this issue, since, as Margaret E. Roberts puts it, "if a book is missing from a library shelf, is it lost, not ordered, or removed by the government? If a social media post does not appear in a news feed, is it because the algorithm predicts you might not be interested in it, or because of government

[17] Langvardt (2017), pp. 1353–1388.

[18] Oppenheim and Smith (2004), p. 160; Cf. "Censorship is the suppression of certain views in favour of other views (. . .)" Bajomi-Lázár (2017), p. 63.

[19] For a detailed history of political censorship, see Sect. 2.3.

[20] For more on the situation in Central Eastern Europe, see Codreanu et al. (2021).

[21] Bennett and Naim (2015).

[22] Cf. Balkin (2019), pp. 159–162.

manipulation?"[23] Or, for example, if a manuscript of a book is rejected, an editorial (professional) decision is made, or perhaps there is an accusation of quasi 'pre-censorship' for fear of possible adverse consequences. Even so, Matthew Bunn's question is certainly worth reflecting on: "is an author 'censored' whenever and by whatever means she feels herself censored?"[24] Of course, there may be (mainly) economic interests behind this, namely private companies putting their own profit-making interests before fundamental rights.[25] The main question here is the discretion given to the platforms over third-party content.

This became tangible with the advent of the Internet and the giant platforms, where, in the early stages of development, as we shall see later, the state outsourced (or, as the international literature puts it, 'privatised') content moderation that left the decision to publish content entirely to the service providers.[26] As Jack M. Balkin put it, "digital speech flows through an elaborate privately-owned infrastructure of communication. Today, our practical ability to speak is subject to the decisions of private infrastructure owners, who govern the digital spaces in which people communicate with each other. This is the problem of private governance of speech."[27]

As a significant part of content is nowadays channelled through these giant companies, they certainly have a "significant influence (...) in shaping the choice of content available to the public".[28] Helberger and his colleagues distinguish between two types of influence: "one is due to direct journalistic and editorial influence on content, and the other is due to the ability to control the resources, media and services that are essential for the flow of information."[29] It is therefore clear that this type of media not only emerged in the Internet era, but also became of paramount importance. There had been previous attempts by publishing companies to sway journalists and editors into not publishing certain content, but the online world has brought with it a whole new range of possibilities for this type of influence. „Yet today, users of social media are subject to a regime of private censorship that was only recently unimaginable."[30]

---

[23] Roberts (2018), pp. 9–10.

[24] Bunn (2015), p. 40.

[25] For more on the economic power of platforms, see Busch et al. (2021), pp. 15–17.

[26] There is no consensus in the literature as to what term should be used: even documents issued by the same organisations give different names and definitions of ISPs (online platforms, gatekeepers, intermediary service providers, etc.), as they are of very broad types and cover a wide range of activities. On the issue of classification, the European Parliament pointed out that "would be very difficult to arrive at a single, legally relevant and future-proof definition of online platforms at EU level, owing to factors such as the great variety of types of existing online platforms and their areas of activity, as well as the fast-changing environment of the digital world." 2016/2276(INI), p. 6.; for a recent example of classification, see Bertolini (2021), pp. 7–23.

[27] Balkin (2018), p. 1153.

[28] Polyák (2020), p. 132.

[29] Helberger et al. (2015), pp. 50–71.

[30] Langvardt (2017), p. 1355.

Of course, one might ask why we should bother with private companies at all, since the benefits of more speech are outweighed by the absence of certain content. Benjamin F. Jackson summarised[31] the problems with this type of thinking in three points:

- users have no alternative these days to exercise their freedom of expression elsewhere,[32]
- modern communication tools are clustered around communication nodes, which means that if a particular type of speech is blocked, it can have a fatal impact on that type of message,
- online censorship (especially of political messages) can easily trigger harassment or bullying in real life.

Such actions are what Jack M. Balkin calls *collateral censorship*, which, in his view, has led communicating humanity from the classical era of censorship into a new era, which he calls the new school of free speech:[33] “the state holds one private party A liable for the speech of another private party B, and A has the power to block, censor, or otherwise control access to B’s speech. This will lead A to block B’s speech or withdraw infrastructural support from B. In fact, because A’s own speech is not involved, A has incentives to err on the side of caution and restrict even fully protected speech in order to avoid any chance of liability.”[34] We will see many examples of this later.[35]

2.1.3 Self-Censorship

It could be argued that this third type of censorship is the most difficult to define,[36] although it is, as Julian Petley puts it, the most effective of all forms of censorship.”[37] As early as the 19th century, English philosopher and economist John Stuart Mill, in his book *On Liberty*,[38] argues that freedom of expression can be threatened not only by legislation but also by social pressure.[39] His ideas were echoed in the work of

[31] Jackson (2014), pp. 132–133.

[32] On user feelings and thoughts, see West (2018), pp. 4366–4383.

[33] Balkin (2014), pp. 2306–2307.

[34] Ibid., p. 2309.

[35] It is worth pointing out at the beginning of the book that the liability of tech companies is legally secondary to the primary liability of the content creator, but because the identity of the content creator is not always clear on the internet, many documents confuse these levels of liability. For the sake of simplicity and clarity, I will leave this distinction aside in the further discussion of the liability of tech companies. On the advantages and disadvantages of secondary liability, see Sartor (2017), pp. 10–12.; Ullrich (2021), pp. 108–115.

[36] Schimpfössl et al. (2020), pp. 3–4.

[37] Petley (2009), p. 33.

[38] Mill (1859).

[39] Threet (2018), pp. 539–565.

Pierre Bourdieu, who argued that self-censorship or impersonal censorship is stronger and more significant than overt, formal repression.[40]

The phenomenon is perhaps most vividly described by John Keane in his book *The Media and Democracy*: "Censorship (. . .) can echo within us, take up residence within our selves, spying on us, a private amanuensis who reminds us never to go too far. The internal censor warns us that too much is at stake – our reputation, our families, our career, our jobs, legal action against our company. It makes us zip our lips, tremble and think twice, with a smile."[41] In these situations, we consciously (or often even unconsciously) hold back our own opinions for fear of a real or unreal consequence, a punishment. This, of course, inevitably leads to a *chilling effect,*[42] which makes us hesitate to exercise our freedom of speech in accordance with the law.[43] Hayes and his collegues have also produced a scale[44] of the propensity to self-censor one's speech, which they have described as „withholding of one's true opinion from an audience perceived to disagree with that opinion."[45]

2.2 Content Management or Censorship on the Internet?

In the context of censorship, it is worth examining how this is, and can be, displayed on the Internet. It is generally accepted that the internet has affected our lives in different ways, not only providing instant access to an incredible amount of information, but also transforming our notions of the state, the economy and education, as well as our human relationships and anxieties about the world today.[46] Zaryn Dentzel writes: "Out of all the plethora of communication opportunities that the Internet has opened up, I would highlight the emergence of social media and the way they have intricately melded into our daily lives. Social media have changed our personal space, altering the way we interact with our loved ones, our friends, and our sexual partners; they have forced us to rethink even basic daily processes like studying and shopping; they have affected the economy by nurturing the business start-up culture and electronic commerce; they have even given us new ways to form broad-based political movements."[47]

---

[40]Bourdieu (1991), pp. 77–79.

[41]Keane (1991), p. 39.

[42]Pech (2021); Baumbach (2018), pp. 92–114.; Townend (2017), pp. 73–82.; UNHRC (2011), pp. 26., 28.

[43]It is worth noting here that this can also be related to Elisabeth Noelle-Neumann's theory of the spiral of silence. Noelle-Neumann (1974), pp. 43–51.

[44]Hayes et al. (2005), pp. 306–307.

[45]Ibid., p. 299.

[46]Badouard (2021), pp. 49–58.

[47]Dentzel (2014), pp. 242–243.

In Cengiz and others v Turkey, the ECtHR stated that "the Internet has now become one of the principal means by which individuals exercise their right to freedom to receive and impart information and ideas." [48] Indeed, the Internet has become not only our primary means of communication, but also a platform where, at least at first glance, the ideas put forward by John Stuart Mill in his book *On Liberty* can become a reality.[49] Again quoting the ECtHR, "the Internet plays an important role in enhancing the public's access to news and facilitating the dissemination of information in general. User-generated expressive activity on the Internet provides an unprecedented platform for the exercise of freedom of expression." [50]

However, it is now becoming increasingly clear what new challenges even democratic states face in relation to this new medium. If we follow Jack M. Balkin's above line of thought, we can say that, with the emergence and spread of the Internet, there have been many cases, in addition to classical political censorship, where it is also difficult to decide whether we can really talk about censorship. In his writings, he consistently argues for the use of the term *speech control* rather than censorship,[51] which shows how the scope of speech and the resulting content control has changed according to some views. "Traditional or 'old-school' techniques of speech regulation have generally employed criminal penalties, civil damages, and injunctions to regulate individual speakers and publishers",[52] but the twenty-first century has fundamentally rewritten these. All this, as will be seen in a moment, makes it very difficult to determine whether we are talking about content regulation or censorship in individual cases.

2.3 Tools for Internet Content Management

Under the heading of content restrictions to be discussed in the context of Internet governance, the literature refers to a variety of solutions: both legal and illegal cases can be included. The simplest case is where the restriction is imposed for simple traffic management or network security reasons, which is of course—in principle—lawful. In order to manage the ever-increasing amount of traffic on Internet networks optimally, some form of traffic management is inevitably required.[53] To give an example of the almost unimaginable exponential growth in data traffic, "by 2022, traffic is expected to reach 150,000 GB of traffic per second, a 1,000-fold increase

[48] *Cengiz and Others v Turkey* App nos 48226/10 and 14027/11 (ECtHR, 1 December 2015), [49.].

[49] Gordon (1997), pp. 235–249.

[50] *Cengiz and Others v Turkey* App nos 48226/10 and 14027/11 (ECtHR, 1 December 2015), [52.].

[51] Balkin (2014), p. 2299.; Cf. based on Heidegger's work, Judith Butler suggests the general use of the term exclusion instead of censorship. Butler (1998), p. 255.

[52] Balkin (2014), p. 2299.

[53] Sethi and Behera (2017), pp. 369–375.

compared to the 156 GB in 2002, 20 years earlier. Ten years before that, in 1992, global internet traffic was 100 GB per day."[54]

However, there are also interventions that are less clear-cut. Cases where private market companies restrict or slow down access to certain content are in principle illegal under the EU's Net Neutrality Regulation,[55] but there may be legitimate cases. However, to which category we should attribute, for example, price mark-ups (whether justified or not), changes to the content displayed on the home screens of the most visited social media users, or to the algorithms used to determine search engine rankings is questionable. In these cases, it is not possible to give a single, clear answer, and the issues involved need to be examined on a case-by-case basis. Third, two types of content restriction by the State can be identified: on the one hand, when Internet access providers restrict certain content as they are obliged to by the State (by court or by law),[56] and, on the other hand, when States restrict or make Internet access to certain services inaccessible, or even build up a completely alternative service portfolio in order to maintain their own power, in a censorial manner. Nils Muižnieks, the then acting Commissioner for Human Rights of the Council of Europe, wrote that "Internet blocking is a widespread phenomenon in Council of Europe (CoE) member states."[57] While most states try not to use the option of restricting websites, as it is very similar to and in many cases difficult to separate from the implementation of censorship, "they do not necessarily object to voluntary filtering by ISPs to create a safe online environment for their users."[58]

In addition, and to underline the complexity of the issue, it should be noted that without access to the internet, the situation of marginalised groups in any society will continue to deteriorate, and this is also true for less developed countries.[59] "The Internet offers a key means for such groups to obtain information, assert their rights, and participate in public debates concerning social, economic and political changes to improve their situation."[60] Addressing the digital divide between the world's states (and the different groups within each state) is a much-debated issue and has attracted the attention of world leaders, as exemplified by the Declaration of Principles and Plan of Action adopted at the 2003 World Summit on the Information

[54] World Bank (2021).

[55] Regulation (EU) 2015/2120.

[56] See, for example: (A) a Brazilian court ordered Facebook and Twitter to suspend the social media accounts of individuals under investigation for 'false news, false accusations, spreading threats' and other illegal conduct that 'affect the honour and safety of the members and families of the Supreme Court'. *Inquérito 4.781, Distrito Federal* (May 26, 2020) or (B) a German court ruled that Facebook can block access to its platforms from associations that are classified as 'hate organizations'. *Ein Prozent v Facebook Ireland Ltd*, Oberlandesgericht Dresden, 4 U 2890/19, 16 June 2020.

[57] CoE (2018).

[58] Koltay (2019), p. 137.

[59] Korpisaari (2022), p. 358.

[60] UNHRC (2011), p. 62.

Society in Geneva,[61] and the Connect the World Plan adopted at the 2005 International Telecommunication Union Forum.[62]

References

Badouard R (2021) Ce que peux l'État face aux plateformes (What the State can face with the platforms). Pouvoirs – revue française d'études constitutionnelles et politiques 2021(177)

Bajomi-Lázár P (2017) Manipulál-e a média? (Is the media manipulating?) Médiakutató 18(4)

Balkin JM (2014) Old-School/New-School speech regulation. Harv Law Rev 127(8)

Balkin JM (2018) Free speech in the algorithmic society. The new school of big data, private regulation and the regulation of expression. Columbia Law Rev 118(7)

Balkin JM (2019) The American system of censorship and free expression. In: Peleg I (ed) Patterns of censorship around the world. Routledge, London

Barendt E (2007) Freedom of speech. Oxford University Press, Oxford

Bateman T (2022) Tonga is finally back online. Here's why it took 5 weeks to fix its volcano-damaged Internet cable. Euronews, 23 Feb. https://www.euronews.com/next/2022/02/23/tonga-is-finally-back-online-here-s-why-it-took-5-weeks-to-fix-its-volcano-damaged-interne

Baumbach T (2018) Chilling effect as a European Court of Human Rights' concept in media law cases. Bergen J Crim Law Crim Just 6(1)

Bennett P, Naim M (2015) 21st-century censorship. Columbia J Rev 14(1)

Bertolini A (2021) Liability of online platforms. European Parliamentary Research Service, European Union, Brussels

Bourdieu P (1991) Language and symbolic power. Harvard University Press, Cambridge

Bradbury R (1991) Fahrenheit 451. Ballantine Books, New York

Bunn M (2015) Reimagining repression: new censorship theory and after. Hist Theory 54(1)

Busch C, Graef I, Hofmann J, Gawer A (2021) Uncovering blindspots in the policy debate on platform power. Bruxelles, Observatory on the Online Platform Economy, European Commission

Butler J (1998) Ruled out: vocabularies of the censor. In: Post RC (ed) Censorship and silencing: practices of cultural regulation. Getty Research Institute for the History of Art and the Humanities, Los Angeles

Codreanu I, Ganea L, Godársky I, Hanáková E, Klíma M, Kužel R, Mračka M, Polyák G, Toma M, Urbán Á, Zamfirescu I (2021) Four shades of censorship: state intervention in the Central Eastern European Media Markets. Mérték Médiaelemző Műhely, Budapest

Council of Europe (CoE) (2018) Arbitrary Internet blocking jeopardises freedom of expression. Commissioner for Human Rights

Dentzel Z (2014) How the internet has changed everyday life. In: Castells M et al (eds) Change: 19 key essays on how internet is changing our lives. Turner, Madrid

European Parliament resolution of 15 June 2017 on online platforms and the digital single market (2016/2276(INI)), OJ C 331, 18.9.2018, p. 135–145

Freshwater H (2004) Towards a redefinition of censorship. In: Müller B (ed) Censorship & cultural regulation in the modern age. Critical Studies, No. 22. Rodopi, Amsterdam

Garton Ash T (2016) Free speech: ten principles for a connected world. Atlantic Books, London

Gordon J (1997) John Stuart Mill and the "Marketplace of Ideas". Soc Theory Pract 23(2)

Green J, Karolides NJ (2005) Encyclopedia on censorship. Facts on File, Inc, New York

[61] Pyati (2005), p. 73.

[62] ITU (2005).

Hayes AF, Glynn CJ, Shanahan J (2005) Willingness to self-censor: a construct and measurement tool for public opinion research. Int J Public Opin Res 17(3)
Hegyi W (2018) György: Mos és res publica (Mos and res publica). Gondolat Kiadó, Budapest
Helberger N, Kleinen-von Königslöw K, van der Noll R (2015) Regulating the new information intermediaries as gatekeepers of information diversity. Info 17(6)
International Telecommunication Union (ITU): Connect the World (2005). https://www.itu.int/dms_pub/itu-s/opb/gen/S-GEN-CTW-2005-PDF-E.pdf
Jackson BF (2014) Censorship and freedom of expression in the age of Facebook. New Mexico Law Rev 44(1)
Keane J (1991) The media and democracy. Polity Press, Cambridge
Koltay A (2019) New media and freedom of expression: rethinking the constitutional foundations of the public Sphere. Hart Publishing, Oxford
Korpisaari P (2022) From Delfi to Sanchez – when can an online communication platform be responsible for third-party comments? An analysis of the practice of the ECtHR and some reflections on the Digital Services Act. J Media Law 14(2)
Langvardt K (2017) Regulating online content moderation. Georgetown Law J 106(5)
Lessig D (2015) Censorship and the climate of opinion. In: Jones D (ed) Censorship. A world encyclopedia. Routledge, London
Mendel T (2010) Restricting freedom of expression: standards and principles. Centre for Law and Democracy, Halifax
Mill JS (1859) On liberty. John W. Parker, London
Noelle-Neumann E (1974) The spiral of silence. A theory of public opinion. J Commun 24(2)
Oppenheim C, Smith V (2004) Censorship in libraries. Inf Serv Use 24(4)
Pech L (2021) The concept of chilling effect. Its untapped potential to better protect democracy, the rule of law, and fundamental rights in the EU. Open Society European Policy Institute, Brussels
Petley J (2009) Censorship. A beginner's guide. Oneworld Publications, Oxford
Polyák G (2020) A forgalomirányító szolgáltatások médiaszabályozási kérdései (Media regulation issues for traffic management services). In: Polyák G (ed) Algoritmusok, keresők, közösségi oldalak és a jog: A forgalomirányító szolgáltatások szabályozása (Algorithms, search engines, social networking sites and the law: regulating traffic management services). HVG-ORAC Lap- és Könyvkiadó Kft., Budapest
Pyati K (2005) Ajit: WSIS: Kinek a víziója az információs társadalomról? (WSIS: Whose vision of the information society?) Információs Társadalom 5(4)
Regulation (EU) 2015/2120 of the European Parliament and of the Council of 25 November 2015 laying down measures concerning open internet access and amending Directive 2002/22/EC on universal service and users' rights relating to electronic communications networks and services and Regulation (EU) No 531/2012 on roaming on public mobile communications networks within the Union, OJ L 310, 26.11.2015, pp 1–18
Riordan J (2016) The liability of intermediaries. Oxford University Press, Oxford
Roberts ME (2018) Censored. Distraction and Diversion Inside China's Great Firewall. Princeton University Press, Princeton
Rosenfeld S (2001) Writing the history of censorship in the age of enlightenment. In: Gordon D (ed) Postmodernism and the enlightenment. New perspectives in eighteenth-century French intellectual history. Routledge, New York
Sartor G (2017) Providers liability: from the ecommerce directive to the future. in-depth analysis for the directorate-general for internal policies. European Parliament, Strasbourg
Schimpfössl E, Yablokov I, Zeveleva O, Fedirko T, Bajomi-Lázár P (2020) Self-censorship narrated: journalism in Central and Eastern Europe. Eur J Commun 35(1)
Sethi PC, Behera P (2017) Network traffic management using dynamic bandwidth on demand. Int J Comput Sci Inf Secur 15(6)
Smith S (2019) Freedom of expression. Foundational documents and historical arguments. Oxbridge Research Associates, Oxford

Sorabji R (2021) Freedom of speech and expression: its history, its value, its good use, and its misuse. Oxford University Press, Oxford

Threet D (2018) Mill's social pressure Puzzle. Soc Theory Pract 44(4)

Tótfalusi I (2001) Magyar Etimológiai Nagyszótár. Arcanum, Budapest

Townend J (2017) Freedom of expression and the chilling effect. In: Tumber H, Waisbord S (eds) The Routledge companion to media and human rights. Routledge, Abingdon

Ullrich C (2021) Unlawful content online. Towards a new regulatory framework for online platforms. Nomos, Baden-Baden

UNHRC (2011) Report of the Special Rapporteur on the promotion and protection of the right to freedom of opinion and expression. UN Doc A/HRC/17/27

West SM (2018) Censored, suspended, shadowbanned: user interpretations of content moderation on social media platforms. New Media Soc 20(11)

World Bank (2021) World Development Report: Data for Better Lives. 2021, https://wdr2021.worldbank.org/stories/crossing-borders/

Zetter K (2008) Undersea Cables Cut; 14 Countries Lose Web – Updated. Wired, 19 Dec. https://www.wired.com/2008/12/mediterranean-c/

Chapter 3
Snapshots from the History of Political Censorship in Europe and United States of America

> "A brief history of censorship would by no means be brief."
> *[Atwood (2010), p. 59.]*

3.1 Ancient Cases

Taboos, repressions, and unspeakable ideas probably appeared in societies very early: almost certainly as early as when speech emerged.[1] "The compulsion to silence others is as old as the urge to speak", writes Eric Berkowitz in his book in 2021.[2] Of course, due to the relative scarcity of sources, we do not know of all cases, but the beginnings are probably to be found in ancient Greece, where perhaps the most famous is the case of Socrates, who in 399 BC was poisoned for corrupting young people and for impiety, which he willingly consumed rather than allow his thoughts to be censored. Plato, from whose writings we learn the famous trial of his master Socrates, "evidently idealises the behaviour and death of Socrates at the trial and after the verdict",[3] in his work on the *State,* thus: "In Plato's State (. . .) there is no freedom in the political sense of the word. The modern idols of freedom of the press, freedom of speech, freedom of assembly, etc., would be, in Plato's eyes, the pathetic aberrations of political obtuseness. In his state there is strict censorship, all-embracing surveillance."[4] To support this, he makes moral, religious and political arguments, thus formalising the chain of reasoning:

- To have a good society, we must have good citizens.
- To have good citizens, children must be well educated.
- To be well educated, children must be exposed to good material and shielded from bad material.

---

[1] Cf. "Until writing was invented, man lived in acoustic space: boundless, directionless, horizonless, in the dark of the mind, in the world of emotion, by primordial intuition, by terror. Speech is a social chart of this bog." McLuhan and Fiore (2001), p. 48.

[2] Berkowitz (2021), p. 10.

[3] Horváth (2003), p. 12.

[4] Huszti (1927), p. 40.

G. Gosztonyi, *Censorship from Plato to Social Media*, Law, Governance and Technology Series 61, https://doi.org/10.1007/978-3-031-46529-1_3

- So, to have a good society, children must be exposed to good material and shielded from bad material.
- It is the obligation of the State to educate its citizens.
- So the State should allow only good material and suppress bad material.
- The State's censorship applies also to art.
- So the State should allow only good art and suppress bad art.[5]

According to him, the opinions of the ancient Greek community were shaped by law, and members of the community could be punished for saying things that offended public sensibilities, undermined common morals or subverted the institutional system.[6] In all this, Béla Mester notes that "in some of his works, the Athenian philosopher contradicts the censorship he himself demanded, since he often quotes approvingly from works which he orders to be banned elsewhere."[7]

On the Roman Empire, Andor Maros writes "Aelius Saturninus was thrown down from Capitoline Hill for some of his more daring poems, Pacunianus was strangled in prison, and Scaurus was condemned to death by the Emperor Tiberius for one of his tragedies."[8] In 12 BC, books were also burned, probably for political reasons; their content was denied and claimed to be religious.[9] The morals of religion and the community have always been under special protection, and those who violated them were severely punished. This was no different in the ancient emergence of Christianity: on the one hand, Christian persecution was both physical and spiritual, and then, as the religion grew stronger, it became vital for early Christian leaders to counter heretical threats. One important step in this direction was the Nicene-Constantinopolitan Creed, which took a stand against the doctrines of the Arian movement, which was considered heretical.[10]

3.2 The Spread of Printing and Censorship of Books

Even before the invention of the printing press, written content was becoming more and more common, making the word a more dangerous source of information: content deemed dangerous, heretical or undesirable could be spread more widely. However, while it took a good three quarters of a year for scribes to copy a book, everything changed with Johannes Gensfleisch zur Laden zum Gutenberg.[11] Printing

[5]Hicks (2012).

[6]Naddaff (2002).

[7]Mester (2003a), p. 58.

[8]Maros (1947), p. 12.

[9]Cramer (1945), p. 167.

[10]Maxwell (2015).

[11]McLuhan (1962).

with movable type and the letterpress[12] was a technical innovation in the mid-15th century[13] that could produce roughly 100 times the volume of the book as in the previous example in the same amount of time.[14] It is safe to say that this stage in the development of the media still has a living impact on our everyday lives. At the same time, it also greatly facilitated the spread of Protestant Reformation ideas, which both the Roman Catholic Church and governments did their utmost to prevent. In 1529, the first list of books banned by the government on the orders of Henry VIII was published in England[15] and by the mid-16th century, England had also established which printing houses (London, Oxford and Cambridge) could print books with a state-issued licence.[16] In France, in 1535, Francis I issued a list of banned books, followed by the *Edict of Chateaubriant* (1551), which prohibited the sale, importation or printing of any book not approved by the Faculty of Theology of the University of Paris.

Until the eighteenth century, censorship in Europe was characterised by concepts such as the Inquisition and book burning, alongside the desire for total control and censorship of book printing. The Roman Catholic Church, on the orders of Pope Paul IV, published from 1559 the *Index Librorum Prohibitorium*[17] (or *Index* for short), which contained a list of banned books.[18] The list had three parts:

- the names of writers whose works had all been banned;[19]
- individual works, with the names of the authors;
- anonymous authors and their works.

In 1564, at the *Council of Trent*, the ten principles for the censorship of books were published. A summary of these ten rules below shows which were the works of writing most feared by the Catholic Church.

1. "All books condemned by popes or councils before 1515 remain banned.
2. All heretical guidebooks and theological books written by heretics are forbidden.

[12]It is now generally accepted that the predecessor of book printing, tablet printing, was invented in China. For more details, see Carter (1955).

[13]Barbier (2012).

[14]It should be noted, however, that due to the shortage of paper at the time and the relative novelty and underdevelopment of the technology, only 180 copies of the famous Gutenberg Bible were produced. Andrews (2015).

[15]Green and Karolides (2005), p. 603.

[16]A Licensing Act was passed in England in 1662, but was allowed to lapse in 1695. Briggs and Burke (2020), p. 84.

[17]Newth (2010).

[18]The last one was published in 1948 (!), and was officially discontinued by Pope Paul VI in 1966. Schwenk (2020). It is important to note, however, that although it was not subsequently attributed canonical or canonical implications, it continued to be taken into account in ecclesiastical circles as a moral guide. Petley (2009), p. 35.

[19]After 1596, this category was abolished, so that afterwards "only" works were banned, not authors.

3. Bible translation by heretics is prohibited; translation of other texts by heretics requires approval.
4. Vernacular translations of the Bible by Catholic scholars require approval.
5. Compilations of earlier works edited by heretics require correction and approval.
6. Theological writings in the vernacular require correction and approval.
7. Obscene or immoral works are prohibited. Classical works are for adults.
8. Books that are generally acceptable but contain heretical details shall be corrected.
9. Any books containing magic, superstition, astrology or occult practices are prohibited.
10. The bishop and the inquisitor require that all books be approved before publication."[20]

On the basis of the above rules, the list of books was reviewed again and again by the Sacred Congregation of the Index, which met regularly from 1571 onwards and included the official theologian of the papal court *(Magister Sacri Palatii)*.[21] As a result, a list of books to be destroyed, the *Index Expurgatorius*, was published. Thomas James, the librarian of the Bodleian Library at the University of Oxford, wryly described the publication as "an invaluable reference work to be used by the curators of the Bodleian library when listing those works particularly worthy of collecting."[22] Consequently, in 1627 Thomas James published the *Index Generalis*, which listed the books that libraries in England should certainly acquire from the Index Expurgatorius.[23]

However, the situation was far from easy: in addition to the list of the Roman Catholic Church, various lists were drawn up in Spain, England, the Low Countries and the Holy Roman Empire, on which works promoting heretical ideas or ideologically dangerous doctrines could be placed, according to the issuer's view.[24] The fate of the publications was, in good cases, to be made inaccessible, in worse cases to be destroyed, and in the most extreme cases to punish (even physically) the author. Hence, "it has of course never been possible to make a summary assessment of the number of books and other works of literature and art which have been the victims of censorship, either in connection with the Inquisition or later independently of it, over the last 500 years, especially as many records and judgments were destroyed ex officio after the cases had been closed."[25] The censorship of the time thus operated through the 'joint exercise' or collaboration between the State and the Church, in

[20] Busäus (1664).

[21] Pillari (2017), p. 11.

[22] Green and Karolides (2005), p. 257.

[23] The list, known only as the 'James Index', was used by Oxford University in the 20th century. Ibid., p. 257.

[24] Just to give you an example, some of the authors who have been included in the various Indexes are Luther, Erasmus, Boccaccio, Galileo, Machiavelli, Descartes, Malebranche, Spinoza, Montaigne, Bacon, Hobbes, Voltaire, Rousseau, Hume, Bentham, Mill.

[25] Pruzsinszky (2014), p. 9.

many cases concealing from posterity whether events were really motivated by religious differences, ideology or pure politics.

3.3 Censorship in the 17th–18th Centuries

A change in the tides can first be observed around the seventeenth century, when the struggle for the freedom of printing and the printed press, which was becoming increasingly important, became intertwined with the fight against censorship. It "appeared first and most vigorously in Britain (from where it spread rapidly to America, and less energetically, to the Continent)."[26] John Keane divided the contemporary arguments against censorship into four groups:[27]

1. The theological argument is based on the premise that God has given individuals the faculty of reason to exercise it, so that censorial restrictions on it stifle the freedom of thought and judgment that God has granted. In this line of thought, the writings of Henry Burton, Henry Robinson and William Walwyn are worth highlighting. However, the most complete summary of such ideas was given by John Milton, who in 1644 addressed the English Parliament in favour of freedom of (unlicensed) printing. This was the famous *Areopagitica*, in which, using the rules of ancient rhetoric,[28] he persuaded the two houses of parliament that "the censorship of books is A) an unchristian thing . . .; consequently B) its existence can only be explained by some papal intrigue; for C) there is no such thing in either the biblical or the pagan ancient tradition, and cannot be legitimated on that ground."[29]

John Milton's point is, moreover, that censorship needs to be combatted, not only because it does not exist in tradition, but also because the literacy (or lack of literacy) of the recipient, the reader, plays a role in the reading of books, not only the words but also their range of meaning. This would mean not only banning books but also the modes of interpretation, which is obviously an impossible undertaking: "infection which is from books of controversy in religion is more doubtful and dangerous to the learned than to the ignorant; and yet those books must be permitted untouched by the licenser. It will be hard to instance where any ignorant man hath been ever seduced by papistical book in English, unless it were commended and expounded to him by some of that clergy: and indeed all such tractates, whether false or true, are as the prophecy of Isaiah was to the eunuch, not to be understood without a guide."[30]

2. The main idea of the second line of argument is that, with civilisation, individuals have acquired various liberties, which entitle them to stand up for their interests in the political sphere and to exercise their natural rights against the state.

---

[26] Keane (1991), p. 8.

[27] Ibid., pp. 10–20.

[28] Blasi (1995), p. 5.

[29] Mester (2003b), pp. 33–34.

[30] Milton (2008), p. 25.

Freedom of the press and the fullest possible expression of ideas—in other words, the prohibition of censorship—can usher in an age in which good government and the rule of law can be established, following the unpredictable mediaeval legal system. The proponents of this theory include John Locke, John Asgill, John Trenchard and Thomas Gordon, who published under the name 'Cato', as well as Matthew Tindall. The latter pointed out, in connection with the prohibition of censorship, that "like a faithful centinel,[31] a free press prevents all surprize, and gives timely warning of any approaching danger."[32]

3. Third, it is worth highlighting the utilitarian argument, according to which the most important goal of governments is to be able to provide happiness for as many people as possible. According to the proponents of this theory (William Godwin, James Mill, Jeremy Bentham), the most important purpose of the press and the content it publishes is to act as a counterweight to tyrannical government, since it can use the power of publicity to create legal norms that maximise the happiness of the people through government. This, of course, requires that the press should operate under as little control and scrutiny as possible, so that citizens have access to the widest possible range of information and, in today's terms, data of public interest.

4. The fourth set of arguments linked the expansion of press freedom and the abolition of censorship to the concept of justice. Although the foundations of the argument were laid by Leonard Busher and Joseph Priestley, the most lasting influence was the ideas expressed by John Stuart Mill in his book *On Liberty*.[33] Mill's position is that it is the duty of the press to ensure that all opinions in society are presented, because, in the event of a clash of views, the view that contains the truth will prevail over erroneous ideas. János Frivaldszky pointed out that, in Mill's view, "it is socially harmful to ban opinions which appear to be wrong or false; on the one hand because they may be true and correct, of which history offers glaring examples, and on the other hand because, even if they are wrong, it is good for the correct doctrine or the doctrine which is held to be correct to defend the arguments in its support in debates against those propounding an doctrine based on false premises. Furthermore, there may be partial truths in false doctrines which can contribute to the ... social search for truth."[34]

This was already a forerunner of ideas which posited freedom of expression as a fundamental right, and that human rights, freedom and human dignity should not be allowed to be enjoyed by only a few, as in earlier times. As such, the freedom of expression campaigners of this era (Paine, Tindall, Burke etc.) were both challenging the pre-existing system of state-church censorship and placing this struggle under the umbrella of a larger struggle.

---

[31] Cf. "It is the job of the press ... to always be suspicious, and ... as the 'watchdog of democracy' (*public watchdog*) to 'snarl' when it perceives abuses of power" Bajomi-Lázár (2006), p. 51.

[32] Keane (1991), p. 14.

[33] Mill (1859). See in details Gunatilleke (2021).

[34] Frivaldszky (2016), p. 300.

In 1753, Pope Pius V ordered the Sacred Congregation for the Index to begin a major revision of the censorship system in the bull 'Sollicita ac Provida'. The result was „the first major redirection of ecclesiastical censorship for two centuries and the church's first acknowledgement that it could not and should not attempt to control the entire volume of worldwide printing.[35] Patrizia Delpiano notes, however, that this did not mean the end of the desire for control (in today's terms, content control), but merely a refinement of the method: after the censorship decision, it allowed for a new censorship decision to be requested (appeal phase) and even for a verbal defence. At the same time, the system relied heavily on the institution of self-censorship, as authors were given the opportunity to 'improve their texts' between the two decision points.[36] All these processes led to the first in the world, Sweden in 1766,[37] followed by Denmark-Norway[38] in 1770, to enact laws banning censorship and protecting the freedom of the press. György Képes quotes the reasoning: „nationwide debate promotes rational decisions."[39]

Standing on the theoretical foundations of the Enlightenment, the Declaration of the Rights of Man and of the Citizen of 1789 was the first legal document to state clearly in point XI that "The free communication of thoughts and of opinions is one of the most precious rights of man: any citizen thus may speak, write, print freely, except to respond to the abuse of this liberty, in the cases determined by the law." In 1791, the United States of America also amended its Constitution, adopted in 1787 and enacted in 1789, and the First Amendment stated that "Congress shall make no law respecting an establishment of religion, or prohibiting the free exercise thereof; or abridging the freedom of speech, or of the press; or the right of the people peaceably to assemble, and to petition the Government for a redress of grievances." This is the highest level of legal document prohibiting the state from adopting censorship rules, and it is mainly this and the lack of a centuries-old 'tradition' of censorship that explains the different regulatory paths in Europe and the US. Moreover, as Péter Smuk notes, "a recurrent turn in American judicial reasoning, which became successful in the dissenting opinion of Judge Oliver Wendell Holmes (*Abrams v United States*), sets out the basic premise of the conditions and mechanism of competition of opinions and state intervention: the market rather than the state should regulate."[40]

This has led to the prohibition of prior censorship in more and more countries - not, of course, independently of the growing importance of the printed (daily) press. As William Blackstone put it: "The liberty of the press is indeed essential to the nature of a free state: but this consists in laying no previous restraints upon publications, and not in freedom from censure for criminal matter when published.

[35] Green and Karolides (2005), p. 258.

[36] Delpiano (2018), p. 56.

[37] Nordin (2017–2018), pp. 137–144.; Laursen (2005), pp. 100–121.

[38] Képes (2015), p. 48.

[39] Képes (2019), pp. 223–224.

[40] Smuk (2019), pp. 48–49.

Every freeman has an undoubted right to lay what sentiments he pleases before the public: to forbid this is to destroy the freedom of the press: but if he publishes what is improper, mischievous or illegal, he must take the consequence of his own temerity."[41]

3.4 Changes in the 19th and 20th Centuries

The French Revolution, American democracy, urbanisation, and industrialisation, among many others, together brought revolutions and then civil rights systems across Western Europe. All this went hand in hand with increased freedom of access to information, changes in education systems and the development of literacy. The political, social, societal, cultural, and legal changes of the era brought a temporary improvement in the censorship situation: by the second half of the 19th century, prior censorship was banned throughout Europe.[42] This was another 'war': for souls. As the Hamburg *Echo* newspaper put it, "In waging our war, we do not throw bombs. Instead, we throw our newspapers amongst the masses of the working people. Printing ink is our explosive."[43] And this war was fought by governments and their political opponents. Robert Justin Goldstein shows that a classic era of no prior censorship was slowly dawning in Europe in the nineteenth century.[44]

The situation was complicated, however, by the fact that a number of laws—often conflicting within the same country—were passed in relation to the press during the period. "In Spain between 1810 and 1883, at least fifteen major press laws and decrees were promulgated. By 1851, the French laws had become so complicated that (...) two judges published a handbook on them to aid befuddled lawyers and journalists."[45] It should be pointed out, however, that although the legal prohibition of prior censorship appeared in many countries, in many of them printed newspapers had to be submitted to the state authorities before or at the same time as distribution (e.g. Austria, Germany, Russia and France). Thus, although we can speak of a press free of censorship on paper, the real realisation of press freedom was far from materialising.[46]

Thus, while it is true that the (almost) general development of the late nineteenth century was not perfect, but had a positive impact on the situation of freedom of expression, the historical events of the twentieth century led to significant changes. The overall situation of the press in Europe in the twentieth century is difficult to draw, but it is certain that the two world wars and the many conflicts, both large and

[41] Blackstone (1897), p. 636.

[42] Gosztonyi (2023).

[43] Cited by Goldstein (2000), p. 1.

[44] Goldstein (1989), p. 38.

[45] Ibid., p. 39.

[46] In addition, some countries have set high deposits to start a newspaper and imposed special taxes, which can be seen as indirect censorship at worst, or as a hindrance to publication at best.

small, in Europe made it very difficult for freedom of expression to be fully effective.[47] The two great totalitarian empires, the Nazi[48] and the Soviet,[49] were also at the forefront of the political repression of opinion. All this was compounded by the emergence of new media and, as Jürgen Wilke put it, "temporary progress was followed by repeated setbacks. In the 20th century, the new media (film, radio and television) were also censored and controlled."[50]

As briefly outlined above, the United States of America has followed a different regulatory path[51] to the Old Continent: rather than legislation, it is judicial practice that has shaped the scope, limits and constraints on freedom of expression. Without delving deeply into these chapters of legal history,[52] it is worth quoting Ken Wachsberger: "The history of books censored for depicting sexual acts—whether the chosen word was 'pornography,' 'erotica,' or 'obscenity'— is a fascinating ride through our country's court system."[53] So while classical press censorship has not significantly affected everyday life in America,[54] examples of other types of restrictions abound. In the well-known McCarthy era (late 1940s-mid 1950s), communist content was targeted, and later films, comic books and music tracks deemed violent were also allowed to bleed through the filters of government agencies.[55]

The political turbulence in Europe throughout the century did not spare the press and freedom of expression, and only the emergence of European cooperation in the second half of the century brought improvements. The regime changes of 1989 also brought about a better situation for the Eastern European states after the Soviet influence, so that—as we shall see later—the emergence of the internet in Europe and America was now in a situation free of political censorship. The 'privatised' regulation of speech is therefore a different story. Paraphrasing Margaret Atwood, one could easily say that the brief history of censorship is by no means be brief.

References

Andrews E (2015) 7 Things You May Not Know About the Gutenberg Bible. History, 23 Feb (Updated 22 Aug 2018), https://www.history.com/news/7-things-you-may-not-know-about-the-gutenberg-bible

Atwood M (2010) Don't tell us what to write. Index Censorship 39(4)

[47] On wartime censorship, see Eggleston (1941), pp. 313–323.; Kelemen (2022), pp. 31–44.

[48] Merziger et al. (2019), pp. 135–152.

[49] Kruglikova and Alexeev (2019), pp. 153–171.

[50] Wilke (2013), p. 1.

[51] On the US debates on the absolutist and deliberative defence of free speech, see Török (2017), pp. 722–725.

[52] For details see Beattie (2009), pp. 22–27.

[53] Quoted in Steele (2020), p. 7.

[54] Of course, war censorship is an exception to this rule, see Price (1942), pp. 837–849.

[55] Steele (2020), pp. 12–13.

Bajomi-Lázár P (2006) Média és társadalom (Media and society). PrintXBudavár Zrt. – Médiakutató Alapítvány, Budapest
Barbier F (2012) Histoire du livre (History of book). Armand Colin (Collection U), Paris
Beattie S (2009) Community, space and online censorship: regulating Pornotopia. Routledge, London – New York
Berkowitz E (2021) Dangerous ideas. A brief history of censorship in the west, from the ancients to fake news. Beacon Press, Boston
Blackstone W (1897) Commentaries on the laws of England: In one volume, together with a copious glossary of legal terms employed; also, biographical sketches of writers referred to; and a chart of descent of English sovereigns. West Publishing Co, St. Paul
Blasi V (1995) Milton's Areopagitica and the Modern First Amendment. Yale Law School Occasional Papers, https://digitalcommons.law.yale.edu/ylsop_papers/6/
Briggs A, Burke P (2020) A social history of the media 4th edn. Revised and updated with Espen Ytreberg). Polity Press, Cambridge
Busäus J (1664) Sacros. Concilium Tridentinum: Editio reformata cum indice librorum prohibitorum ex praescripto Concilii (Sacred. The Council of Trent: A reformed edition with a list of books prohibited by the provisions of the Council). Johann Busäus, Cologne
Carter TF (1955) The invention of printing in China and its spread westward. Columbia University Press, New York
Cramer F (1945) Bookburning and censorship in ancient Rome: a chapter from the history of freedom of speech. J Hist Ideas 6(2)
Delpiano P (2018) Church and censorship in Eighteenth-Century Italy. Governing reading in the age of enlightenment. Routledge, London
Eggleston W (1941) Press censorship. Can J Econ Polit Sci 7(3)
Frivaldszky J (2016) A politikai véleménynyilvánítás szükségessége, joga és felelőssége a közjó és a jó kormányzás szemszögéből (The need, right and responsibility of political expression from the perspective of the common good and good governance). In Medias Res 5(2)
Gosztonyi G (2023) From feudal censorship to freedom of the press in Hungary in 1848 through the work of József Irinyi. In: Švecová A, Lanczová I, Gajarský A (eds) Právno-historické trendy a výhľady VII. (Legal-Historical Trends and Perspectives VII). Nakladatelství Leges, Prague
Goldstein RJ (1989) Political censorship of the arts and the press in nineteenth-century Europe. Palgrave Macmillan, New York
Goldstein RJ (2000) Introduction. In: Goldstein RJ (ed) The war for the public mind: political censorship in nineteenth-century Europe. Praeger Publishers, Westport
Green J, Karolides NJ (2005) Encyclopedia on censorship. Facts on File, Inc, New York
Gunatilleke G (2021) Justifying limitations on the freedom of expression. Human Rights Rev 22(1)
Hicks S (2012) Plato on censoring artists. http://www.stephenhicks.org/2012/01/21/plato-on-censoring-artists-a-summary
Horváth B (2003) A géniusz pere. Szókratész – Johanna (The trial of genius. Socrates – Johanna). Attraktor, Budapest
Huszti J (1927) Platon eszményi állama (Plato's ideal state). Széphalom 1(1)
Keane J (1991) The media and democracy. Polity Press, Cambridge
Kelemen R (2022) Az első világháborús sajtórendészet szervezete (The organisation of the press police during the First World War). In: Gosztonyi G (ed) A velünk élő történelmi cenzúra (The historical censorship that lives with us). Gondolat Kiadó, Budapest
Képes G (2015) Felvilágosult abszolutizmus Dániában (Enlightened absolutism in Denmark). In: Tevesz L (ed) Államhatalom és társadalmi autonómia viszonya a nyugati keresztény civilizációban (The relationship between state power and social autonomy in Western Christian civilisation). ELTE Eötvös Kiadó, Budapest
Képes G (2019) A Dán Királyság alkotmánytörténete a kezdetektől 1848-ig (Constitutional history of the Kingdom of Denmark from the beginning to 1848). ELTE Eötvös Kiadó, Budapest

Kruglikova O, Alexeev K (2019) The Russian revolution and the establishment of the authoritarian media system. In: Arnold K, Preston P, Kinnebrock S (eds) The handbook of European communication history. Wiley Blackwell, Hoboken
Laursen JC (2005) Censorship in the Nordic Countries, Ca. 1750–1890: transformations in law, theory, and practice. J Mod Eur Hist 3(1)
Maros A (1947) A cenzúra (Censorship). Népszava Könyvkiadó, Budapest
Maxwell DR (2015) The Nicene Creed in the Church. Concordia J 41(1)
McLuhan M (1962) The Gutenberg galaxy. The making of typographic man. University of Toronto Press, Toronto
McLuhan M, Fiore Q (2001) The medium is the Massage. An inventory of effects. Ginko Press, Corte Madera
Merziger P, Balbi G, Barrera C, Sipos B (2019) Crises, rise of fascism and the establishment of authoritarian media systems. In: Arnold K, Preston P, Kinnebrock S (eds) The handbook of European communication history. Wiley Blackwell, Hoboken
Mester B (2003a) A cenzúra és az elmék fölötti uralom. Elmetartalmakra vonatkozó metaforáink gondolatszabadságot érintő következményeiről (Censorship and the domination of minds. On the implications of our metaphors for the freedom of thought). Világosság 44(5–6)
Mester B (2003b) Néhány sajátos szókép John Milton Areopagiticájában (Some peculiar idioms in John Milton's Areopagitica). Világosság 44(11–12)
Mill JS (1859) On liberty. John W. Parker, London
Milton J (2008) Areopagitica. Speech to the Parliament of England for the unlicensed right to print. Arc Manor, Rockville
Naddaff R (2002) Exiling the poets: the production of censorship in Plato's Republic. University of Chicago Press, Chicago
Newth M (2010) Index Librorum Prohibitorum. Beacon for Freedom of Expression, http://www.beaconforfreedom.org/liste.html?tid=415&art_id=556
Nordin J (2017–2018) The Swedish Freedom of Print Act of 1776 – background and significance. J Int Media Entertain Law 7(2)
Petley J (2009) Censorship. A beginner's guide. Oneworld Publications, Oxford
Pillari A (2017) The Current Juridic and Moral Value of the Index of Forbidden Books. http://www.valtorta.org.au/JCL-Thesis-on-the-Index-and-Valtorta.pdf
Price B (1942) Governmental censorship in war-time. Am Polit Sci Rev 36(5)
Pruzsinszky S (2014) Halhatatlan cenzúra (Immortal censorship). NMHH Médiatudományi Intézet, Budapest
Schwenk K (2020) Lifting the Veil: Abolishing Censorship at the Vatican. San Diego State University Library, https://library.sdsu.edu/scua/new-notable/lifting-veil-abolishing-censorship-vatican
Smuk P (2019) A kormány beszéde. Az Első Alkotmánykiegészítés paradigma és a 'government speech' alkotmányos korlátai az Egyesült Államokban (Speech by the Government. The First Amendment paradigm and the constitutional limits of 'government speech' in the United States). Iustum Aequum Salutare 15(4)
Steele JE (2020) A history of censorship in the United States. J Intellect Freedom Priv 5(1)
Török B (2017) A szólásszabadság védelmének dinamikája (Dynamics of the protection of freedom of expression). Magyar Jog 64(2)
Wilke J (2013) Censorship and Freedom of the Press. Leibniz Institute of European History, Mainz

Chapter 4
The Spread of Social Media and the Emergence of New Forms of Content Regulation

4.1 The Emergence of Web 1.0 and Web 2.0

Although data suggest that the spread of social media has only happened in the last decade, the development of the online world did not start with them. The old, one-way, so-called Web 1.0 applications were just a new way of presenting traditional media in a new environment.[1] "Web 1.0, the 'golden age', from the perspective of Web 2.0, was about being online, showing off, brochure-like (rarely updated) websites for companies, portfolios and other presentation sites for individuals, news sites, a kind of online representation of the paper world, where email or telephone was the obvious form of feedback."[2] As the quote shows, the internet of the 1990–2000 period is hardly comparable to the digital world we live in today.[3] On the one hand, there were obvious technological limitations to the traditional presentation of traditional media products, but the more important difference is that we are talking about a straight line of information that has been the norm for centuries, a one-way flow of information from the content creator to the content consumer, controlled and with no (or little) need for feedback. It is clear that the key here is the passivity of the consumer, i.e. the primary 'task' of receiving the information. This is closely connected to László Ropolyi who argues that the internet conceives "in four – easily distinguishable, but obviously connected – contexts: we regard it as a system of technology, as an element of communication, as a cultural medium, and as an independent organism."[4]

---

[1] On the early history of the internet, see Naughton (2016), pp. 5–28.; Campbell-Kelly and Garcia-Swartz (2013), pp. 18–33.

[2] Herendy (2010), pp. 41–55.

[3] Szűts (2013), pp. 59–60.

[4] Ropolyi (2021), p. 82.

G. Gosztonyi, *Censorship from Plato to Social Media*, Law, Governance and Technology Series 61, https://doi.org/10.1007/978-3-031-46529-1_4

In contrast, technological advances,[5] the first dotcom bubble burst in 2000[6] and the subsequent crisis of confidence have pushed internet companies in a direction where the role of the user has been transformed, with a focus on shared knowledge, co-creation and collective action. While some of the companies that have been at the forefront of these changes were founded a few years earlier (Google 1998; Napster 1999; Blogger 1999; Wikipedia 2001), the big bang was still a few years away.[7] Even though Myspace, Last.fm, Picasa and Facebook were founded in 2004, and Flickr, del.icio.ust and YouTube a year later in 2005, the real take-up of Web 2.0 required a significant mass of users capable of going online. "In fact, it is only in Web 2.0 that the number of content uploaders will expand dramatically, with a changed and stable infrastructure and a simple user interface that potentially turns every downloader into an uploader."[8] Within a few years (by December 2007), 20% of the world's population would have access to the internet:

Date	Number of users	% of world population[9]
December 1995	16 million	0.4%
December 1996	36 million	0.9%
December 1997	70 million	1.7%
December 1998	147 million	3.6%
December 1999	248 million	4.1%
December 2000	361 million	5.8%
August 2001	513 million	8.6%
September 2002	587 million	9.4%
December 2003	719 million	11.1%
December 2004	817 million	12.7%
December 2005	1,018 billion	15.7%
December 2006	1,093 billion	16.7%
December 2007	1,319 billion	20.0%

This then maintained its exponential nature, rising to 30% in another four years, 40% in two and a half years, and then to 50% and 60%, as the table below shows.

Date	Number of users	% of world population[10]
June 2011	2.110 billion	30.4%
December 2013	2.802 billion	39.0%
June 2016	3,696 billion	49.5%

(continued)

[5]"In 2012, 20 (!) typical households – with broadband internet – will generate more information traffic than the entire internet in 2008." Hámori (2015), p. 133.

[6]Murdock (2020).

[7]Slumkoski (2012), pp. 153–162.

[8]Csordás (2005).

[9]https://www.internetworldstats.com/emarketing.htm.

[10]https://www.internetworldstats.com/emarketing.htm.

Date	Number of users	% of world population
June 2020	4.833 billion	62.0%
July 2023	5.385 billion	67.9%

Moreover, the 68% figure for mid-2023 still indicates huge growth potential in Africa, Asia, Latin America and the Middle East (by this time, almost 90% of the population in North America and Europe already has access, so further growth is not realistic).[11]

Region	Population	Number of users	Users as a percentage of total population (%)[12]
Africa	1,394,588,547	652,865,628	46.8%
Asia	4,352,169,960	2,934,186,678	67.4%
Europe	837,472,045	750,045,495	89.6%
North America	372,226,482	349,572,583	93.4%
Middle East	268,302,801	211,796,760	78.9%
Latin America	664,099,841	543,396,621	81.8%
Oceania and Australia	43,602,955	31,191,971	71.5%
Total	7,932,791,734	5,385,798,406	67.9%

It is also linked to the famous thesis by Manuel Castells on the information society, according to which the user activity that is emerging as a result of technological progress can only really be exploited by privileged groups of the public who have the resources (computer, bandwidth, legal background, etc.). In Castells' words, they are the interactive ones, who are able to make use of the tools of computer-mediated communication (CMC).[13] In this context, a major public task can be imagined and expected, since both the development of media literacy[14] and access to appropriate technology and the fight against fake news[15] put non-privileged social groups at a significant disadvantage in their daily lives, and thus social inclusion cannot be achieved to the extent required.

However, after these parenthetical thoughts, back to the emergence of Web 2.0. The now tangible volume of users could engage in an endless stream of two-way[16] communications, which were primarily community-based and proclaimed the primacy of user-generated content. Continuous content sharing,[17] continuous content reviews (e.g. commenting, recommending, linking) and continuous content

[11] However, the difference between urban and rural populations can significantly skew the data on internet access. Zandt (2021).

[12] https://www.internetworldstats.com/emarketing.htm.

[13] Castells (2010), pp. 385–394.

[14] Nagy (2018), pp. 187–222.

[15] Bogrea (2023).

[16] Later still, even in the course of multi-directional (P2P) communication.

[17] Cf. on the Internet:'Sharing is caring'.

classification (e.g. tagging) enabled the creation of a communication space in which the now active consumer could become an empowered actor. What we call media complety changed.[18] Although there has been no clear and universally accepted definition of Web 2.0 since Tim O'Reilly's conceptualisation,[19] the triple attribute set he based on the work of Christopher Alexander[20] has become the basis for all attempts at definition. According to O'Reilly, the main characteristics of new media are:

- "The little guy can become big at any time – either by internal development or by merging (The Long Tail),
- Data is the Next Intel Inside,
- Participatory Design (Users Add Value),
- Loose organisational structure (The Perpetual Beta),
- It is based on cooperation, not control (Cooperate, Don't Control)."[21]

Building on the above, Jonathan Obar and Steve Wildman later summarised attempts to define it in earlier years, with a decade of development as a basis:

- "Social media means Web 2.0 web applications,
- User-generated content is the lifeblood of social media,
- Users create service-specific profiles for a website or application,
- Social media facilitates the development of online social networks by linking a user's profile to the profiles of other individuals or groups."[22]

This also means that social networking sites represent only a small—albeit still huge in terms of user numbers—slice of Web 2.0 applications. According to the Web 2.0 glossary of the Hungarian-language Wikipedia incarnation,[23] the following types can be grouped:

- Social networking sites (Facebook, LinkedIn, Orkut, MySpace)
- Photo sharing sites (Instagram, Flickr, Indafoto, Picasa, Photobucket, SmugMug, Zooomr)
- Video sharing portals (YouTube, Google Videos, IndaVideo)
- Blogs, microblogs (Twitter, Jaiku.com, Plurk)
- Online office applications (Google Calendar, Google Docs, Google Spreadsheets, Zoho, ThinkFree Online)
- Auction sites (Marketplace, eBay, Vatera)
- Podcasts
- Wikipedia and other wikis

---

[18] Zeno-Zencovich (2019).

[19] Karambiri (2009), p. 30.

[20] Alexander (1977).

[21] O'Reilly (2005).

[22] Obar and Wildman (2015*), pp. 745–750.*

[23] https://hu.wikipedia.org/wiki/Web2.0.

- Forums
- Online storage providers (Dropbox, Google Drive, Box.net)
- Online map applications (Waze, Google Maps, Yahoo! Maps)
- Sites that engage in or support online retail (PayPal, Abaqoos)
- Social music recommendation sites (Pandora.com, Last.fm)
- Pre-written licence agreements (Creative Commons, GPL)
- Link sharing services (del.icio.us, Diigo, Linkzilla)
- Services that rate other sites (Digg)
- News sources (feeds, RSS)
- Custom homepages (iGoogle, Netvibes, Google Reader) supporting news remixing
- Communities for sharing internet access (Fon, Meraki)
- Virtual worlds (Second Life) and online games (MMORPG)
- Unified access control systems (OpenID, TypeKey)
- Mashups and the services that support their creation
- Version control softwares (CVS, SVN, Git, Mercurial, Bazaar) supporting the collaborative development of open source software
- Pastebins
- Internet-based science programmes (SETI@Home, Galaxyzoo) and meteorological communities[24]

Of these, the average user only knows and uses the most popular ones. Even so, the list is an excellent illustration of the potential that still lurks in Web 2.0. "The massive increase in the number of users creating content is leading to a democratisation of creation, consumption, expression and communication, and a qualitative change in the way we learn about the world."[25]

If we were to summarise this, we should refer to Shayne Bowman and Chris Willis 2003, who distinguished between what they call the *broadcast model* and the *intercast model*. The first is used to describe classical media services (television, radio) as well as Web 1.0 in the 1990s, while the second is used to describe Internet communication and Web 2.0 as it is used today.[26]

The fundamental difference between the two is the way they are organised, since broadcast communication is a top-down type of organisation, where—as we have seen above—the consumer, the receiver, is a passive actor, while in the intercast model we are talking about a self-organising, active type of consumer, the receiver. This clearly implies a difference in the direction of communication, i.e. the possibility of a two-way or multi-directional, now real dialogue, replacing the former one-way communication. The basic characteristics of the two models are set out in the table below:

---

[24] I have selected the examples in the article and changed their order, giving priority to the more popular services. *Author.*

[25] Cserpes (2011), p. 194.

[26] Bowman and Willis (2003), p. 10.

	Broadcast model	Intercast model
	Web 1.0	Web 2.0
How is it organised 1.	Hierarchical	Networked
How is it organised 2.	From top to bottom	Self-organising
Communication direction	One-way	Bi-directional/multi-directional
Type of communication 1.	Monologues	Dialogue
Type of communication 2.	From one to many	From many for many

So is it a brave new world? Indeed, in the early to mid-2000s, many people thought that Web 2.0 would bring a democratising form of communication that would be accessible and available to all, contributing to a better understanding of the world and to the un-indoctrinated development of the masses. In 2006, *Time* magazine awarded the title of 'Person of the Year' to the millions of users who were almost becoming journalists and editors in the process of creating content on the Internet. The designation they used was 'You'. Even the now iconic front page mimicked a Mac computer and the YouTube framework running on it.[27]

As Lev Grossman wrote in the magazine's usual editorial explainer, "The new Web is a very different thing. It's a tool for bringing together the small contributions of millions of people and making them matter. Silicon Valley consultants call it Web 2.0, as if it were a new version of some old software. But it's really a revolution."[28] While the decision has been attacked by many,[29] he was certainly right in realising that the media, their environment and their ecosystem would change significantly in the coming years. Grossman continued, "for seizing the reins of the global media, for founding and framing the new digital democracy, for working for nothing and beating the pros at their own game, TIME's Person of the Year for 2006 is you."[30] Dan Glimour summed it all up by calling it the 'new wave of journalism':

- "My readers know more than I do.
- That is not a threat, but rather an opportunity.
- We can use this together to create something between a seminar and a conversation, educating all of us.
- Interactivity and communications technology - in the form of e-mail, weblogs, discussion boards, web sites and more - make it happen."[31]

It would be easy to say they were wrong, because it would not become true. They were right in the basics: a brand new form of communication has indeed been created, the like of which humanity has never seen before in its history. For the first time, it was indeed possible to put communication, real dialogue, in the hands of

[27] http://content.time.com/time/covers/0,16641,20061225,00.html.

[28] Grossman (2006).

[29] Kedrosky (2006).

[30] Grossman (2006).

[31] Bowman and Willis (2003), p. 13.

the masses and not just in the hands of a privileged elite few.[32] If we think about the history of communication,[33] there has always been a threshold of entry that has prevented the masses from participating. Even if we do not go back to the beginning of the media, we only have to think of the codes before the printing of books, where access to paper, special ink and literacy all prevented participation.[34] Of course, the invention of printing contributed significantly to the development of the dissemination of information, but it took a few more years to make another qualitative leap. The emergence of the classical press and of monthly, weekly and then daily newspapers enabled a new (but still closed) circle of people to access information.[35] Then, in the 20th century, the spread of telephony,[36] radio[37] and television[38] allowed newer and newer layers of people to enter the communication process, but, as we have seen above, only as passive recipients. Thus, although radio, television or newspapers have become a significant part of everyday life, the possibility of transmitting information has been extended, but it has not become a forum for feedback, i.e. dialogue.

4.2 The Problems of Web 2.0, or the Myth of the Lawless Space Is Disappearing

The real dialogue—or, as Judge Stewart Dalzell wrote, "a never-ending, worldwide conversation" [39]—had to wait until the advent of Web 2.0 for the possibility of real communication via mass media,[40] so we should not be surprised at the optimism that surrounded it. This was reinforced—perhaps anticipating later problems—by the myth[41] that the Internet is an ancient, unregulated, lawless space. where communicators would be able to assert this unprecedented freedom of communication in a self-regulated way, independent of state regulation. As Anna Zanathy notes, "*Cyberlibertarianism*, as the theory's name implies, rejected the intervention of

[32] Speier (1952), pp. 305–317.; Foley Dabbaraccio (2021).

[33] Barbier and Lavenir (2009).

[34] Giles (1996), p. 613.

[35] King et al. (2019).

[36] Balni and Bert (2019), pp. 105–114.

[37] MacLennan (2020), pp. 191–207.

[38] Ellis (2003), pp. 278–285.

[39] *ACLU v Reno*, 929 F. Supp. 824 (E.D. Pa. 1996).

[40] An interesting project on the interface between old and new media was carried out in 2016 in the small Italian town of Civitacampomarano, called Web 0.0: "The provocative idea is to show that these virtual functions, considered by the vast majority of the population as necessary and essential to everyday life, also exist in the country, where the connection is hard to reach: this is a sort of Internet 'in real life'." http://www.biancoshock.com/web-00.html.

[41] Tambini et al. (2008), p. 294.

any state or international organisation and focused exclusively on self-regulation by users. It was based on the premise that, since the Internet is not subject to physical or geographical boundaries, cyberspace is by its very nature *de facto* unsuitable for legal regulation in the traditional sense."[42] As recently as 2008, the British politician and former Liberal Democrat leader Paddy Ashdown stated that "Is the internet a lawless space? Of course. Effectively, there are no laws, except in places like China. I'm a liberal, so I believe in the free flow of information (...)."[43] And this in the context of the adoption of a national report which already stated that terrorist and violent content on the internet was on the rise.[44]

In response to the problems of cyberlibertarianism, cyberpaternalism emerged as a system of thought that took the opposite approach to the regulatory issues of the internet.[45] They argued that the internet is nothing more than physical computers connected by cables, hence state regulation of the internet can be derived from the physicality of the internet and supranational regulation is not necessary. "According to those who advocate paternalistic regulation, there is no reason to regulate the internet within the framework of the presumptions surrounding freedom of expression: this claim no longer makes sense to them; there is no primacy of expression, there is nothing special about it."[46] A different view to both was taken in 1996 by Frank H. Easterbrook, who argued that the Internet did not need a separate, specific legal regime, as it was just the "The Law of the Horse",[47] and that it was enough to apply the rules already existing and in force in cyberspace.

The myth of a lawless space[48] was not sustainable for long: year by year, month by month, even day by day, it became increasingly apparent that this brave new world of Aldous Huxley's was anything but brave and new. For a long time, moreover, the lawless space was not really lawless at all, but a space free of state regulation, where rules were made by individuals and private companies, and where questions and problems were raised responsibly and with good reason.[49] The clash between private companies and the state and the various fundamental rights was not long in coming, as we shall soon see...

---

[42] Zanathy (2021a), p. 44.

[43] Espiner (2008).

[44] Ibid., p. 66.

[45] Murray (2011), pp. 195–221.

[46] Sajó and Clare (2016), p. 30.

[47] The term 'The Law of the Horse' comes from Gerhard Gasper, who argued that it is unnecessary to teach the application of legal provisions to specific cases as a separate subject in law school, i.e. for example, in the case of damage caused by a horse, it is not necessary to introduce 'The Law of the Horse' as a special subject in the curriculum, but that it is sufficient to teach general civil law rules. Easterbrook (1996), pp. 207–216. For more details see Gosztonyi (2021).

[48] Suzor (2019), pp. 1–2.

[49] Klein (2018), pp. 41–50.

4.2.1 *"If You Are Part of the Media, Will You Finally Be a Star?"*[50]

The changed media environment and the drastic lowering of the entry threshold have changed everything we call media. Today, if you can participate in global communication with an internet-connected mobile phone or computer, the Marshall McLuhan 'global village' was truly born.[51] But, as Péter Nádori put it, "the analogies drawn from previous relations have proved inadequate: the comment, the reblog, the tweet, the Tumblr post, the search hit, from a fixed perspective, can be equated with the reader's letter, the manifesto nailed to a light pole, the speech of the lone soapbox-speaker, the database query, or even the conversation between friends, but with the change of perspective, the qualities that break down the imposed frames become apparent."[52] Unfortunately, with all the difficulties that we know so well even from the news:

- Excessive atomisation of the internet and online communities;[53]
- The quality of of the knowledge created by the community;[54]
- The difficulty of obtaining reliable information (fake news, deepfake);[55]
- Economic risks that could lead to a second dotcom bubble;[56]
- The issue of information overload, where an unprecedented volume and wealth of information collides with a scarcity of attention of users;[57]
- The issue of junk content (data pollution, digital pollution, advertisements, pop-ups) that slows down web traffic;[58]
- An important feature of the early internet was anonymity, but today it has become a hotbed of abuse (cyberbullying, online inhibition, flame wars, revenge porn);[59]
- Censorship by private companies and states;
- Self-censorship.

As the world-renowned Polish philosopher-sociologist Zygmunt Bauman put it in a 2016 interview: "Social media does not teach us to have a dialogue because it is so easy to avoid debates... Most people don't use social media to find common ground with others, not to broaden their horizons but, on the contrary, to create a comfort

[50] Courtesy of Mátyás 'Doransky' Dobó.

[51] McLuhan (1962), p. 31. See also Bayer (2019), p. 8.

[52] Nádori (2014), p. 306.

[53] Brooks (2021).

[54] Grabner-Kräuter and Bitter (2015), pp. 48–68.

[55] Vaccari and Chadwick (2020), pp. 1–13.

[56] Kilmann (2021).

[57] IDF (2020).

[58] Ben-Shahar (2019), pp. 104–159.

[59] Namasudra et al. (2018).

zone where the only voice they hear is the echo of their own voice,[60] where the only image they see is a reflection of their own face. Social media are very useful, they give you pleasure, but it's really a trap."[61] And so, despite the expectations of many that they too would finally become stars, Andy Warhol's fifteen minutes of fame[62] have still reached only a few.

4.2.2 Web 3.0 as an Empty Buzzword or a Promise of a Solution?

Understanding Web 1.0 as an opportunity for a communications revolution, Web 2.0 s brought the realisation of collaboration and collective knowledge creation. But this realisation is being eroded in many places: by the people involved, by the (lack of) legal environment and by technological over-development. In terms of the development of new media in a person's lifetime, we have passed adolescence and have now come of age.[63] But trust is still missing. Just think of the problems described above, for which neither social science, nor media science, nor jurisprudence have yet been able to provide coherent answers. This brings us to the term that has recently become increasingly common: Web 3.0. The following nodes are emerging:

- An increased proportion of higher quality community content;
- Full freedom of communication (by which we mean both improving the legal environment and improving the technological and infrastructural conditions);
- Full personalisation (using the positive side of artificial intelligence).

What is certain is that "the Web 3.0 is envisioned to be associated with the evolution to an 'Intelligent Web',[64] and that we are talking about an artificial intelligence-driven system with a much higher degree of self-learning and self-awareness than we have today. Although there have been numerous scientific papers,[65] conferences and presentations on the subject, it is still not entirely clear whether we are talking about a genuine new innovation, a new type of AI, or merely a clever marketing gimmick.[66] The fact that—accepting the unimaginable and almost inconceivable scale of technological progress—there is now talk of not just

---

[60] Zanathy (2021b), pp. 95–99.

[61] de Querol (2016).

[62] Piechucka (2014).

[63] It is interesting to think about how many years it took for the new types of communication (books, newspapers, radio, television, internet) to become widespread. On this question, see LTE (2016).

[64] Yen et al. (2015), p. 5008.

[65] Hiremath and Kenchakkanavar (2016), pp. 705–710.; Prabhu (2016), pp. 54–62.

[66] Marlinspike (2022).

Web 3.0, but even Web 4.0 and Web 6.0,[67] is a reason for strong scepticism. In addition, the so-called semantic web, a "common framework that allows data to be shared and reused across application, enterprise, and community boundaries",[68] underpins Web 3.0 and is still evolving and is not yet a definitive change.[69]

From a legal point of view, it is worth mentioning a flagship project of the European Union, which is based on the same technology. The EU Open Data Portal[70] provides access to a wide range of datasets published and continuously updated by the European Union institutions, agencies and other bodies, as well as by the participating Member States. The datasets on the website are freely available for use. The portal is established by Article 5 of Commission Decision 2011/833/EU of 12 December 2011 on the re-use of Commission documents.[71]

4.3 Web 2.0 and Regulatory Issues

Let's go back from the doubtful future to the present: as we have seen, (A) a significant number of users have emerged and are now actively participating, (B) applications have been developed to serve the expressive needs of these users (social media being the main one, of course), and (C) all of this was surrounded by an almost vacuum of legal space in the first period. It is not particularly surprising that, as a result of these three circumstances, it was the private companies providing the services that established and set the conditions for participation by the users of the services. For a few years, this set-up was convenient and satisfactory for all concerned: the states could 'wash their hands' of any questionable issue by pointing to a tech company; the tech companies could act essentially free of external control, mainly in the interests of profit maximisation, while the masses of users could participate in an unprecedented media environment, almost entirely independent of the previous set of rules governing traditional media.

The new media have completely transformed our lives—both our private lives and our social lives—and no one was prepared for such a huge change. "Early commentators questioned how governments would respond to the spread of the Internet and whether an international approach to internet governance would develop."[72] While most shared Steve Hanley's thoughts that "Stymied legislative bodies find the Internet difficult to regulate, however, the present hands off approach

67 Khanzode et al. (2016), pp. 1–11.; Solanki and Dongaonkar (2016), pp. 75–78.

68 WWWC (2013).

69 Perhaps it would be more appropriate to use the term 'Next Generation Internet' (NGI), promoted by the European Union, which - wittily – uses the term 'Internet of Humans' (IoH) instead of 'Internet of Things' (IoT). https://www.ngi.eu/about/.

70 https://data.europa.eu/.

71 2011/833/EU.

72 Paslawsky (2017), p. 1487.

is creating a mockery of well-established law. Each country connected to the Internet may opt to either ignore Internet regulation or implement a system that supports an international scope and uphold each nations established jurisprudence",[73] a clear need for regulation has only come after the problems have multiplied. In addition, it should be pointed out that while the internet was born in the US and was based on the fullest guarantees of freedom of expression and privacy,[74] in Europe these were still only just accepted (albeit with modifications), but the internet soon spread to (legal) cultures where all these values are measured in different ways.[75]

Thus, the legal challenge is multidimensional: to bring within a legal framework a mass communication tool that is now used by millions and billions of people—on several continents—and is operated and owned by (mostly) American companies with a (basically) American approach, and to address (legal) issues that are reflected differently in different legal cultures (and even in different laws between countries with similar legal cultures). And then we are only talking about the legal situation, not the differences between social and political arrangements. Moreover, the internet has developed its own set of standards over the years, which users accept by their own implicit behaviour—by using it.[76]

Thus, regulatory states could easily find themselves in a situation where the subject matter of regulation could only be interpreted "at different and sometimes overlapping levels: from the local to the supra-national and global."[77] Thus "the vertical, centralized and state-based modes of traditional regulation have been complemented by collaborative horizontal arrangements, leading to 'a complex ecology of interdependent structures' with 'a vast array of formal and informal mechanisms working across a multiplicity of sites'".[78]

As to the moment when they could no longer do so, there is no consensus. It has to be sometime in the early 2010s, when events took place for the previously anonymous and voiceless masses to become active shapers of social media. Examples include the WikiLeaks scandal of 2010, the Arab Spring of early 2011, the London riots of 2011 and the Occupy Wall Street movement. However, the presentation and dissemination of terrorist attacks to the general public has also been greatly amplified by social media: the terrorist attacks of 11 September 2001 in New York, the Boston Marathon bombing, the mass bombing of the Bataclan Theatre in Paris, the attack on the mosques of Christchurch in New Zealand, and of course the Islamic State's rampage have all been significantly influenced by the tools and possibilities of the new media. And, unfortunately, this is also true of the presentation of natural disasters, whether you call it Hurricane Harvey, Irma, Maria or a magnitude 7.0 earthquake in Haiti or a huge tsunami in the Solomon Islands.

---

[73]Hanley (1998), pp. 1023–1024.

[74]Forgó (2016).

[75]Paslawsky (2017), p. 1489.

[76]Ibid., p. 1541.

[77]Raboy and Padovani (2010).

[78]Hintz (2015), p. 111.

Some of the coverage was live on social media, some was after the fact, but in neither case was the mass impact missed. Moreover, the 2016 US presidential election and the referendum on the UK's withdrawal from the European Union, *Brexit*, came later. After that, by the mid-2000s, political actors and the states they governed could no longer look the other way: they could not allow the so-called 'privatised' regulation by social media companies,[79] in other words, the outsourcing of the state's regulatory needs, to continue. As Jack M. Balkin put it in his seminal work, "Nation states, understanding this, have developed new techniques for speech regulation. In addition to targeting speakers directly, they now target the owners of private infrastructure, hoping to coerce or co-opt them into regulating speech on the nation state's behalf."[80] At this moment, then, the ideas of the first paragraph of John Perry Barlow's famous manifesto from 1996, "Governments of the Industrial World, you weary giants of flesh and steel, I come from Cyberspace, the new home of Mind. On behalf of the future, I ask you of the past to leave us alone. You are not welcome among us. You have no sovereignty where we gather."[81]

4.4 The Intertwined American and European Sovereignty

"The 2010s will be remembered for a new era in the development of capitalism, one of mind-boggling scale. Apple, Amazon and Microsoft are closing the decade as the world's first trillion-dollar companies. Last year,[82] Apple's revenue was larger than Vietnam's GDP, while Amazon's research and development spending alone is almost as much as Iceland's GDP. Facebook boasts 2.4 billion users, a population larger than that of every continent except Asia."[83] Jay Owens' late 2019 article accurately describes a change we have seen since the 2010s: the rise of giant tech companies that countries are trying to bring under the umbrella of state regulation in some way—by words, by begging, or even by force. However, we have seen that new media and regulation are not always easy to bring together on the same platform.

The 'big two'—Europe and the United States—have tried and failed to regulate the market in recent years. In 2010, the European Commission decided to open an antitrust investigation into allegations that Google had abused its dominant position in online searching, in violation of Article 102 of the Treaty on the Functioning of the European Union (TFEU).[84] However, the case was only concluded in 2017,

---

[79] Ibid., pp. 109–126.

[80] Balkin (2018), p. 1153.

[81] Barlow (1996).

[82] 2018 – T*he author.*

[83] Owens (2019).

[84] Consolidated versions of the Treaty on European Union and the Treaty on the Functioning of the European Union.

when the European Commission found that "the more favourable positioning and display by Google Inc. ('Google'), in its general search results pages, of its own comparison shopping service compared to competing comparison shopping services, infringes Article 102 TFEU and Article 54 of the EEA Agreement."[85] The fine imposed amounted to €2,424,495,000. In the US, Facebook reached an agreement with the Federal Trade Commission (FTC) in 2011 regarding the illegal disclosure of user data.[86] The FTC has also taken action against Google on the same grounds.[87] These early years—in which it became increasingly clear that states would take some kind of action against the overreach of tech giants—were more about using soft-power; in other words, seeking out the possibility of settlements and getting tech companies to make independent commitments to comply with the law.

The stakes have been rising since the mid-2010s: "The debate on platform regulation picks up from 2014. First, with the fall-out from the Facebook/WhatsApp deal,[88] which kick-started a public debate on mergers and acquisitions by digital platforms. Then in 2018, the Cambridge Analytica scandal[89] ramps up the volume of the debate on privacy by large platforms, and provides the political lever for starting to design regulatory frameworks for the big digital platforms, at least in Europe."[90] Moreover, all this has happened after the adoption of the European Union's General Data Protection Regulation (commonly known as the GDPR[91]), making regulation of the internet (and the platform providers that underpin social media) seem more realistic than ever before. But before planning for the 2020s, it is worth looking at the way in which the US and the European Union have tried to regulate new media liability issues, and the codification processes that, 20–25 years ago set up two different types of liability regimes.

4.4.1 Communication Decency Act

As we have seen, the myth of a lawless space has been dispelled and it is becoming increasingly apparent that, in line with US litigation patterns, internet companies will be exposed to lawsuits in which they will be held liable for providing a forum for infringing content, and the litigation costs and the penalty imposed will make it impossible for them to grow.

---

[85] C(2017) 4444.

[86] https://www.ftc.gov/news-events/press-releases/2011/11/facebook-settles-ftc-charges-it-deceived-consumers-failing-keep.

[87] https://www.ftc.gov/about-ftc/foia/frequently-requested-records/foia-records/google/2012-00465.

[88] Deutsch (2022).

[89] Hu (2020), pp. 1–6.

[90] Abate (2020).

[91] Regulation (EU) 2016/679.

In the first key case, Don Fitzpatrick published a daily newsletter in the early nineties called 'Rumorville', which published news and gossip about journalists and the industry in which they worked. The newsletter was available to CompuServe users who subscribed to the CompuServe Journalists' Forum, one of a number of CompuServe's electronic forums and electronic bulletin boards, which was operated by third parties. Robert Blanchard and his company, Cubby, developed a similar newsletter called 'Skuttlebut'. Both Fitzpatrick and CompuServe were smeared by Cubby for spreading false information. [92] The grounds for suing CompuServe were that Cubby claimed that it was acting as a publisher and was therefore responsible for the content it placed on the site. The court found that, because CompuServe had no prior knowledge of the content that Fitzpatrick would be publishing on Rumorville, it was merely a distributor, not a publisher. The court ruled that "CompuServe has no more editorial control over such a publication than does a public library, book store, or newsstand."

A few years later, in the autumn of 1994, an unknown user on a forum of the then very popular—now defunct—Prodigy company made comments about Stratton Oakmont and its president, Daniel Porush, that they were committing fraud. The company and its president sued the anonymous commenter. [93] The legal question was whether Prodigy was a publisher, in which case it would be liable for the content it posted even if it did not post it, or merely a distributor, in which case it would be exempt from liability and the person who posted the content would bear the consequences alone. In the course of the court proceedings, Prodigy was found to have guidelines for users on what content is not desirable; it employed human moderators and had a (rudimentary but functioning) filtering system to weed out offensive content, hence, although the court noted in its judgment that forums are in principle distributors, Prodigy was a publisher by virtue of its editorial activity in relation to the forum, which gave it liability. Prodigy appealed against the judgment, but we will never know what the outcome of the appeal would have been: in October 1995, the parties reached an out-of-court settlement.

This was a major change from the CompuServe ruling and stirred up public opinion in the US legal community. The divergent rulings in the two cases raise the question of whether it is worthwhile to moderate or censor, since, if the Internet company does not do so, it is merely a distributor; that is, it is exempt from liability. This, however, contradicts the need to curb problematic content on the Internet, since a lack of law and liability would have perpetuated the Wild West (or, in Alfred

[92] *Cubby, Inc. v Compuserve Inc.*, 776 F. Supp. 135 (S.D.N.Y. 1991).

[93] *Stratton Oakmont, Inc. v Prodigy Servs.* , (N.Y. Sup. Ct. May 24, 1995).

C. Yen's words, "western frontier"[94]), where anything goes, whether good or bad.[95]

To solve this problem, Republican Chris Cox and Democrat Ron Wyden have proposed an amendment to the Telecommunications Act.[96] The Telecommunications Act was a huge step forward in itself, amending the Communications Act of 1934 after sixty years, and providing a new regulatory framework for a significantly changed communications environment. For the first time, the Internet appeared as a subject of regulation,[97] but the key was the Cox-Wyden section, which was incorporated into Section 230(c)(1) of Chapter V of the Act (commonly known as the Communications Decency Act).[98] Twenty-six short words in English completely rewrote the history of the Internet:[99] "No provider or user of an interactive computer service shall be treated as the publisher or speaker of any information provided by another information content provider." In addition, Section 230(c)(2) also includes 'good Samaritan' protections against civil liability for the removal or moderation of speech the service provider deems obscene or offensive, even constitutionally protected speech, so long as they act in good faith.

With these two regulatory solutions, the state in fact—as we have seen earlier—'privatised' the issue of protecting freedom of expression and the decisions to remove illegal or harmful content. To put it simply, we could say that all the tools needed to remove content have been placed, in good faith, in the hands of the service providers. "It gave internet startups and their investors the confidence that they could fill their platforms with content from ordinary users, without attracting any legal liability for anything those users might write."[100] It does not take much courage to say that this legal regulation has enabled the internet to grow exponentially over the last two decades. It also meant progress, but it has embedded the problems of the present, too. Because—and this is where we come to the issue of economic censorship—if operators considered that a user or a piece of content was not in their interests, they had the legal power to remove it. It was not called censorship, but, in reality, that is what happened. And it is the same with the infamous paedophile comments on

---

[94] Yen (2002), p. 1210. It is very interesting to read his comments on his own study almost twenty years later: Yen (2020), pp. 134–148. "These companies — Facebook, YouTube, Twitter, Google, and their competitors and successors — are the new governors of digital expression. They develop and enforce their terms of service, end-user license agreements, and internal company policies, applying them to end- users and community members. They operate in many different countries but are privately owned. Some of them are richer than some of the countries in which they do business." Balkin (2018), p. 1188.

[95] Levy (2017).

[96] For details, see Cox (2020).

[97] Cf. however, "The word 'internet' appears only 11 times in that law, and 10 of them are in Section 230." Milton (2021).

[98] It follows that although Section 230 is part of the Telecommunications Act, it is referred to in both legal and common parlance as CDA230, referring to Chapter V (Communications Decency Act). Communications Decency Act (CDA), Pub. L. No. 104-104 (Tit. V), 110 Stat. 133 (8 Feb, 1996).

[99] Kosseff (2019).

[100] Reynolds (2019).

YouTube, the swastika shoes sold on Amazon or the video footage of the Christchurch massacre. Even though these companies have grown to have unimaginable economic power, CDA230 gives them almost unlimited immunity—whether they restrict content or users upload unacceptable content. The flip side of the question, however, is whether the aforementioned Wild West would really have come about without CDA230. Knowing the history of communication, let there be no doubt...

To answer the above, it is worth looking at the story of Kenneth Zeran through his court case. [101] After the Oklahoma City bombing, an unknown person started selling merchandise glorifying it with a message on the forum on which it was advertised saying "Ask for Ken" and "Due to high demand please call back if busy." The phone number belonged to Zeran, who had no idea what had happened. To this day it has not been possible to find out who posted the message, but Zeran received hundreds of threatening phone calls.[102] He Zeran sued AOL for not doing everything possible to remove the original message and copies of it from its platform. AOL's position was that CDA230 gives it full immunity for content uploaded by third parties, even if it knew the content was illegal. The US Court of First Instance and the US Court of Appeals upheld AOL under CDA230(c)(1) and did not consider the applicability of CDA230(c)(2). Immunity appears complete on this basis.[103]

This immunity[104] has been challenged several times over the years, [105] while the need to amend the CDA has been reinforced after 2020. This was based on the then President Donald Trump's signing into law of the Fight Against Online Sex Trafficking Act (FOSTA),[106] which created an exemption from the CDA230. Under the Act, the relevant section cannot be invoked if the content in question gives rise to civil or criminal liability for conduct that promotes or facilitates sex trafficking or prostitution. The adoption of the law has been widely criticised, with the Electronic Frontier Foundation stating that the bill "silences online speech by forcing Internet platforms to censor their users."[107] The law is also retroactive, which even the

[101] *Zeran v America Online, Inc.*, 129 F.3d 327 (4th Cir. 1997), cert. denied, 524 U.S. 937 (1998). In details see: Gosztonyi (2022).

[102] Another reason is that Oklahoma's KRXO Radio scanned the news and urged their listeners to feel free to call the number provided. *Zeran v Diamond Broadcasting, Inc.*, 19 F. Supp. 2d 1249 (W.D. Okla. 1997), 203 F.3d 714 (10th Cir. 2000).

[103] However, it should be stressed that "The private platforms regulated or protected by Section 230 are not government actors and therefore are not subject to First Amendment constraints. But, like the First Amendment, Section 230 operates as a constraint on defamation law." Cohen et al. (2021), p. 5.

[104] Citron and Wittes (2018), pp. 453–473.

[105] *Force v Facebook, Inc.*, 934 F.3d 53, 64 (2d Cir. 2019), cert. denied, 140 S. Ct. 2761 (2020); *Marshall's Locksmith Serv. Inc. v Google, LLC*, 925 F.3d 1263, 1267 (D.C. Cir. 2019); *Enigma Software Grp. U.S.A v Malwarebytes, Inc.*, 946 F.3d 1040, 1052 (9th Cir. 2019), cert. denied, 141 S. Ct. 13, 208 L. Ed. 2d 197 (2020).

[106] Allow States and Victims to Fight Online Sex Trafficking Act of 2017. The Act is often referred to as the FOSTA/SESTA Act in the United States, as an earlier version was known as the Stop Enabling Sex Traffickers Act (SESTA).

[107] Harmon (2018).

Ministry of Justice has not agreed with.[108] Critics argue that the law is more flawed in terms of content, since it does not protect victims in the main, but for us it is the violation of freedom of expression that is more problematic. "No matter what methods platforms use to mitigate their risk, one thing is certain: when platforms choose to err on the side of censorship, marginalized voices are censored disproportionately."[109] It seems that the law being passed was more for political reasons (according to a report published in June 2021,[110] only one such exception to CDA230 has been used in three years), and adding more exceptions to the CDA230 is causing more problems than it solves.[111] The issue of censorship is back on the agenda. As Nicolas P. Suzor put it, platforms are "judges, jurors and executioners"[112] at the same time."

4.4.2 The TWF and AVMS Directives

The European internal market,[113] also known as the Single Market, was created on 1 January 1993 and has brought many benefits to the then 12—now many more—Member States and their citizens, as well as to other countries through various agreements within the framework of the European Economic Area. The Single Market is based on the 'four freedoms'[114]—free movement of persons, services, goods and capital—enshrined in the TFEU. However, as Perry Keller writes, "the media sector has presented a huge challenge for the project of creating a European Single Market."[115] The reasons for this are several: first, European media regulation sees the media market not only as an economic issue but also as a cultural and human rights issue; second, broadcasting in Europe has traditionally been organised with considerable state support and intervention, making it more difficult for national governments to create common European rules in this field; and, third, common European rules have hardly been able to keep pace with fast technological evolution. Despite this, audiovisual media services and the internet, as we now call them, were from the outset clearly categorised as goods (e.g. print media, CDs, DVDs) and services (e.g. radio, television), and their free movement often clashed with the

[108] https://www.eff.org/files/2018/03/19/doj-sesta.pdf.

[109] Harmon (2018).

[110] GAO-21-385.

[111] Although this book avoids an examination of copyright issues, it is worth examining, tangentially related to the topic, the US removal rules for copyright infringement in the Copyright Act of 1998. The Digital Millennium Copyright Act (DMCA), Pub. L. No. 105-304, 112 Stat. 2860 (Oct. 28, 1998). Urban et al. (2017), pp. 15–19.; Chemerinsky and Chemerinsky (2022), p. 93.

[112] Suzor (2019), p. 73.; Cf. "at extreme, they become the police, judge, jury and excecutioner". McNamee (2011), p. 4.

[113] European Parliament (2012).

[114] Barnard (2019), pp. 28–30.

[115] Keller (2011), p. 115.

historically closed national will in this area. At the time, media companies seeking a more favourable regulatory environment pushed for single European regulatory framework, as it would allow them to operate in a more favourable economic, regulatory (and possibly political) environment than their national counterparts. The European Court of Justice has confirmed in several cases[116] that, as a general rule, no legal restrictions can be imposed on cross-border television broadcasting. As Petra Lea Láncos puts it: "European integration and in particular, the development of EU media law can also be explained through the theory on competition between national legal systems."[117] It was in these circumstances, after lengthy negotiations and consultations, that the Television without Frontiers (TWF) Directive was born.[118] "The TWF Directive, the forerunner to the AVMS Directive, is the main regulatory instrument for the audiovisual sector in Europe."[119] It lays down two key points that have subsequently been used to regulate internet services: the principle of free movement of services and the country of origin principle."[120]

Already with this directive, the difference from the competition-based approach to regulation in the United States of America was apparent: the media in Europe play a prominent role in maintaining and transmitting democratic rules, as well as in maintaining, developing and disseminating cultural, social and societal aspects. Moreover, while technological developments brought changes to the TWF relatively quickly onto the agenda,[121] the European Commission's 1999 formulation has remained unchanged throughout the process: "The audiovisual media play a central role in the functioning of modern democratic societies. Without the free flow of information; such societies cannot function. Moreover, the audiovisual media play a fundamental role in the development and transmission of social values. This is not simply because they influence, to a large degree, which facts about and which images of the world we encounter, but also because they provide concepts and categories—political, social, ethnic, geographical, psychological and so on—which we use to render these facts and images intelligible. They therefore help not only to determine what we see of the world but also how we see it. The audiovisual industry is therefore not an industry like any other and does not simply produce goods to be sold on the market like other goods."[122]

With all these principles in mind, while ensuring competition in the market, and with the exponential technological development of the industry, it became clear over

---

[116]"Conditions affecting the structure of foreign broadcasting bodies cannot therefore be regarded as being objectively necessary in order to safeguard the general interest in maintaining a national radio and television system which secures pluralism." *Stichting Collectieve Antennevoorziening Gouda and others v Commissariaat voor de Media*. CJEU, C-288/89, 1991, I-04007, [25].

[117]Láncos (2022), p. 50.

[118]Council Directive 89/552/EEC.

[119]Katsirea (2014), p. 297.

[120]Herold (2008), pp. 5–24.; Polyák and Szőke (2009), pp. 83–97.

[121]Drijber (1999), p. 87.

[122]COM/99/0657 final, [8].

time that the TWF's patchwork approach would not yield sufficient results, and a new directive was needed, which would now not only affect the television segment but the entire industry, which has now become audiovisual. In 2010, this became the Audiovisual Media Services Directive,[123] in which the word 'internet' appears only three times (and basically all of them in an innocuous context). Although the situation with video-sharing services and on-demand audiovisual media services changed later, it soon became clear that the rules on the internet could not be properly dealt with in the TWF-AVMS framework by 'rewriting' the old rules.

4.4.3 Directive on Electronic Commerce

The regulation of internet services in Europe has not been without its problems. Already when the TWF was amended in 1997, it was suggested that the new audiovisual regulation should cover this area, but this proposal failed in the European Parliament.[124] A formal distinction has thus emerged between traditional media services, where the provider determines the time of consumption of the content, and Internet-based services, where the consumer can determine this. Thus was born the concept of 'information society services', which has become one of the key concepts in the twenty years since the adoption, on 8 June 2000, of the Directive on electronic commerce (ECD),[125] which regulated digital services.[126] The ECD underlines[127] that the concept itself is not a product of the text from 2000, as it was already found in earlier Directives,[128] and provides a definition of the concept with a definitive intent, namely what services are covered and what services are not. It stresses that "information society services span a wide range of economic activities which take place on-line."[129]

It falls within this broad range:[130]

- selling goods online;
- online contracting;
- offering online information (as a commercial activity);
- offering commercial communications;
- providing tools allowing for search, access and retrieval of data;

---

[123] Directive 2010/13/EU.

[124] Keller (1998), p. 188.

[125] Directive 2000/31/EC.

[126] It should be noted here that the DSA legislation analysed later in the book (see Sect. 6.1) supersedes some parts of the ECD, but to understand the current legislation it is necessary to look at the history.

[127] Directive 2000/31/EC, Recital 17.

[128] Directive 98/34/EC; Directive 98/84/EC.

[129] ECD, Recital 18.

[130] Ibid.

- transmission of information via a communication network;
- providing access to a communication network;
- hosting information provided by a recipient of the service;
- video-on-demand services;
- providing commercial communications by electronic mail.

But it does not include:[131]

- delivery of goods as such;
- provision of services offline;
- television broadcasting;
- radio broadcasting;
- using of electronic mail or equivalent individual communications by natural persons (when acting outside their trade, business or profession);
- contractual relationship between an employee and their employer;
- activities which, by their very nature, cannot be carried out at a distance and by electronic means (e. g. statutory auditing of company accounts or medical advice requiring the physical examination of a patient).

The ECD thus contributes to the proper functioning of the internal market by ensuring the free movement of information society services between Member States. As can be seen from the above list, Internet service providers (including the then nascent social media) were brought within the scope of the ECD in the early 2000s, rather than the TWF Directive. However, it is clear throughout from the careful wording of the regulation that it reflects "the policy consensus that the internet should not be brought under existing media regulatory regimes",[132] thus forming a kind of transition between the early internet's legal vacuum and traditional state regulation.

On a key issue for the internet, namely who can be held liable for infringing content, the European Union has developed a different regime from the CDA230 rules outlined above.[133] The central element is Section 4 of the ECD, entitled 'Liability of intermediary service providers'. The rules use a threefold set of definitions, the first two of which ('mere conduit' and 'caching') give service providers similar immunity from liability as under the US system.

For simple transmission, the provider:

- does not initiate the transmission;
- does not select the receiver of the transmission; and
- does not select or modify the information contained in the transmission.[134]

In the case of caching, the provider

[131] Ibid.

[132] Keller (2011), p. 151.

[133] Wendehorst (2016), pp. 30–33.

[134] ECD, Section 4, Article 12.

- does not modify the information;
- complies with conditions on access to the information;
- complies with rules regarding the updating of the information, specified in a manner widely recognised and used by industry;
- does not interfere with the lawful use of technology, widely recognised and used by industry, to obtain data on the use of the information; and
- acts expeditiously to remove or to disable access to the information it has stored upon obtaining actual knowledge of the fact that the information at the initial source of the transmission has been removed from the network, or access to it has been disabled, or that a court or an administrative authority has ordered such removal or disablement.[135]

If these conditions are met, the service provider exemption also applies to infringing content. More interesting, however, is the issue of the liability of hosting providers, the rules for which are set out in Article 14. Under this, the provider is in principle liable for the content hosted on it and is exempted from liability if:

- it does not have actual knowledge of illegal activity or information and, as regards claims for damages, is not aware of facts or circumstances from which the illegal activity or information is apparent; or
- upon obtaining such knowledge or awareness, acts expeditiously to remove or to disable access to the information.[136]

The (relative)[137] novelty of the European system is therefore this commonly used 'notice and take-down system' (NTDS),[138] which has thus introduced a multi-step system of conditions and procedures: the intermediary service provider must be aware of content that is manifestly illegal and must take steps to remove it within a specified time. It can therefore be concluded that, in contrast to the US legislation, the European Union has opted for a different model (also known as the *safe harbour model*[139]), which focuses on a non-automatic exemption.[140] Although there have been debates since the adoption of the Directive on a number of issues (such as when to declare that the provider has actual knowledge; what is 'manifestly illegal content'; what is the time limit within which the provider must act; and whether we are talking about an active or passive type of provider, but some have suggested

[135] Ibid., Article 13.

[136] Ibid., Article 14.

[137] The procedure already appears in the 1998 US DMCA, but it applies only to copyright infringement there. For a comparison, see Peguera (2009), pp. 481–512.

[138] De Streel et al. (2020), p. 10.

[139] Madiega (2020), pp. 1–2.

[140] It is important to note, however, ECD, Section 4, Article 14(3), which states: "This Article shall not affect the possibility for a court or administrative authority, in accordance with Member States' legal systems, to require the service provider to terminate or prevent an infringement, nor does it affect the possibility for Member States of establishing procedures governing the removal or disabling of access to information."

that there should be more than one type of procedure for different types of content).[141] An examination of these issues—without which it is not possible to determine whether content has been lawfully removed or whether there are censorship effects—is covered in Sect. 9 of the book.

In addition to the NTDS, the provisions of Article 15 of the ECD should be highlighted,[142] as it is stated, in addition to the above provisions, that Member States shall not impose a general obligation on service providers to *(a) monitor the* information they transmit or store or (b) investigate facts or circumstances indicating illegal activity ('no general obligation to monitor').[143] This rule does not oblige service providers, and therefore not social media either, to monitor content posted on their sites on a continuous basis.[144] It should be borne in mind, however, that the regulation was adopted in 2000, and that, in the 2020s, a growing number of Member States have considered changing this rule.[145]

4.4.4 *Towards a Digital Single Market as the Co-Regulation Period*

In this process, it has become increasingly clear to all parties involved that the rules of the European Single Market need to be translated into the digital space. This process of making the digital marketplace as complete as possible began in 2015, when the European Commission published its Communication on a Digital Single Market Strategy for Europe.[146] The document states that "A Digital Single Market is one in which the free movement of goods, persons, services and capital is ensured and where individuals and businesses can seamlessly access and exercise online activities under conditions of fair competition, and a high level of consumer and personal data protection, irrespective of their nationality or place of residence. Achieving a Digital Single Market will ensure that Europe maintains its position as a world leader in the digital economy, helping European companies to grow

[141] Although this book avoids examining copyright issues, it is worth considering the European removal rules for copyright infringement in the 2019 Copyright Directive as a tangential link to the topic. Directive (EU) 2019/790. See Romero-Moreno (2019); Mezei and Lábody (2022); Grad-Gyenge (2022).

[142] Oster (2017), pp. 234–236.

[143] However, it must be stressed – as has been addressed in subsequent case law – that ECD, Recital 47 states that "this does not concern monitoring obligations in a specific case and, in particular, does not affect orders by national authorities in accordance with national legislation."

[144] van Hoboken et al. (2018), pp. 45–47.

[145] Article 28(b) of the AVMS is also a new challenge for reconciling the prohibition on general monitoring obligations and the safe harbour regime. C/2020/4322.

[146] COM(2015) 192 final.

globally."[147] Zoltán Angyal has identified three pillars[148] within which the sixteen targeted actions are located:

- making online products and services more accessible to European consumers;
- creating the conditions and a level playing field for digital networks and innovative services to flourish; and
- maximising the growth potential of the digital economy.

The second pillar is the most important one for this book's topic, as it involves reviewing the framework for audiovisual media and adapting it to the twenty-first century, analysing the role of internet platforms in the digital single market and assessing how to tackle illegal content on the internet. By 2015, both television broadcasting and on-demand audiovisual media services will be covered by the AVMS Directive, which sets common minimum standards for both services. However, as the document states, "the Commission will examine whether the current system of rules applying to broadcast and to on-demand services should be adapted. It will also consider whether the current scope or the rules should be broadened to encompass new services and players that are currently not considered as audiovisual media services under the Directive and/or providers that fall outside its current geographical scope."[149] In relation to the increasing market power and concentration of platform providers,[150] the Communication identified a number of concerns:[151] from the lack of transparency in the use of information obtained to the advertising of their own products to the detriment of competitors, to the unpredictability of pricing problems. In addition, it identified a number of areas[152] where the Commission will begin to investigate, which have been given legal form in subsequent draft regulations:

- transparency of search results (paid links and/or advertising);
- the use of data collected by the platforms;
- the relationship between platforms and users;
- limiting the ability of individuals and entrepreneurs to switch from one platform to another; and
- the most effective ways to combat illegal content on the internet.

---

[147] Ibid., 1.

[148] Angyal (2020), p. 6.

[149] COM(2015) 192 final, 3.2.

[150] The situation has not improved, but rather deteriorated: by the middle of 2022; four of the seven leading social media platforms (Facebook, WhatsApp, Instagram and Messenger) were be owned by the very same company.

[151] COM(2015) 192 final, 3.3.1.

[152] Ibid., 3.3.2.

Two important steps in this investigation were the adoption and signing of two Codes of Conduct.[153] To quote Petra Lea Láncos: "the regulatory choice of soft law is strategical to provide a frame of reference for the Member States without taking a step towards harmonisation in a field pertaining to the realm of interventionist measures."[154] The first was the EU Code of Conduct on countering illegal hate speech online, whereby four tech mammoths (Facebook, Microsoft, Twitter, YouTube[155]) committed to, among other things, reviewing valid reports of unlawful hate speech within 24 hours and removing or making such content inaccessible.[156] For removal of this type of content, the Code found the NTDS to be an appropriate solution. In 2018, Facebook, Google, Twitter and Mozilla,[157] some of the world's biggest tech companies, also signed the EU Code of Practice on Disinformation. The adoption of the Codes was preceded by a recent European Commission Communication on online misinformation[158] which indicated the responsibility of platform providers on the issue. As such, there was no—well communicated—alternative for tech companies than signing the Code by.[159] Moreover, the Codes[160]—which are only applicable to signatories—cannot be considered as a real regulatory, definitional solution from a legal point of view, as it is important to underline that they "shall apply within the framework of existing laws of the EU and its Member States and must not be construed in any way as replacing, superseding or interpreting the existing and future legal framework."[161] For example, the commitments undertaken by the signatories include:

- scrutiny of ad placements;
- examining political and issue-focused advertising;
- the integrity of services;
- reinforcing informed consumer behaviour; and
- strengthening the role of the research community.[162]

[153] Self-regulation and co-regulation have gained prominence in those years as alternatives to more restrictive forms of government regulation.

[154] Láncos (2022), p. 60.

[155] TikTok also joined the Code of Conduct on countering illegal hate speech online in 2020 and LinkedIn in 2021.

[156] The sixth evaluation in 2021 found that "while the average of notifications reviewed within 24 hours remains high (81%), it has decreased compared to 2020 (90.4%). At 62.5% the average removal rate was also lower than in 2019 and 2020." Reynders (2021).

[157] Microsoft also joined the Code of Practice on Disinformation in 2019 and TikTok in 2020.

[158] COM(2018) 236 final.

[159] Colliver (2019).

[160] A Strengthened Code of Practice on Disinformation was issued on 16 June 2022 with a more diverse range of stakeholders. Their commitments include demonetising the dissemination of disinformation, guaranteeing transparency of political advertising, enhancing cooperation with fact-checkers, and facilitating researchers access to data. https://ec.europa.eu/newsroom/dae/redirection/document/87585.

[161] Ibid., Preamble, (q).

[162] Twitter already left it in 2023. DW (2023).

At the same time, as Matteo Monti comments on the document, "in the European scenario, both at the EU level and the level of the Member States, there seems to be a trend that encourages and favours the privatisation of censorship."[163] However, it is positive that, in their commitments, the signatories are investing in technical tools to help achieve these goals and are developing active partnerships with civil society, governments, educational institutions and other stakeholders.[164]

This active, proactive role on the part of the European Union is "shifting the balance of power away from the US and towards Europe for the first time in the internet's history."[165] And because the companies that adopted the two codes of conduct also had to modify their own terms of service to comply with their voluntary commitments, "these companies essentially agreed to apply European rules to every one of their users globally."[166] Service providers have thus moved from a period of pure self-regulation to, in the words of Christopher T. Marsden, "the incoming tide of Internet co-regulation."[167]

4.4.5 Amendment of the AVMS Directive

The explosion in the use of social media video-sharing platforms[168] and on-demand audiovisual media services has made it clear that the previous legal approach of adopting legislation that is relevant to the current situation but does not take technological developments into account is no longer a viable option. Recent years have made it clear that, in the media field, 8–10 years is now like 40–50 years. As Klára Gellén put it, "the definition of the scope is one of the most sensitive issues of the AVMS Directive. Sometimes it is very difficult to distinguish the nature of a service and whether it falls within the scope of media regulation."[169] Similarly, the regulatory differences between traditional media services and internet-based services had to be reconsidered,[170] as all the indications were that convergence would be strengthened in this area.[171] As a consequence, on-demand audiovisual media services were moved from the scope of the 2000 ECD to the AVMS in order to operate within a single legal framework.[172] It should be noted that the legislator was already struggling to reconcile traditional broadcasting and communications with the

---

[163] Monti (2020), p. 219.

[164] Wilman (2020).

[165] Reynolds (2019).

[166] Ibid.

[167] Marsden (2011), p. 5.

[168] Sorbán (2019), p. 213.

[169] Gellén (2018), p. 82.

[170] See in more detail Cabrera et al. (2018).

[171] On the country-of-origin principle, see Kokoly (2020), pp. 83–103.

[172] On the fragmented European regulation of video-sharing platforms, see Capello (2021).

ever-changing terminology of the internet, "following the creation of the AVMS Directive in 2010, media convergence (again[173]) made it necessary to update the legal framework, and an amendment to the AVMS was finally adopted in November 2018.[174] The scope of the Directive (with additional elements[175]) has been extended to include social media platforms as important actors in entertainment and education."[176] While there are indeed some social media platforms that are now automatically covered by the AVMS (such as YouTube, Vimeo or streaming and its different variants: VOD, Catch-Up TV, OTT), it is not yet clear which social media platforms will be excluded from the scope.[177]

The crucial question here is to define what these platforms' essential function is. The European Commission has issued a non-binding guidance[178] on the subject in July 2020, which will allow a decision to be taken on the applicability of the AVMS rules based on a common assessment of quantitative and qualitative criteria. The following can be summarised in this context:

- "Economic relevance of the audio-visual content for the platform;
- The amount, use and reach of the audio-visual content for the platform;
- Relevance of monetization or revenue generation from the audio-visual content;
- Tools aiming at enhancing the visibility and attractiveness of audio-visual content."[179]

Transposed into national law, it does not seem realistic at this stage that all Member States will consider exactly the same services to be covered, so the administrative and judicial practice will be very interesting in the future. Ireland is particularly worthy of consideration in this respect, as a number of US social media platforms are based in the country. In implementing AVMS, Ireland could adopt a new law that would clearly extend its scope to all social media providers.[180] The new Media Authority, as indicated by Cathrine Martin, Irish Minister (also) responsible for Media, "will have a role in regulating certain companies with a European headquarters established in Ireland on a pan-EU basis. This includes a number of major global companies such as Apple, YouTube and Facebook."[181] The Irish implementation sought to clarify the European Commission's guidance and used the following delimitation questions:

[173] Interpretative insertion by the author.

[174] Directive (EU) 2018/1808.

[175] Interpretative insertion by the author.

[176] Kelemen (2021).

[177] Kukliš (2021).

[178] C/2020/4322.

[179] König (2020).

[180] Ireland was the last country to notify the European Commission of the transposition of the AVMS in its national legislation. Sboarina (2023).

[181] Newstalk (2020).

- "The relationship between the audiovisual content and the main activity of the service (e.g., is the video-sharing element a 'standalone' feature or does it merely facilitate economic transactions?);
- The quantitative and qualitative relevance of audiovisual content for the activities of the service (e.g., are there a significant number of videos with a large reach?)
- Monetisation or revenue generation from the audiovisual content (e.g., do customers pay for access? Do videos have advertisements?)
- Availability of tools enhancing the visibility or attractiveness of content (e.g., are the videos promoted on the website? Are tools such as filters, sharing options and live chats specifically linked to the videos?)"[182]

4.4.6 A New European Regulatory Framework at the Horizon

With the GDPR, the European Union has set an excellent agenda that has been elaborated and is seen as worthy of emulation by many parts of the world,[183] it is no wonder that it has also set an exemplary approach to regulating tech companies.[184] In many respects, the actions outlined above have shown the European continent to be much more active and proactive than in previous years.

The problem that had to be faced, however, is that "the way the E-commerce Directive has been implemented across the EU varies greatly and that national jurisprudence on online liability today remains very fragmented."[185] This is compounded by the 'Good Samaritan paradox',[186] whereby platform providers prefer to remain passive, losing the possibility of immunity from liability if they are active. Twenty years have passed since the adoption of the ECD on 8 June 2000, and it still governs digital services today. In a market that is changing so rapidly, this is not a short time, as regulatory solutions that seemed forward-looking in 2000 have often lost their relevance today. This has been seen in practice, with the European Union following the US and other countries in taking action against the perceived or real dominance of digital giants. For example, in 2017 Facebook was fined €110 million,[187] and, between 2017 and 2019, Google was fined a record €8.2 billion for systematic and systemic breaches of competition rules,[188] while in late 2020 Amazon was prosecuted for antitrust violations. [189] The fact that these fines have been

[182] Andrews et al. (2021).

[183] Li et al. (2019), pp. 1–6.; Hoofnagle et al. (2019), pp. 65–98.; Feiler et al. (2018).

[184] De Gregorio (2019).

[185] Madiega (2020), Summary.

[186] Strömbäck (2020).

[187] Kharpal (2017).

[188] Weissmann (2019).

[189] *AT.40462*, Amazon.com, *Inc.; Amazon Services Europe SARL; Amazon EU SARL; Amazon Europe Core SARL.*

handed down shows that mammoth companies—typically American—that were previously thought to be untouchable have entered waters that are now considered dangerous not only legally but also politically. Fines may represent a fraction of the annual revenues of these companies, and they are typically appealed in the various courts, but the path that many countries around the world have taken clearly shows the political will, that the regulation of digital services cannot remain in the same mould as it was twenty years ago.[190]

Alexandre De Streel and his colleagues considered the following to be necessary for the creation of the new framework:[191]

- providing sufficient and effective safeguards for all fundamental rights (in particular freedom of expression, the right to privacy, non-discrimination and the right to a fair trial/effective remedy);
- strengthening the Internal Market and alleviate national regulatory fragmentation;
- ensuring a level playing field between online and offline activities;
- ensuring that what is illegal offline is illegal online;
- ensuring the rules are technologically and commercially neutral;
- ensuring that all stakeholders involved in the removal of illegal content online have appropriate incentives to minimise the risk of mistakes (both in terms of *over-removal /overblocking* and under-removal/*underblocking*);
- ensuring the proportionality of rules, which may require the use of different regulations and regulatory tools, either according to the type of content (and its potential negative impact on society) or according to the size of the platforms (and their means and social reach);[192] while keeping this multi-layered regulatory framework coherent;
- ensuring that the rules are sufficiently general to adapt easily to rapidly and often unpredictably evolving technologies and business models; and
- ensuring effective enforceability both for traditional public enforcement mechanisms and alternative private enforcement mechanisms (such as self- and co-regulation and out-of-court dispute resolution[193]).

[190] In addition to fines, another avenue has been actively pursued by European countries, which believe that the current international tax system does not take sufficient account of the digitalisation of the economy. Under the current international tax rules, multinational companies generally pay corporate tax in the country where production takes place, rather than where consumers or, especially in the case of the digital sector, users are located. As a consequence, "About half of all European OECD countries have either announced, proposed, or implemented a DST. Austria, France, Hungary, Italy, Poland, Portugal, Spain, Turkey, and the United Kingdom have implemented a Digital Services Tax (DST). Belgium, the Czech Republic, and Slovakia have published proposals to enact a DST, and Latvia, Norway, and Slovenia have either officially announced or shown intentions to implement such a tax." Asen and Bunn (2021). See also Pérez Bernabeu (2022).

[191] De Streel et al. (2020), pp. 77–78.

[192] On this topic, Anett Pogácsás argues that measures should not only be necessary and proportionate, but also effective. Pogácsás (2020), pp. 165–177.

[193] Cf. Commission Recommendation (EU) 2018/334, II.

The task facing the European Union's rule-making bodies was clearly no small one. However, as the Italian MEP Annalisa Tardino said at the European Parliament's meeting on 10 February 2021, which dealt with the digital regulation package[194] that had been published shortly before, "Decisions on what will be published in the digital realm should not be made based on guidelines created by platforms, but a law that lays down clear procedure and rules."[195] It was the intention to create these legal standards that led the legislator to create a new regulatory framework.

References

2011/833/EU: Commission Decision of 12 December 2011 on the reuse of Commission documents, OJ L 330, 14.12.2011, pp 39–42

Abate S (2020) A reflection on a decade of regulating digital platforms – will 2021 be the year of internet regulation converging with media and telecoms regulation? In: Wright E (ed) International comparative legal guides. telecoms, media & internet 2021, 14th edn. Global Legal Group, London

Alexander C (1977) A pattern language. Towns, buildings, construction. Oxford University Press, Oxford

Allow States and Victims to Fight Online Sex Trafficking Act of 2017

Andrews P, Treacy L, Donohue C (2021) Update on Implementation of Audio-Visual Media Services Directive in Ireland. McCann FitzGerald Knowledge, 19 Apr. https://www.mccannfitzgerald.com/knowledge/antitrust-competition/update-on-implementation-of-audio-visual-media-services-directive-in-ireland

Angyal Z (2020) Úton a digitális egységes piac felé (Towards the digital single market). Miskolci Jogi Szemle 15(3)

Asen E, Bunn D (2021) What European OECD countries are doing about digital services taxes. Tax Foundation, 22 Nov. https://taxfoundation.org/digital-tax-europe-2020/

Balkin JM (2018) Free speech in the algorithmic society. The new school of big data, private regulation and the regulation of expression. Columbia Law Rev 118(7)

Balni G, Bert CB (2019) Towards a telephonic history of technology. Hist Technol 35(2)

Barbier F, Lavenir CB (2009) Histoire des médias de Diderot à Internet (History of the media from Diderot to the Internet). Armand Colin (Collection U), Paris

Barlow JP (1996) A Declaration of the Independence of Cyberspace. 8 Feb. https://www.eff.org/cyberspace-independence

Barnard C (2019) The substantive law of the EU. The four freedoms 6th edn. Oxford University Press, Oxford

Bayer J (2019) Between Anarchy and Censorship. Public discourse and the duties of social media. CEPS Papers in Liberty and Security in Europe, 2019(3). https://www.ceps.eu/wp-content/uploads/2019/05/LSE2019-03_Between-Anarchy-and-Censorship.pdf

Ben-Shahar O (2019) Data pollution. J Legal Anal 11(1)

Bogrea Ş (2023) Fake news laws in the pandemic times: a human rights perspective. In: Gosztonyi G, Lazar E (eds) Media regulation during the Covid-19 pandemic: a study from Central and Eastern Europe. Ethics International Press, Cambridge

[194] See Chap. 6. LINK

[195] European Parliament News (2021).

Bowman S, Willis C (2003) We media. How audiences are shaping the future of news and information. The Media Center at The American Press Institute, https://www.hypergene.net/wemedia/download/we_media.pdf

Brooks D (2021) Can we build trust in online communities? Weave, https://weareweavers.org/weavers/can-we-build-trust-in-online-communities/

Cabrera B, Francisco J, Cappello M, Fontaine G, Rabie I, Valais S (2018) The legal framework for video-sharing platforms. European Audiovisual Observatory, Strasbourg

Campbell-Kelly M, Garcia-Swartz DD (2013) The history of the internet: the missing narratives. J Inf Technol 28(1)

Capello M (ed) (2021) Mapping of national rules applicable to video-sharing platforms: Illegal and harmful content online. European Audiovisual Observatory, Strasbourg

Castells M (2010) The rise of the network society, the information age: economy, society and culture, vol. 1. Blackwell Publishing, Oxford

Chemerinsky E, Chemerinsky A (2022) The golden era of free speech. In: Bollinger LC, Stone GR (eds) Social media, freedom of speech and the future of our democracy. Oxford University Press, Oxford

Citron DK, Wittes B (2018) The problem isn't just backpage: revising section 230 immunity. Georgetown Law Technol Rev 453

Cohen T, Dreeben M, Drummond Hansen M et al (eds.) (2021) CDA section 230: its past, present, and future. O'Melveny. Los Angeles

Colliver C (2019) Cracking the code: an evaluation of the EU code of practice on disinformation. Institute for Strategic Dialogue, https://www.isdglobal.org/wp-content/uploads/2020/06/isdCracking-the-Code.pdf

Commission Recommendation (EU) 2018/334 of 1 March 2018 on measures to effectively tackle illegal content online, C/2018/1177, OJ L 63, 6.3.2018, pp 50–61

Communication from the Commission Guidelines on the practical application of the essential functionality criterion of the definition of a 'video-sharing platform service' under the Audiovisual Media Services Directive 2020/C 223/02, C/2020/4322, OJ C 223, 7.7.2020, pp 3–9

Communication from the Commission to the Council, the European Parliament, the Economic and Social Committee and the Committee of the Regions Principles and guidelines for the Community's audiovisual policy in the digital age. COM/99/0657 final

Communication from the Commission to the European Parliament, the Council, the European Economic and Social Committee and the Committee of the Regions – A Digital Single Market Strategy for Europe. COM(2015) 192 final

Communication from the Commission to the European Parliament, the Council, the European Economic and Social Committee and the Committee of the Regions – Tackling online disinformation: a European Approach. COM(2018) 236 final

Communications Decency Act (CDA), Pub. L. No. 104-104 (Tit. V), 110 Stat. 133 (Feb. 8, 1996)

Consolidated version of the Treaty on the Functioning of the European Union, OJ C 326, 26.10.2012, pp 47–390

Council Directive 89/552/EEC of 3 October 1989 on the coordination of certain provisions laid down by Law, Regulation or Administrative Action in Member States concerning the pursuit of television broadcasting activities, OJ L 298, 17.10.1989, pp 23–30

Cox C (2020) The origins and original intent of section 230 of the communications decency act. J Law Technol, 27 Aug. https://jolt.richmond.edu/2020/08/27/the-origins-and-original-intent-of-section-230-of-the-communications-decency-act

Cserpes A (2011) Marketing és menedzsment a közművelődésben (Marketing and Management in Public Culture). Keresztury Dezső Általános Művelődési Központ, Zalaegerszeg

Csordás A (2005) A feltölthető világ – Web 2.0 (The uploadable world – Web 2.0). Magyar Narancs, 17 Nov. https://magyarnarancs.hu/tudomany/afeltolthetovilag-web20-64804/?pageId=64

De Gregorio G (2019) The e-Commerce Directive and GDPR: towards convergence of legal regimes in the algorithmic society? European University Institute Working Paper RSCAS, 36

de Querol R (2016) Zygmunt Bauman: "Las redes sociales son una trampa". El País, 9 Jan. https://elpais.com/cultura/2015/12/30/babelia/1451504427_675885.html

De Streel A, Defreyne E, Jacquemin H, Ledger M, Michel A (2020) Online platforms' moderation of illegal content online. Law, practices and options for reform. Study for the committee on internal market and consumer protection, policy department for economic, scientific and quality of life policies. European Parliament, Luxembourg

Deutsch AL (2022) WhatsApp: The Best Facebook Purchase Ever? Investopedia, 29 March. https://www.investopedia.com/articles/investing/032515/whatsapp-best-facebook-purchase-ever.asp

Directive (EU) 2018/1808 of the European Parliament and of the Council of 14 November 2018 amending Directive 2010/13/EU on the coordination of certain provisions laid down by law, regulation or administrative action in Member States concerning the provision of audiovisual media services (Audiovisual Media Services Directive) in view of changing market realities, PE/33/2018/REV/1, OJ L 303, 28.11.2018, pp 69–92

Directive (EU) 2019/790 of the European Parliament and of the Council of 17 April 2019 on copyright and related rights in the Digital Single Market and amending Directives 96/9/EC and 2001/29/EC, PE/51/2019/REV/1, OJ L 130, 17.5.2019, pp 92–125

Directive 2000/31/EC of the European Parliament and of the Council of 8 June 2000 on certain legal aspects of information society services, in particular electronic commerce, in the Internal Market ('Directive on electronic commerce'), OJ L 178, 17.7.2000, pp 1–16

Directive 2010/13/EU of the European Parliament and of the Council of 10 March 2010 on the coordination of certain provisions laid down by law, regulation or administrative action in Member States concerning the provision of audiovisual media services (Audiovisual Media Services Directive), OJ L 95, 15.4.2010, pp 1–24

Directive 98/34/EC of the European Parliament and of the Council of 22 June 1998 laying down a procedure for the provision of information in the field of technical standards and regulations, OJ L 204, 21.7.1998, pp 37–48

Directive 98/84/EC of the European Parliament and of the Council of 20 November 1998 on the legal protection of services based on, or consisting of, conditional access, OJ L 320, 28.11.1998, pp 54–57

Drijber BJ (1999) The revised television without frontiers directive: is it fit for the next century? Common Mark Law Rev 36(1)

DW (2023) EU: Twitter leaves voluntary pact on fighting disinformation. DW, 5 May. https://www.dw.com/en/eu-twitter-leaves-voluntary-pact-on-fighting-disinformation/a-65751487

Easterbrook FH (1996) Cyberspace and the law of the horse. University of Chicago Legal Forum, 1996(1)

Ellis J (2003) Television and history. Hist Workshop J 56(1)

Espiner T (2008) Internet is a 'lawless space', says expert. ZDNet, 28 Nov. https://www.zdnet.com/article/internet-is-a-lawless-space-says-expert/

EU Code of Conduct on countering illegal hate speech online

EU Code of Practice on Disinformation

EU Strengthened Code of Practice on Disinformation

European Parliament (2012) History: European Single Market. 28 June. https://multimedia.europarl.europa.eu/en/history-european-single-marketV001-0021ev

European Parliament News (2021) Social media and democracy: we need laws, not platform guidelines. European Parliament News, 10 Feb. https://www.europarl.europa.eu/news/en/headlines/society/20210204STO97129/social-media-and-democracy-we-need-laws-not-platform-guidelines

Feiler L, Forgó N, Weigl M (2018) The EU General Data Protection Regulation (GDPR): A Commentary, 2nd edn. Globe Law and Business, London

Foley Dabbaraccio A (2021.) Communication in History: The Key to Understanding, http://www.uwgb.edu/nationalhistoryday/files/pdf/2021%20Theme%20Narrative.pdf

Forgó N (2016) Privacy and internet governance. Proceedings of the 8th ACM Conference on Web Science (WebSci '16). Association for Computing Machinery, New York

Gellén K (2018) Az audiovizuális médiaszolgáltatásokról szóló irányelv reklámjogi szabályainak változásairól az egységes digitális piaci stratégia törekvéseinek tükrében (On changes to the advertising rules of the Audiovisual Media Services Directive in the light of the Digital Single Market strategy). In Media Res 7(1)
Giles MW (1996) From Gutenberg to gigabytes. scholarly communication in the age of cyberspace. J Polit 58(3)
Gosztonyi G (2021) A ló joga, avagy szükséges-e internetjogot oktatni? (The law of the horse, or is it necessary to teach internet law?) JOG.történet, 2 Nov. https://mtajogtortenet.elte.hu/blog/gosztonyi-gergely-internetjog-oktatasa
Gosztonyi G (2022) Zeran v AOL, avagy az ítélet, amely létrehozta az internetet (Zeran v AOL, or the judgment that created the internet). JOG.történet, 14 Feb. https://mtajogtortenet.elte.hu/blog/gosztonyi-gergely-zeran-itelet
Grabner-Kräuter S, Bitter S (2015) Trust in online social networks: a multifaceted perspective. Forum Soc Econ 44(1)
Grad-Gyenge A (2022) Alapjogi kérdések a DSM-irányelv 17. cikke kapcsán (Fundamental rights issues in relation to Article 17 of the DSM Directive). Fundamentum 26(3).
Grossman L (2006) You Yes, You Are TIME's Person of the Year. Time Magazine, 25 Dec. https://content.time.com/time/magazine/article/0,9171,1570810,00.html
Hámori B (2015) A Barnaby Rich-szindróma a XXI. században. A figyelem, mint szűkös jószág (Barnaby Rich syndrome in the 21st century. Attention as a scarce commodity). Köz-gazdaság 10(3)
Hanley SM (1998) International internet regulation: a multinational approach. John Marshall J Inf Technol Priv Law 16(4)
Harmon E (2018) How Congress Censored the Internet. Electronic Frontier Foundation, 21 March. https://www.eff.org/deeplinks/2018/03/how-congress-censored-internet
Herendy C (2010) A kereső, a dokumentumok és a user (The search engine, documents and the user). Médiakutató 11(1)
Herold A (2008) Country of origin principle in the EU market for audiovisual media services: consumer's friend or foe? J Consum Policy 31(1)
Hintz A (2015) Social media censorship, privatized regulation, and new restrictions to protest and dissent. In: Dencik L, Leistert O (eds) Critical perspectives on social media and protest: between control and emancipation. Rowman & Littlefield, London
Hiremath BK, Kenchakkanavar AY (2016) An Alteration of the Web 1.0, Web 2.0 and Web 3.0: A Comparative Study. Imp J Interdiscip Res 2(4)
Hoofnagle CJ, van der Sloot B, Borgesius FZ (2019) The European Union general data protection regulation: what it is and what it means. Inf Commun Technol Law 28(1)
Hu M (2020) Cambridge analytica's black box. Big Data Soc 7(2)
Interaction Design Foundation (IDF) (2020) Information Overload, Why it Matters and How to Combat It. Interaction Design Foundation, 17 June. https://www.interaction-design.org/literature/article/information-overload-why-it-mattersand-how-to-combat-it
Karambiri Z (2009) Les responsabilités liées aux contenus postés dans les blogs (Responsibility for content posted on blogs). Revue du Droit des Technologies de l'Information, 8(36)
Katsirea I (2014) The television without frontiers directive. In: Donders K, Pauwels C, Loisen J (eds) The Palgrave handbook of European media policy. Palgrave Macmillan, London
Kedrosky P (2006) I Call "Market Top" on "You". 16 Dec. https://web.archive.org/web/20080207013442/http://paul.kedrosky.com/archives/2006/12/16/i_call_market_t.html#
Kelemen L (2021) A közösségi platformok szabályozása az Európai Unióban (Regulation of community platforms in the European Union). Médiatudományi Intézet Blog, 1 March. https://nmhh.hu/cikk/218445/A_kozossegi_platformok_szabalyozasa_az_Europai_Unioban
Keller P (1998) The new television without frontiers directive. In: Barendt ME (ed) Yearbook of media and entertainment law. vol III: 1997/98. Clarendon Press, Oxford
Keller P (2011) European and international media law. Liberal democracy, trade, and the new media. Oxford University Press, Oxford

Khanzode K, Chhaya A, Sarode RD (2016) Evolution of the World Wide Web: From Web 1.0 to 6.0. Int J Digital Libr Serv 6(2)
Kharpal A (2017) Facebook fined $122 million by EU for giving 'misleading information' about its takeover of WhatsApp. CNBC, 18 May. https://www.cnbc.com/2017/05/18/facebook-fine-eu-whatsapp-takeover.html
Kilmann C (2021) Are We Experiencing Another Dot-Com Bubble? Bacon Bits, 18 Feb. https://medium.com/bacon-bits/are-we-about-to-experience-another-dot-com-bubble-dc480fc75320
King A, Easley A, Morton J (2019) The Routledge Handbook to Nineteenth-Century British Periodicals and Newspapers. Routledge, Abingdon
Klein T (2018) A web 2.0. egyes szabályozási kérdései – különös tekintettel az alkotmányjogi vonatkozásokra (Some regulatory issues of web 2.0 – with a special focus on constitutional aspects). In: Klein T (ed) Tanulmányok a technológia- és cyberjog néhány aktuális kérdéséről (Studies on some current issues in technology and cyber law). NMHH Médiatudományi Intézet, Budapest
Kokoly Z (2020) Exceptions to the Principle of Free Transmission and Retransmission of Audio-visual Media Content – Recent European Case-Law. Acta Univ. Sapientiae, Legal Stud 9(1)
König M (2020) Does the AVMS-Directive apply to social media platforms? Will we get more European content on video-sharing platforms? – EU releases Guidelines on the AVMS-Directive. Lexology, 8 July. https://www.lexology.com/library/detail.aspx?g=4401ab6c-cfc0-4eb0-889d-b1410e94c489
Kosseff J (2019) The 26 words that created the internet. Cornell University Press, New York
Kukliš Ľ (2021) Video-sharing platforms in AVMSD: a new kind of content regulation. In: Parcu PL, Brogi E (eds) Research handbook on EU media law and policy. Edward Elgar Publishing, Cheltenham
Láncos PL (2022) The many facets of EU soft law. Pázmány Press, Budapest
Levy S (2017) The internet isn't the wild wild west anymore. It's Westworld. Wired, 1 Apr. https://www.wired.com/2017/04/the-internet-isnt-the-wild-wild-west-anymore-its-westworld
Li H, Yu L, He W (2019) The impact of GDPR on global technology development. J Glob Inf Technol Manage 22(1)
LTE (2016) Evolution of communication. 11 July. https://www.youtube.com/watch?v=oxTUC5I22LU
MacLennan AF (2020) Celebrating a hundred years of broadcasting – an introduction and timeline. J Radio Audio Media 27(2)
Madiega T (2020) Reform of the EU liability regime for online intermediaries. Background on the forthcoming Digital Services Act. European Parliamentary Research Service. https://www.europarl.europa.eu/RegData/etudes/IDAN/2020/649404/EPRS_IDA(2020)649404_EN.pdf
Marlinspike M (2022) My first impressions of web3. moxie.org, 7 Jan 2022, https://moxie.org/2022/01/07/web3-firstimpressions.html
Marsden CT (2011) Internet co-regulation: European law, regulatory governance and legitimacy in cyberspace. Cambridge University Press, Cambridge
McLuhan M (1962) The Gutenberg galaxy. The making of typographic man. University of Toronto Press, Toronto
McNamee J (2011) The slide from self-regulation to corporate censorship. European Digital Rights, Brussels
Mezei P, Lábody P (2022) Több jogdíj, kevesebb vélemény? – Irányváltás az online tartalommegosztó szolgáltatók szerzői jogi felelősségében (More royalties, fewer opinions? – A change of direction in the copyright liability of online content sharing providers). Fundamentum 26(3)
Milton M (2021) Updated Internet Regulations? IG Institutions, Platform Governance, 22 March. https://www.internetgovernance.org/2021/03/22/updated-internet-regulations
Monti M (2020) The Eu code of practice on disinformation and the risk of the privatisation of censorship. In: Giusti S, Piras E (eds) Democracy and fake news. Information manipulation and post-truth politics. Routledge, London

Murdock J (2020) The Dotcom Bubble Crash Was 20 years ago today—could it happen again? Newsweek, 10 Oct. https://www.newsweek.com/dotcom-bubble-crash-20-anniversary-technology-companies-ever-happen-again-1491385
Murray AD (2011) Nodes and Gravity in Virtual Space. Legisprudence 5(2)
Nádori P (2014) Megoldás a komment-dilemmára? (A solution to the comment dilemma?) In Medias Res 3(2)
Nagy K (2018) Műveltség – Média – Szabályozás. A médiaműveltség médiapolitikai jelentősége és szabályozási keretei (Literacy – Media – Regulation. Media Policy Significance and Regulatory Framework of Media literacy). Gondolat Kiadó, Budapest
Namasudra S, Devi D, Choudhary S, Patan R, Kallam S (2018) Security, privacy, trust, and anonymity. In: Namasudra S, Chra Deka G (eds) Advances of DNA computing in cryptography. Chapman and Hall/CRC, London
Naughton J (2016) The evolution of the Internet: from military experiment to general purpose technology. J Cyber Policy 1(1)
Newstalk (2020) YouTube, Netflix and Facebook could face millions in fines for breaches of proposed new laws. Newstalk, 9 Dec. https://www.newstalk.com/news/online-safety-bill-ireland-1119712
O'Reilly T (2005) What Is Web 2.0. Design Patterns and Business Models for the Next Generation of Software. 30 Sep. https://www.oreilly.com/pub/a/web2/archive/what-is-web-20.html
Obar J, Wildman S (2015) Social media definition and the governance challenge: an introduction to the special issue. Telecommun Policy 39(9)
Oster J (2017) European and international media law. Cambridge University Press, Cambridge
Owens J (2019) The tech giants dominated the decade. But there's still time to rein them in. The Guardian, 25 Dec. https://www.theguardian.com/commentisfree/2019/dec/25/2010s-tech-giants-google-amazon-facebook-regulators
Paslawsky A (2017) The growth of social media norms and government's attempts at regulation. Fordham Int Law J 35(5)
Peguera M (2009) The DMCA safe harbors and their European counterparts: a comparative analysis of some common problems. Columbia J Law Arts 32(4)
Pérez Bernabeu B (2022) Taxation of digital business and social media: contribution of the court of justice to the compatibility with EU fundamental freedom. In: Psychogiopoulou E, de la Sierra S (eds) Digital media governance and supranational courts. Selected issues and insights from the European judiciary. Edward Elgar Publishing, Cheltenham
Piechucka A (2014) Fifteen minutes of fame, fame in fifteen minutes: andy warhol and the dawn of modern-day celebrity culture. https://depot.ceon.pl/bitstream/handle/123456789/8734/08pjas8.pdf?sequence=1&isAllowed=y
Pogácsás A (2020) Modern jogérvényesítés vagy modern cenzúra? A weboldalak blokkolásának újabb tanulságai (Modern law enforcement or modern censorship? Recent lessons on website blocking). In Medias Res 9(1)
Polyák G, Szőke GL (2009) The country of origin principle and competition among national regulatory régimes in East Central Europe. Central Eur J Commun 2(1)
Prabhu D (2016) Application of Web 2.0 and Web 3.0: an overview. Int J Res Libr Sci 2(1)
Raboy M, Padovani C (2010) Mapping global media policy: concepts, frameworks, methods. Commun Cult Crit Special Iss Media Gov New Policies Chang Media Landscape, 3(2)
Regulation (EU) 2016/679 of the European Parliament and of the Council of 27 April 2016 on the protection of natural persons with regard to the processing of personal data and on the free movement of such data, and repealing Directive 95/46/EC (General Data Protection Regulation), OJ L 119, 4.5.2016, pp 1–88
Reynders D (2021) Countering illegal hate speech online. 6th evaluation of the Code of Conduct. European Commission, 7 Oct. https://ec.europa.eu/info/sites/default/files/factsheet-6th-monitoring-round-of-the-code-of-conduct_october2021_en_1.pdf

Reynolds M (2019) The strange story of Section 230, the obscure law that created our flawed, broken internet. Wired, 24 March. https://www.wired.co.uk/article/section-230-communications-decency-act

Romero-Moreno F (2019) 'Notice and staydown' and social media: amending Article 13 of the Proposed Directive on Copyright. Int Rev Law Comput Technol 33(2)

Ropolyi L (2021) An 'Aristotelian' philosophy of the internet. WebSci '21: 13th ACM Web Science Conference. Association for Computing Machinery, New York

Sajó A, Clare R (2016) A bírói érvelés és az új technológiák – Gondolati keretek, újdonság, alapjogok és az internet (Judicial reasoning and new technologies – Thought frameworks, novelty, fundamental rights and the internet). Fundamentum 20(2–4)

Sboarina L (2023) Audiovisual Media Service Directive: transposition into member states national legislations is now finalised. Cullen International, 9 March. https://www.cullen-international.com/news/2023/03/Audiovisual-Media-Service-Directive%2D%2Dtransposition-into-member-states-national-legislations-is-now-finalised.html

Slumkoski C (2012) History on the Internet 2.0: the rise of social media. Acadiensis 41(2)

Solanki MR, Dongaonkar A (2016) A journey of human comfort: Web 1.0 to Web 4.0. Int J Res Sci Innov 3(9)

Sorbán K (2019) A videómegosztóplatform-paradoxon, avagy az új európai szabályok alkalmazhatósága a globalizáció és az eltérő tagállami implementáció keresztmetszetében (The video sharing platform paradox, or the applicability of new European rules in the intersection of globalisation and divergent national implementation). In Medias Res 8(2)

Speier H (1952) International political communication: Elite vs. Mass. World Polit 4(3)

Strömbäck P (2020) Good Samaritan Paradox Paradox. Netopia, 12 June. http://www.netopia.eu/good-samaritan-paradox-paradox/

Summary of Commission decision of 27 June 2017 relating to a proceeding under Article 102 of the Treaty on the Functioning of the European Union and Article 54 of the EEA Agreement (Case AT.39740 — Google Search (Shopping)) (notified under document number C(2017) 4444), OJ C 9, 12.1.2018, p. 11–14

Suzor NP (2019) Lawless. The secret rules that govern our digital lives. Cambridge University Press, Cambridge

Szűts Z (2013) A világháló metaforái (Metaphors of the web). Osiris Kiadó, Budapest

Tambini D, Leonardi D, Marsden C (2008) Codifying cyberspace. Communications self-regulation in the age of internet convergence. Routledge, London – New York

The Digital Millennium Copyright Act (DMCA), Pub. L. No. 105-304, 112 Stat. 2860 (Oct. 28, 1998)

United States Government Accountability Office (2021) Report to Congressional Committees. Sex trafficking. Online Platforms and Federal Prosecutions. GAO-21-385

Urban JM, Karaganis J, Schofield BL (2017) Notice and Takedown in Everyday Practice. Version 2. University California Berkeley Public Law Research Paper, https://ssrn.com/abstract=2755628

Vaccari C, Chadwick A (2020) Deepfakes and disinformation: Exploring the impact of synthetic political video on deception, uncertainty, and trust in news. Social Media + Society, Jan-March 2020

van Hoboken J, Quintais JP, Poort J, van Eijk N (2018) Hosting intermediary services and illegal content online. An analysis of the scope of article 14 ECD in light of developments in the online service landscape: final report. European Commission, Luxembourg

Weissmann CG (2019) Google hit with another EU antitrust fine: The grand total now comes to €8.2B. Fastcompany, 20 March. https://www.fastcompany.com/90322678/google-hit-with-another-eu-antitrust-fine-the-grand-total-now-comes-to-e8-2b

Wendehorst C (2016) Platform intermediary services and duties under the E-Commerce directive and the consumer rights directive. J Eur Consum Mark Law 5(1)

Wilman F (2020) The responsibility of online intermediaries for illegal user content in the EU and the US. Edward Elgar Publishing, Cheltenham

World Wide Web Consortium (WWWC) (2013) What is the Semantic Web? 11 Dec. https://www.w3.org/2001/sw/
Yen AC (2020) Revisiting the Western Frontier. IDEA – The Law Review of the Franklin Pierce Center for Intellectual Property, 60(1)
Yen AC (2002) Western frontier or feudal society?: Metaphors and perceptions of cyberspace. Berkeley Technol Law J 17(4)
Yen NY, Zhang C, Waluyo AB, Park JJ (2015) Social media services and technologies towards Web 3.0. Multimed Tools Appl 74
Zanathy A (2021a) "Kiberjog" vagy Netikett: Az internet szabályozására vonatkozó jogtörténeti elméletek ("Cyberlaw" or Netikett: Legal historical theories on the regulation of the internet). Joghistória 26(1–2)
Zanathy A (2021b) Burst the Bubble: how to defend freedom of expression from algorithmic personalization. Int J Sci Res Publicat 11(7)
Zandt F (2021) 50 Percent Of Rural America Without Internet Access. statista.com, 17 Aug. https://www.statista.com/chart/25549/households-with-internet-access-by-area-and-region/
Zeno-Zencovich V (2019) What do we mean by 'Media' Today? In: Weaver RL, Koltay A, Cole MD, Friedland SI (eds) Free speech and media law in the 21st century. Carolina Academic Press, Durham

Chapter 5
Regulatory Options in the United Stated of America

The question that many people asked at the end of 2010 was whether, given the multiplying problems, there was enough political will and courage in policymakers to regulate the internet, social media and the tech giants, and whether these tech moguls were really interested in change or just playing for time. As the US Supreme Court put it—coming to the same conclusion as the ECtHR in *Cengiz and others v Turkey*—"while in the past there may have been difficulty in identifying the most important places (in a spatial sense) for the exchange of views, today the answer is clear. It is cyberspace – the 'vast democratic forums of the Internet' in general." [1]

5.1 The Position of Platforms

The image of Facebook CEO Mark Zuckerberg at his Senate hearing in 2019 is burned into the retinas of many, when he "called . . . for regulators to play a 'more active role' in establishing rules that govern the internet."[2] As a follow-up, in the *Washington Post, he* wrote "The internet needs new rules. Let's start in these four areas",[3] but it could be seen as a manifesto in its content. The letter begins by acknowledging that "technology is a major part of our lives, and companies such as Facebook have immense responsibilities" and then identifies four areas (harmful content, election integrity, privacy and data portability) where regulators need to take urgent action if they are not to lag behind the proliferation of problems and the volume of new media:

- On harmful content, he notes that "lawmakers often tell me we have too much power over speech, and frankly I agree. I've come to believe that we shouldn't

[1] *Packingham v North Carolina*, 137 S. Ct. 1730, 198 L. Ed. 2d 273 (2017).

[2] Bing (2019).

[3] Zuckerberg (2019).

G. Gosztonyi, *Censorship from Plato to Social Media*, Law, Governance and Technology Series 61, https://doi.org/10.1007/978-3-031-46529-1_5

make so many important decisions about speech on our own."[4] He stresses that removing all harmful content from the internet is a technically impossible task, but that a more uniform set of rules could help to bring clarity. Of course, transparency on this issue—from both governments and tech companies—would be a basic requirement.

- On the integrity of elections, he argues in favour of regulating political advertising and bringing political campaigns under a stricter legal framework.
- In the context of data protection, he proposes to enact legislation similar to the GDPR in the US.[5]
- Fourth he draws attention to the portability of data, which is difficult to achieve today between different services and applications.[6]

As a final thought, he shares with the public that "the rules governing the Internet allowed a generation of entrepreneurs to build services that changed the world and created a lot of value in people's lives. It's time to update these rules to define clear responsibilities for people, companies and governments going forward."[7] The big tech companies have been visibly moving forward over the last few years, as they sense changes coming in both the US and the EU. One important step in this process was Facebook's 2020 White Paper,[8] in which four key issues were identified:

- How can content regulation best reduce the amount of harmful content while preserving freedom of expression?
- How could regulation improve the public accountability of internet platforms?
- Does regulation require internet companies to meet certain performance targets?
- Should regulation specify which harmful content should be banned on internet platforms?

The company argues that "consistent with human rights norms, internet platforms generally respect the laws of the countries in which they operate, and they are also free to establish their own rules about permissible expression, which are often more restrictive than laws. As a result, internet companies make calls every day that influence who has the ability to speak and what content can be shared on their platform."[9] The company points out that the decisions of large content providers are often not sufficiently communicated to the public, and that the daily volume of decisions means that mistakes are inevitable, and notes that the categories of illegal content—although often synonymous in the public mind—and harmful content are

[4]Ibid.

[5]On this, see also Mercer (2020), pp. 20–25.

[6]It should be noted that the DMA discussed in Sect. 6.2 also addresses this issue.

[7]Zuckerberg (2019).

[8]Bickert (2020).

[9]Ibid., p. 3.

very different (what is harmful is not necessarily illegal).[10] The White Paper highlights four problems with internet regulation:[11]

- The legal environment and speech standards differ around the world, and, as the biggest tech companies operate in an international environment, this can cause inconsistencies.
- Both technology and speech are dynamic; in other words, technology is constantly changing, as is speech, as we use tools and speak differently to our friends, in a job interview or in an online intergovernmental meeting.
- The implementation will always be imperfect, since it will have to be applied in many languages and dialects, and with the full range of human communication tools, from irony to anger to the most merciful lie.
- Companies are merely intermediaries, not content creators.

In early 2020, Věra Jourová, Vice-President of the European Commission, Commissioner for European Values and Transparency, commented on the proposals presented to her, saying that they were "too low in terms of responsibility."[12] The process had been accompanied by a heavily funded media campaign[13] by Facebook, on television, in print and on the internet, but this was criticised by many for its simplistic tone and factual errors.[14]

5.2 Loss of Vision or the Future?

5.2.1 *The Facebook Oversight Board*

In addition to the above, the world's leading social media provider took a more drastic step: on 6 May 2020, it announced the creation of an independent *Oversight Board of* recognised experts to help it tackle problematic content.[15] "As outside experts and civic leaders, we embrace our responsibility to answer some of the most difficult questions around freedom of expression online: what to take down, what to leave up, and why", they say.[16] The Oversight Board has been described by some as the company's own Supreme Court,[17] since it can overrule a private company's

---

[10] Ibid., pp. 6–7.

[11] These points have been interpreted by many critics as a deflection of responsibility and liability.

[12] Pop (2020).

[13] https://about.fb.com/regulations/.

[14] Milton (2021).

[15] One of the direct precursors to this is a long letter by Mark Zuckerberg, in which he explains that "I've increasingly come to believe that Facebook should not make so many important decisions on freedom of expression and safety on our own." Zuckerberg (2018).

[16] https://oversightboard.com/meet-the-board/.

[17] Morgan (2021).

decisions on content regulation. Tamás Pongó said that the body is a „form of organisation very close to a (constitutional) court."[18] Many have begun to hope that the expertise on the panel might improve the quality of the company's decisions.[19] Importantly, however, the Oversight Board will only rule on issues that are complex, significant, globally relevant and can be used to inform the development of Facebook's future rules.[20]

Although the official announcement of the launch of the panel was not due until mid-2020, the selection process had already been underway for a year and a half, with offline and online consultations held around the world.[21] The original plan was to have 40 people in the Oversight Board, but by the mid-2023, it still has only 22 people in it, although those include "a former prime minister of Denmark, a Nobel Peace Prize laureate, a former editor of The Guardian and nine academics from universities around the world."[22] The members were selected from a pool of around 1000 candidates and, having examined the list, no one has so far suggested that they were not selected in an informed manner. Of the members, Nicolas P. Suzor, for example, said, "I was about seizing an opportunity to put my research into practice, after a decade of yelling at tech companies to do better. This is a cool experiment – there's no guarantee that it will work. But I really wanted to do what I could to see how much I could push Facebook to change its governance practices in line with human rights agendas."[23]

In December 2020, the Oversight Board selected the first cases to review the company's decisions, and the first decisions were made in early 2021: four of the first five cases were against Facebook's moderation decision, and one case upheld the moderators' previous decision.[24] Although it is not yet possible to draw a firm conclusion from the only forty-six decisions taken by mid-2023, it can be seen that, in thirty-two cases, the Oversight Board has overturned Facebook's original decision:

Decision of the Oversight Board	Number of cases
Case selected for review but not eligible for investigation.[25]	1

(continued)

[18]Pongó (2020), p. 150.

[19]Lanza and Jackson (2021).

[20]Cf. "In Q2 2022 (1 April to 30 June 2022), the Board received 347,000 appeals from Facebook and Instagram users around the world. In this quarter, the Board published three case decisions." Meta (2022).

[21]Klonick (2020), pp. 2451–2457.

[22]Morgan (2021).

[23]Ibid.

[24]An excellent professional analysis of the very first decisions is provided by Szikora (2021).

[25]"This case concerned a comment on a post, with the user who made the comment appealing Facebook's decision to remove it. However, the post itself, which remained on the platform, was subsequently deleted by the user who posted it. As a result, it would not be possible for the Board to restore the content." 2020-001-FB-UA, https://oversightboard.com/decision/FB-KBHZS8BL/.

Decision of the Oversight Board	Number of cases
The Oversight Board overturned Meta's original decision to remove the Facebook content and requires the reinstatement of the post.	32
The Oversight Board overturned Meta's original decision to remove Facebook content. However, the Oversight Board notes that Facebook has already reinstated the post after it was selected for review.	4
The Oversight Board upheld Meta's decision.[26]	9
Total[27]	46

It can be seen that one case could not have been examined by the Oversight Board for technical reasons, and only nine cases were upheld, so, as a consequence, the 'moderation's effectiveness rate' is about 20%. Of course, this data is by no means generalisable, as it is the Oversight Board that selects the cases it examines, but it shows that the previous criticisms that led to the Oversight Board's establishment had a basis. It is particularly interesting that, in four cases, without waiting for the Oversight Board's decision, which was later condemned, Facebook reinstated the content in question.

The decisions taken in the first months of operation may also provide an outline of the coordinating framework within which the Oversight Board envisages its own activities:

- It was considered important to stress that moderation by artificial intelligence (AI) without any human control is unacceptable from a human rights perspective.
- It was stressed that moderation should not only examine the content in question, but also its textual and visual context.
- In particular, they stressed that Facebook is strongly encouraged to ensure that the rules that users can understand are clear, unambiguous, and predictable.
- It is proposed to translate Facebook's Community Standards into as many languages and dialects as possible.
- The Oversight Board was concerned that Facebook had not applied an exception rule to its own internal policies for several years and that this could have led to the erroneous removal of many other posts.

[26] The decision that received the most attention of all was the indefinite suspension of former US President Donald Trump. The Oversight Board dealt with the issue under the number 2021-001-FB-FBR (https://oversightboard.com/decision/FB-691QAMHJ/). As a detailed examination of the decision is beyond the scope of this book, it is worth mentioning here only Sándor Lénárd's fascinating thought experiment on the relationship between private companies and international human rights treaties, about which he argues "it is possible that the rationale behind the application of international human rights is actually that Facebook wishes to be seen as a state, or at least as a company performing a state function." Lénárd (2021). For some other interesting decisions, see also Lendvai (2023a, b).

[27] 28 Aug 2023.

- In several cases, the panel suggested that it would be more legally justifiable to use less restrictive means of free speech (such as warning messages or even audio alerts) rather than removing content.[28]

The problems, many say, do not lie in the composition of the Oversight Board or its initial decisions, but elsewhere. According to Julie Cohen, the "star-studded panel and lavish funding[29] will prevent regulation while allowing the company to outsource controversial decisions."[30] A similar point was made by Laurence Tribe—a member of the 'Real Facebook Oversight Board'[31] set up by academics and activists in November 2020—that it is "generating a patina of legitimacy that cannot in fact be justified by the board's composition or function."[32] It is their common view that the Oversight Board is merely a body designed to mislead the public (and of course even more so US and European politicians), to serve as a distraction. Tamás Szikora also raises the problem that "until a 'final' decision is taken on certain specific content, content that is subsequently found to be infringing can remain available to the public. This, given the speed of information dissemination on social media, can result in serious harm."[33]

Dipayan Ghosh in the *Harvard Business Review* critiques it, noting that "On its surface, the Oversight Board is a remarkable answer to a novel problem. The firm, which enjoys well over two billion users across the globe, has seen a broad array of serious problems related to the scaled, frictionless dissemination of content that is its core consumer service."[34] He argues that it is not the poor practical implementation of content monetisation that is the cause of the problems, but the very model in which these giant tech companies operate; a model in which they do not distribute content but sell advertising space, and in which content is actually less important.[35] It relies on complex algorithms and the most comprehensive collection of personal data in order to personalise these ads as much as possible and as automatically as possible for its millions of users. As a result, users "are subjected to whatever content the platform believes will maximize profits."[36] To address the problem, the Oversight Board's screening of some problems and some user content is therefore not sufficient, as it does not have access to control, for example, the political campaigns that cause (one of) the main problems. As long as the operating mechanisms of the

---

[28] Gyetván (2023).

[29] The company is spending $130 million to run the Oversight Board and expects this money to last for about six years. Culliford (2019).

[30] Klonick (2021).

[31] Butcher (2020).

[32] Morgan (2021).

[33] Szikora (2020).

[34] Ghosh (2019).

[35] As Siva Vaidhyanathan put it so eloquently, "The problem with Facebook is Facebook." Vaidhyanathan (2018).

[36] Ghosh (2019).

big companies themselves do not change, systemic changes cannot be achieved by looking at individual issues.

Ghosh sees the solution in a significant broadening of the powers of the Oversight Board: it would not only be able to take decisions on content removal, but also on a company's data management practices, acquisition intentions or even consumer protection. Ghosh says the world's biggest company should lead by example in the midst of problems.[37]

5.2.2 *BlueSky of Twitter*

Twitter[38] took a different direction from Facebook in December 2019 by funding a team of five (*BlueSky*) programmers, engineers and designers (all open source) to develop an open and decentralised standard for social media.[39] As they put it, "We'd expect this team not only to develop a decentralized standard for social media, but to also build open community around it, inclusive of companies & organizations, researchers, civil society leaders, all who are thinking deeply about the consequences, positive and negative."[40] The announcement was greeted with great scepticism, saying it was nothing more than a distraction from the criticisms of big tech companies, while others suggested that it was not a case of starting new teams but of funding existing projects (ActivityPub, XMPP, Solid) that were working in this direction.[41] In response, Twitter announced that the team it supports is free to choose whether to propose an existing standard or one under development at the end of the process, or to start working on a new standard.[42]

The project is seen by others as a new opportunity, as it would not only address the issue of content removal, unlike Facebook's solution, but the standards systems behind the whole industry,[43] which could contribute to innovation, the rise of new startups and the concentration of content regulation in the hands of more than a select few tech mammoths.[44] In early 2021, the invited team released a brochure,[45] which "signals that Bluesky is trying to build on what people in the field have already

[37] More on the possible future of the Oversight Board, see Barata (2022); Helfer and Land (2023).

[38] Twitter was rebranded and renamed X in mid-2023, causing serious confusion how to call the company and the app. This book sticks to the original and well-known name. Conger (2023).

[39] De Streel et al. (2020), p. 62.

[40] Price (2019).

[41] Robertson (2019).

[42] https://twitter.com/bluesky/status/1204916413980233728.

[43] We're talking about a process similar to e-mail management, where users see e-mails in the same way, regardless of the service provider they're connected to and the software they're using.

[44] Article-19 (2020).

[45] Graber (2021).

discovered... even if we don't know where it might go from there."[46] Even so, all this leads on to the next question, of what direction US regulation should take.

5.3 "The Internet Has Problems, and Regulation Is Coming"[47]

First, it is worth clarifying the US position on the existence of 'comprehensive internet regulation',[48] as it is presented in Facebook's ads and campaign. While the above described CDA230 regulates a fundamental aspect of the internet, it would be difficult to call it comprehensive. A related question, which also appears in the campaign, is that "nothing has happened since then to regulate the internet."[49] In this regard, Mueller Milton notes that "between the 105th Congress (1997–1998) and the 116th Congress (2019–2021), over 300 bills related to the Internet were enacted by the U.S. Congress."[50] One of the most important of these is the adoption of net neutrality rules in 2015 by the Federal Communications Commission (FCC).[51] Although the latter has been legally challenged (in court proceedings [52]) and revised (by the then new President Trump administration[53]), on 9 July 2021, President Joe Biden ordered the FCC to reinstate net neutrality rules by Presidential Order 14036.[54]

Tom Wheeler, who was the FCC's Chairman from 2013 to 2017, argues[55] that a new regulator should be created, because the FCC is overburdened in many ways (both in terms of cases and jurisdiction) and is not up to the task of providing authority in a fast-changing and problematic area such as the internet. Wheeler cites the new EU's proposed regulations as an example to follow.[56] He argues that what is needed is not just technological regulation, but where "instead of technical standards, there would be behavioral standards."[57] The proposal is that tech companies, in cooperation with stakeholders, would draft a self-regulatory code proposal, which would then be adopted by this new agency, so that a combination of public and self-regulation, i.e. co-regulation, could be observed. In addition, he sees a need to

46 Robertson (2021).

47 Suzor (2019), p. 94.

48 https://about.fb.com/regulations/.

49 Ibid.

50 Milton (2021).

51 Protecting and Promoting the Open Internet, 80 FR 19737.

52 *United States Telecom Ass'n v FCC* 825 F.3d 674 (D.C. Cir. 2016).

53 Collins (2018).

54 Executive Order 14036 Promoting Competition in the American Economy, Sec. 2. (k) (i).

55 Wheeler (2021).

56 See Sect. 6.

57 Wheeler (2021).

change US antitrust rules, as "rigid, top-down, bureaucratic policies that often required prior approval for innovation have been sabotaged by the fast pace of the digital era."[58]

It is also worth noting that, in June 2020, the then Attorney General William Barr's Department published a report[59] on CDA230. The report points out that "platforms that choose to permit online consumer reviews and third-party content would be likely to remove or censor content whenever someone objects in order to minimize liability risks", which inevitably leads to the removal of non-infringing content, and indeed raises accusations of economic censorship.[60] In addition, a contemporaneous letter from the Attorney General suggests that the framework of immunity should be clarified so that platforms "cannot hide behind the shield of Section 230 to censor lawful speech in bad faith and inconsistent with their own terms of service."[61] The letter and report recommend that the following issues be considered by the US Congress and Senate:

- Is it necessary to provide for general immunity, or are there possible exceptions for certain content (child protection, terrorism, cyberbullying, etc.)?
- What are the conditions of good faith and, in this context, can the immunity of service providers acting in bad faith be waived?[62]
- Is it worth differentiating between different service providers (whether by size, function, contribution) or should uniform rules apply? Can a one-person blog and Facebook, Twitter or Google be treated in a uniform legal way?
- In the current situation, where the big fish are eating the smaller fish in the internet ecosystem, does the creation of new rules not lead to a (further) reduction of competition?
- Can the platform provider's own content (and therefore its own speech) be distinguished from content (and therefore speech) uploaded by third parties?
- Should there be long-term rules or temporary rules to deal with the current situation?
- Should defamation be retained as an exception to immunity?
- How can one determine whether a service provider is an author, editor or publisher?
- Is there immunity for knowing about (and not acting on) illegal or harmful content?
- How does this relate to the issue of censorship?

---

[58] Wheeler (2020).

[59] United States Department of Justice (2020).

[60] See *Delfi AS v Estonia* App no. 64569/09 (ECtHR, 16 June 2015), [67.]: "err on the side of caution to avoid possible subsequent liability."

[61] Barr (2020).

[62] For example, in a case where the provider benefited from immunity despite being established for a bad faith purpose because it sold firearms to people who were prohibited from doing so—and one of the customers subsequently killed three people with the purchased firearm (*Daniel v Armslist, LLC*, 386 Wis. 2d 449 [Wis. 2019]).

The questions are more numerous than the answers, and we have seen how this latest issue has been politicised in US politics. On 28 May 2020, then President Donald Trump issued Executive Order 13925[63] to crack down on online censorship. The text itself is at the level of generalities throughout (e.g. "Twitter, Facebook, Instagram, and YouTube wield immense, if not unprecedented, power to shape the interpretation of public events; to censor, delete, or disappear information; and to control what people see or do not see"[64]), but, in the debates around CDA230, the president also voted in favour of internet freedom, free competition and freedom of expression.[65]

The question is now not only what to do with CDA230, but also what are the ways forward in terms of establishing the responsibility of platform providers, the most important issue for the internet in the 2020s. Kyle Langvardt outlines four paths[66] that the regulator can take:

- The state *expressly* defines what content is illegal, harmful or to be removed.
- Users can choose between different methods defined by the service providers, thus reinforcing individual responsibility.
- Mandatory publication of content moderation policies and procedures.
- The 'privatisation' of content hosting, i.e. leaving it entirely up to service providers to decide how to publish content.

As Kyle Langvardt notes, none of the paths is the perfect solution, because:

- Given the nature of the internet and the freedom of communication, the first solution requires continuous state control (even censorship). Moreover, this may run counter to previous legislative practice—one need only think of the obligation to regulate fundamental rights at the highest level of the law. However, if we regulate at a lower level, "eventually someone will be tasked with safety-checking the censorship algorithms, and doing so will require a kind of close, ongoing regulatory intervention in the public sphere that has no clear historical parallel."[67]
- The second solution, where users can choose, for example, whether they are adults or children, can easily lead to the same problem where users are put in situations where they are given false access to certain content by providers,

[63]Executive Order 13925 Preventing Online Censorship.

[64]Ibid., Section 1. Policy.

[65]However, it is difficult to ignore the fact that Donald Trump, as President of the United States of America, has himself contributed to a significant erosion of the real meaning of the word censorship by communicating via Twitter messages. Cf. his post of 3 May 2019: "I am continuing to monitor the censorship of AMERICAN CITIZENS on social media platforms. This is the United States of America -- and we have what's known as FREEDOM OF SPEECH! We are monitoring and watching, closely!!" Romm (2019).

[66]Langvardt (2017), pp. 1353–1388.

[67]Langvardt (2017), p. 1378.

claiming exemption from liability.[68] In addition, when it comes to the content offered, it is easy for service providers to be confronted with different legal and social cultures in different countries, which may mean that what is legal in one country may be illegal in another.

- The third way may naturally raise constitutional issues, on the one hand, whether the algorithms that control moderation are part of the freedom of expression of the companies concerned,[69] and, on the other hand, competition law issues may arise in relation to the ownership of a private company.
- Although it can be said that the vast majority of users have never been censored by any service provider, this is not yet a significant argument in law for a fourth way. The more significant problem is that "under such a system, the shape of free speech will be determined by popular opinion, market pressures, governmental pressures, and managerial conscience."[70] In addition, in this case, service providers would be forced to monitor uploaded content on an ongoing basis.

It seems clear, therefore, that the US path needs to be reviewed,[71] but the direction in which the regulator will go remains to be seen.[72] As Balázs Csáki and Gyula Hatalovics put it, "several representatives from both political parties (Democrats and Republicans) have expressed expectations (or specific proposals)."[73] For those following these developments, it is not news that new regulatory attempts are being made,[74] such as the Online Content Policy Modernization Act (OCPMA), which was introduced in the Senate in September 2020, or the Platform Accountability and Consumer Transparency Act (PACTA), which was introduced in the Senate in March 2021. The proposals are clearly an attempt to break the immunity set up in the CDA230, as they are designed to make portals responsible for the content they post. According to the proposal's critics, "If policymakers aren't careful, they could inadvertently stifle innovation online, reduce the Internet's agility and efficiency, and put companies out of business by forcing intermediaries to assess liability of each new piece of content and service."[75]

The most eloquent summary of the situation was maybe provided by Senator Ron Wyden in 2021: "Mark Zuckerberg knows that rolling back Section 230 will cement Facebook's position as the dominant social media company and make it vastly

[68] It is not a perfect analogy, but the direction is similar: as a general rule, social media should not be used by persons under 13 years of age, and only a self-declaration form is used to check this during the process of registration.

[69] Panzarino (2016).

[70] Langvardt (2017), p. 1387.

[71] Szőke (2021), pp. 105–106.

[72] Citron and Franks (2020), pp. 45–75.; Whitehouse (2022), pp. 115–117.

[73] Csáki-Hatalovics (2021), p. 616.

[74] "In the last two years, there have been at least 18 attempts – via bills, executive orders and other initiatives – to try blow up the rule that has kept Internet intermediaries from being liable from the actions of their users since 1996." Jordan (2020).

[75] Ibid.

harder for new startups to challenge his cash cow."[76] In addition, "often there's a call for a publicly funded state social media platform."[77] Although in the 1990s and 2010s it seemed that US and European regulation could diverge, the time that has passed since then has shown that, without close cooperation between the 'big two', states are doomed to defeat. And in the battle between Silicon Valley and Washington in the United States of America, it is not yet clear who is winning...[78]

References

Article-19 (2020) Why decentralisation of content moderation might be the best way to protect freedom of expression online. 30 March. https://www.article19.org/resources/why-decentralisation-of-content-moderation-might-be-the-best-way-to-protect-freedom-of-expression-online/

Barata J (2022) The decisions of the oversight board from the perspective of international human rights law. Columbia University, New York

Barr WP (2020) Letter on 23 Sep. https://www.justice.gov/file/1319346/download/

Bickert M (2020) Online Content Regulation. facebook.com, Feb. https://about.fb.com/wp-content/uploads/2020/02/Charting-A-Way-Forward_Online-Content-Regulation-White-Paper-1.pdf

Bing C (2019) Facebook CEO calls for updated internet regulations. Reuters, 31 March. https://www.reuters.com/article/us-facebook-privacy-regulation-idUSKCN1RB0RX/

Butcher M (2020) The Real Facebook Oversight Board launches to counter Facebook's Oversight Board. TechCrunch, 30 Sep. https://techcrunch.com/2020/09/30/the-real-facebook-oversight-board-launches-to-counter-facebooks-oversight-board/

Citron DK, Franks MA (2020) The internet as a speech machine and other myths confounding section 230 reform. University of Chicago Legal Forum, 2020(3)

Collins K (2018) Net neutrality has officially been repealed. Here's how that could affect you. The New York Times, 11 June. https://www.nytimes.com/2018/06/11/technology/net-neutrality-repeal.html/

Conger K (2023) So what do we call twitter now anyway? The New York Times, 3 Aug. https://www.nytimes.com/2023/08/03/technology/twitter-x-tweets-elon-musk.html/

Crouch D (2022) HB20: Social Media Censorship and the Supreme Court. PatentlyO, 17 May. https://patentlyo.com/patent/2022/05/social-censorship-supreme.html/

Csáki-Hatalovics GB (2021) A közösségi média személyiségvédelemmel összefüggő kihívásai és szabályozása az Amerikai Egyesült Államokban (Privacy challenges and regulation of social media in the United States of America). In: Czékmann Z, Csák C, Barzó T (eds) "Gondolatok köztere". A közösségi média személyiségvédelemmel összefüggő kihívásai és szabályozása az egyes államokban ("Public space of thoughts". Privacy challenges and regulation of social media in different countries). Miskolci Egyetemi Kiadó, Miskolc

Culliford E (2019) Facebook pledges $130 million to content oversight board, delays naming members. Reuters, 12 Dec. https://www.reuters.com/article/facebook-oversight-idINKBN1YG23E/

[76] Lima (2021).

[77] Owens (2019).

[78] It should also be pointed out that the Texas House Bill 20 treats social media platforms as common carriers and forbid them to censor content on their platforms based on their own views. Although Supreme Court temporarily blocked the law in May 2022, States will likely try again with a slightly different approach. Crouch (2022).

De Streel A, Defreyne E, Jacquemin H, Ledger M, Michel A (2020) Online Platforms' Moderation of Illegal Content Online. Law, Practices and Options for Reform. Study for the committee on Internal Market and Consumer Protection, Policy Department for Economic, Scientific and Quality of Life Policies. European Parliament, Luxembourg

Executive Order 13925 Preventing Online Censorship

Executive Order 14036 Promoting Competition in the American Economy

Ghosh D (2019) Facebook's Oversight Board Is Not Enough. Harvard Business Review, 16 Oct. https://hbr.org/2019/10/facebooks-oversight-board-is-not-enough/

Graber J (2021) Ecosystem Review. matrix.org, Jan. https://ipfs.io/ipfs/QmdFrru4PyHzXGZztEPnYToBR3QovD7fkC1HSyty22LzfD/

Gyetván D (2023) A DSA és a Facebook Oversight Board szerepe a jogorvoslat biztosításában a social media vonatkozásában (The role of the DSA and the Facebook Oversight Board in providing redress for social media). In Medias Res 12(3)

Helfer LR, Land MK (2023) The Facebook oversight board's human rights future. Cardozo Law Rev 44(6)

Jordan K (2020) The Internet Is Built on 'Intermediaries' – They Should Be Protected. Internet Society, 2 Oct. https://www.internetsociety.org/blog/2020/10/the-internet-is-built-on-intermediaries-they-should-be-protected/

Klonick K (2020) The Facebook oversight board: creating an independent institution to adjudicate online free expression. Yale Law J 129(2418)

Klonick K (2021) Inside the Making of Facebook's Supreme Court. The New Yorker, 12 Feb. https://www.newyorker.com/tech/annals-of-technology/inside-the-making-of-facebooks-supreme-court/

Langvardt K (2017) Regulating online content moderation. Georgetown Law J 106(5)

Lanza E, Jackson M (2021) Content Moderation and Self-Regulation Mechanisms. The Facebook Oversight Board and its Implications for Latin America. Inter-American Dialogue, Washington, D.C.

Lénárd S (2021) Kié az utolsó szó? A Facebook Ellenőrző Bizottság döntésének margójára (Who has the last word? In the margins of the Facebook Oversight Board decision). Ludovika Blog, 25 May. https://www.ludovika.hu/blogok/frontierblog/2021/05/25/kie-az-utolso-szo/

Lendvai GF (2023a) Zwarte Piet a Facebook Oversight Board kontextusában – a Zwarte Piet és a kulturális különbségek értelmezése (Zwarte Piet in the context of the Facebook Oversight Board – Zwarte Piet and cultural differences). Arsboni 10(3–4)

Lendvai GF (2023b) "Pure Rat Country" – Reflections on Case Decision 2022-001-FB-UA of Facebook Oversight Board (Knin Cartoon Case). J Digital Technol Law 1(3)

Lima C (2021) Lawmakers rebuff Facebook's proposed internet rules. Politico, 24 March. https://www.politico.com/news/2021/03/24/facebook-proposed-internet-rules-477868/

Mercer ST (2020) The limitations of European Data Protection as a model for global privacy regulation. AJIL Unbound 114

Meta Q2 2022 Quarterly Update on the Oversight Board

Milton M (2021) Updated Internet Regulations? IG Institutions, Platform Governance, 22 March. https://www.internetgovernance.org/2021/03/22/updated-internet-regulations/

Morgan J (2021) Scholars overseeing Facebook: Supreme Court or fairness washing? Times Higher Education, 10 March. https://www.timeshighereducation.com/news/scholars-overseeing-facebook-supreme-court-or-fairness-washing/

Owens J (2019) The tech giants dominated the decade. But there's still time to rein them in. The Guardian, 25 Dec. https://www.theguardian.com/commentisfree/2019/dec/25/2010s-tech-giants-google-amazon-facebook-regulators/

Panzarino M (2016) Apple files motion to vacate the court order to force it to unlock iPhone, Citing Constitutional Free Speech Rights. TechCrunch, 25 Feb, https://guce.techcrunch.com/copyConsent?sessionId=3cc-sessionfcd249e6-9b52-468c-810b-9640bb3f02b7&lang=en-US/

Pongó T (2020) Új korszak az online véleménynyilvánítás korlátozásában? Gondolatok a Facebook Oversight Board működéséről. Iustum Aequum Salutare 16(4)

Pop V (2020) Zuckerberg Tells EU Regulators Facebook Wants More Content Liability. The Wall Street Journal, 7 Feb. https://www.wsj.com/articles/zuckerberg-tells-eu-regulators-facebook-wants-more-content-liability-11581961804/

Price R (2019) Twitter is trying to build a new decentralized social media service that could transform its business—or present new kinds of headaches. Insider, 11 Dec. https://www.businessinsider.com/bluesky-twitter-team-decentralised- socialmedia-2019-12?IR=T/

Protecting and Promoting the Open Internet, 80 FR 19737

Robertson A (2019) Twitter wants to decentralize, but decentralized social network creators don't trust it. The Verge, 12 Dec. https://www.theverge.com/2019/12/12/21012553/twitter-bluesky-decentralized-social-network-developers-reaction-mastodon-activitypub/

Robertson A (2021) Twitter's decentralized social network project takes a baby step forward. The Verge, 21 Jan. https://www.theverge.com/2021/1/21/22242718/twitter-bluesky-decentralized-social-media-team-project-update/

Romm T (2019) Trump warns he'll 'monitor the censorship' on social media after Facebook banned some far-right leaders. The Washington Post, 3 May. https://www.washingtonpost.com/technology/2019/05/03/trump-jr-accuses-facebook-silencing-conservatives-day-after-it-bans-some-far-right-users/

Suzor NP (2019) Lawless. The secret rules that govern our digital lives. Cambridge University Press, Cambridge

Szikora T (2020) Vajon miben hoz érdemi változást a Facebook újonnan felállt felügyeleti szerve? (What will the new Facebook supervisory body change?) Ludovika Blog, 25 May. https://www.ludovika.hu/blogok/itkiblog/2020/05/25/vajon-miben-hoz-erdemi-valtozast-a-facebook-ujonnan-felallt-felugyeleti-szerve/

Szikora T (2021) A Facebook Oversight Board első döntései – meglepetések helyett „papírforma"? (Facebook Oversight Board's first decisions – "paper form" instead of surprises?) Ludovika Blog, 5 Feb. https://www.ludovika.hu/blogok/itkiblog/2021/02/05/a-facebook-oversight-board-elso-dontesei-meglepetesek-helyett-papirforma/

Szőke GL (2021) A közösségi oldalak szabályozási problémái (Regulatory problems on social networking sites). In: Kis Kelemen B, Mohay Á (eds) A technológiai fejlődés jogi kihívásai: Kézikönyv a jogalkotás és jogalkalmazás számára (Legal challenges of technological development: a handbook for lawmakers and practitioners). Pécsi Tudományegyetem Állam- és Jogtudományi Kar, Pécs

Texas House Bill 20

United States Department of Justice (2020) Section 230 – Nurturing Innovation or Fostering Unaccountability? Key Takeaways and Recommendations, June. https://www.justice.gov/file/1286331/download/

Vaidhyanathan S (2018) Antisocial media: how facebook disconnects us and undermines democracy. Oxford University Press, Oxford

Wheeler T (2020) The Justice Department's Antitrust Lawsuit Against Google Isn't Enough to Stop the Abuses of Big Tech. Time, 20 Oct. https://time.com/5901696/google-antitrust-case/

Wheeler T (2021) Facebook says it supports internet regulation. Here's an Ambitious Proposal That Might Actually Make a Difference. Time, 5 Apr. https://time.com/5952630/facebook-regulation-agency/

Whitehouse S (2022) Section 230 reforms. In: Bollinger LC, Stone GR (eds) Social media, freedom of speech and the future of our democracy. Oxford University Press, Oxford

Zuckerberg M (2018) A Blueprint for Content Governance and Enforcement. facebook.com, 15 Nov. https://m.facebook.com/notes/mark-zuckerberg/a-blueprint-for-content-governance-and-enforcement/10156443129621634/

Zuckerberg M (2019) The Internet needs new rules. Let's start in these four areas. The Washington Post, 30 March. https://www.washingtonpost.com/opinions/mark-zuckerberg-the-internet-needs-new-rules-lets-start-in-these-four-areas/2019/03/29/9e6f0504-521a-11e9-a3f7-78b7525a8d5f_story.html/

Chapter 6
Towards a Digital Agenda for the European Union 2020

"If it is not already clear, Facebook is not compatible with democracy." (David Cicilline, the Chairman of the US House of Representatives Subcommittee on Antitrust, Commercial and Administrative Law. Twitter, *17 Feb 2021, https://twitter.com/davidcicilline/status/1362172969699704833/)*

At the very end of 2020, the press was full of headlines such as "A bill has been presented that could significantly erode the power of big technology companies in Europe."[1] There were caustic voices, such as "Digital market warns of misguided EU regulation"[2] but there were also jubilant ones, with headlines such as "European Commission publishes landmark package to regulate digital platforms and services."[3] What is certain is that the Digital Services Package could fundamentally change and define the digital regulatory landscape in the European Union and, in the longer term, create a predictable environment. This chapter aims to interpret the likely future steps by outlining the main regulatory plans contained in the Digital Services Package.

It now seems clear that the internet has become, as the ECtHR pointed out in *Cengiz and others v Turkey*, "the principal means by which individuals exercise their right to freedom to receive and impart information and ideas." [4] As a consequence, in many countries around the world, internet regulation has become a top priority on the political agenda, albeit with different solutions, from Australia[5] to Germany[6] and Canada[7] to Poland[8] and Hungary.[9] In recent years, the world has become familiar

[1] Bobák (2020).

[2] Török (2020).

[3] Cunningham (2020).

[4] *Cengiz and Others v Turkey* App nos 48226/10 and 14027/11 (ECtHR, 1 December 2015), [49.].

[5] Stelter (2021).

[6] Toor (2017).

[7] Meyer (2021).

[8] Easton (2021).

[9] Huszák (2021).

G. Gosztonyi, *Censorship from Plato to Social Media*, Law, Governance and Technology Series 61, https://doi.org/10.1007/978-3-031-46529-1_6

with terms such as *fake news, deepfake, dis- and misinformation, the* spread of which digital platforms worldwide have not yet devoted sufficient resources to preventing. Again quoting the ECtHR, "the Internet plays an important role in enhancing the public's access to news and facilitating the dissemination of information in general. User-generated expressive activity on the Internet provides an unprecedented platform for the exercise of freedom of expression." [10] And the changing political climate has also been felt by the tech giants, who have taken steps to change the tide.[11] However, we should also not forget that the fundamental problems lie in the definition of levels of responsibility, as in many cases these giant platforms have acted as quasi-states[12] and in moderation, acting only on the basis of their own ToS-like documents, as quasi-legislative powers in their own right. This is further complicated by the fact that the case-law of the European Court of Human Rights and the Court of Justice of the European Union (CJEU) is far from being consistent.[13]

6.1 Regulation on Digital Services

The first striking legal difference compared to the previous solution in this area is that the European Union with the Digital Services Act (DSA)[14] legislates not as a directive but as a regulation, by analogy with the GDPR.[15] As could be read in the proposal[16] of the DSA that was published in December 2020: "The Commission has decided to put forward a proposal for a Regulation to ensure a consistent level of protection throughout the Union and to prevent divergences hampering the free provision of the relevant services within the internal market, as well as guarantee the uniform protection of rights and uniform obligations for business and consumers across the internal market.[17] This is necessary to provide legal certainty and transparency for economic operators and consumers alike. The proposed Regulation also ensures consistent monitoring of the rights and obligations, and equivalent sanctions in all Member States, as well as effective cooperation between the supervisory

[10] *Cengiz and Others v Turkey* App nos 48226/10 and 14027/11 (ECtHR, 1 December 2015), [52.].

[11] See Sect. 5.2

[12] Kim and Telman (2015), pp. 723–770.

[13] For details, see Sect. 9.

[14] Regulation (EU) 2022/2065 of the European Parliament and of the Council of 19 October 2022 on a Single Market For Digital Services and amending Directive 2000/31/EC (Digital Services Act), PE/30/2022/REV/1, OJ L 277, 27.10.2022, pp 1–102.

[15] Regulations are legal acts which, once they enter into force, apply automatically and uniformly to all EU countries, without the need for transposition into national law. They are binding in their entirety on all EU countries. See de Witte (2008), pp. 79–108.

[16] Proposal for a Regulation of the European Parliament and of the Council on a Single Market For Digital Services and amending Directive 2000/31/EC, COM/2020/825 final (DSA Proposal).

[17] "The DSA's overarching principle is consumer protection." Petrányi (2022), p. 9.

authorities of different Member States and at Union level."[18] However, sentences in other places in the DSA proposal revealed the real intention without any gloss: "the Internet is by its nature cross-border, the legislative efforts at national level referred to above hamper the provision and reception of services throughout the Union",[19] so an important aim is "empowering citizens and building more resilient democracies across the Union."[20]

The new regulation entered into force on 16 November 2022, and all DSA provisions will apply 15 months after its entry into force on February 2024. Operators designated as *very large online platforms* (VLOPs) and *very large online search engines* (VLOSEs)[21] will already have to comply with stricter obligations from mid-2023.[22] The European Commission will adopt implementing and delegating acts framing the application of the DSA.[23]

It is worth highlighting that the new regulation does not repeal the ECD in its entirety, but builds on its legal solutions.[24] However, some parts of the ECD will be replaced by new provisions[25] (e.g. Articles 12–15 of the ECD[26]). It should already be noted here that some of the rules of the new DSA, the ECD and the AVMS do not seem to be harmonised.[27]

The communication on the Digital Services Act summarises the main changes below:[28]

Benefits for Individuals

- More choice, lower prices
- Greater protection against illegal content
- Enhanced protection of fundamental rights

Benefits for Digital Service Providers

- Legal certainty, harmonised legislation
- More favourable framework conditions for starting and expanding businesses

---

[18] DSA Proposal, Explanatory memorandum, 2.; Moravec et al. (2021), pp. 166–185.

[19] DSA Proposal, Explanatory memorandum, 2.

[20] Ibid., 1.

[21] DSA, Chapter III, Section 5.

[22] The first list of 17 VLOPs and 2 very large online search engines VLOSEs was published in May 2023 and the "sole European-originated company that made the cut is Zalando, a German online fashion retailer." Detrekői (2023). In addition, on 27 June 2023, Zalando filed a legal challenge against the European Commission's decision, challenging the classification. Amazon has also joined this action. Kirton et al. (2023).

[23] European Parliament (2022a).

[24] Libor (2021), p. 21.

[25] DSA, Article 89.

[26] "Articles 12 to 15 of Directive 2000/31/EC are deleted." See Sect. 4.4.3.

[27] Cauffman and Goanta (2021), pp. 3–4.

[28] https://commission.europa.eu/strategy-and-policy/priorities-2019-2024/europe-fit-digital-age/digital-services-act-ensuring-safe-and-accountable-online-environment_en.

Benefits for Business Users of Digital Services

- More choice, lower prices
- Access to EU markets through online platforms

Benefits for Society as a Whole

- Greater democratic control and oversight of systemic online platforms
- Mitigating systemic risks, for example by reducing manipulation and disinformation

All this is expected to lead to a strengthening of human rights, equality, legal certainty, freedom and democracy, and in sum, the rule of law, as uniform liability rules, transparency and predictability in the online environment can reduce the problems of fake news and disinformation discussed above. As Bernát Török put it, "the primary regulatory objective is that the service provider must take responsibility for the aspects in which it structures the communication on its own platform and the way it guides us through the proliferation of content with necessarily limited reception."[29]

6.1.1 *Benefits of the Regulation*

As we have seen above, the main advantage of the DSA is that it seeks to put a regulatory environment that has remained essentially unchanged for 20 years, and which has been overtaken by time and technological progress on a new footing.[30] In particular, it would create a category of *trusted flaggers,*[31] in other words, it would bring the fight against illegal content online back to a level of trust and predictability. It would also give users stronger tools to challenge and appeal against the moderation decisions of platforms, unlike current practice.[32]

It would also put one of the most controversial issues, the algorithms of the platforms, on a new footing, to increase transparency by giving access to them to external experts and auditors.[33] To address systemic risks, the *VLOPs and VLOSEs* will be subject to specific, rather than uniform, liability rules.[34] This category include those +online platforms and online search engines which have a number of average monthly active recipients of the service in the Union equal to or higher than

[29] Török (2021).

[30] Klein (2023), p. 286.

[31] DSA, Article 22.

[32] DSA, Article 10.: "Information provided to the recipient of the service shall include a statement of reasons and the possibilities for redress that exist."

[33] DSA, Article 72.

[34] Capello (2021), pp. 40–47.

45 million.[35] The main reason for singling out giant platforms is the correlation between the size of the service and the potential for harm.[36] Related to this is the need for Member States to designate a competent authority *(digital service coordinator)* to carry out all tasks related to the application and enforcement of the Regulation in that Member State.[37] Among the many other innovations,[38] the DSA requires the development of standards, codes of conduct and crisis management protocols.[39] It is also important to underline that "the DSA would apply to all online intermediary service providers as long as their users (businesses or individuals) have their place of establishment or residence in the EU";[40] in other words, the DSA goes back to the extraterritorial solutions of the GDPR. In addition, *safe harbour model*, which has already been used in the ECD, was transferred to the DSA[41] for harmonisation purposes, by strengthening the rules. At the same time, the NTDS would be replaced by a so-called *Notice and action mechanisms*[42] (NAM),[43] which would differ from the existing legislation on a number of points.[44] Under this, if a four-element notification[45] is received by a service provider, it would be deemed to have been brought to the service provider's actual knowledge of the information[46] and they shall "take their decisions in respect of the information to which the notices relate, in a timely, diligent, non-arbitrary and objective manner."[47] Of particular importance, the DSA also confirms the prohibition on imposing general monitoring[48]— although as we will see in the cons, the picture is not clearly positive on these latter two issues.

Given the now real and meaningful level of fines in previous years, it is not surprising that if an online platform infringes the relevant provisions of the DSA, the Commission can impose a fine of up to 6% of the annual worldwide turnover of the

[35] DSA, Article 33(1).

[36] Broughton Micova (2021), p. 5.

[37] DSA, Article 49(1).

[38] Favro and Zolynski (2021), pp. 217–223.

[39] DSA, Articles 44–48.

[40] Van Canneyt (2021).

[41] DSA, Article 89(2).

[42] DSA, Article 16.

[43] It is worth pointing out that although NAM in the DSA would replace the former NTDS, Aleksandra Kuczerawy notes that there is a conceptual ambiguity in the legislation, as the concept of NAM "covers a variety of mechanisms designed to eliminate illegal or infringing content from the Internet upon request of the right holder." In other words, one type of NAM is the NTDS, another is the NSD, and the third is the "notice and notification system" (NN), i.e. where the service provider, after receiving a notification, also sends a notification to the content uploader requesting the voluntary removal of the content. Kuczerawy (2018), p. 38.

[44] Wilman (2023), p. 47.

[45] DSA, Article 16(2); Kuczerawy (2023), pp. 173–174.

[46] DSA, Article 16(3).

[47] DSA, Article 16(6).

[48] DSA, Article 8; Ződi (2023), p. 188.

provider of intermediary services concerned in the preceding financial year.[49] In addition, the use of so-called *interim measures* (e.g. temporary suspension of service) has been introduced as a real enforcement mechanism, as when there is "an urgency due to the risk of serious damage for the recipients of the service, the Commission may, by decision, order interim measures against the provider of the very large online platform or of the very large online search engine concerned on the basis of a *prima facie* finding of an infringement."[50]

6.1.2 Disadvantages of the Proposed Regulation

A problematic issue is the lack of distinction between and definition of illegal and harmful online content in the document—although it is assumed that this would be remedied by the 2018 EU Code of Practice on Disinformation.[51] According to Euractiv, Patrik Tovaryš, head of the Information Society Services Department at the Czech Ministry of Industry and Trade, pointed out that "there is an absolute need to distinguish between the notion of illegal content and legal but harmful content. This is imperative as there usually is a distinction between criminal conduct, such as sharing terrorist content, and sharing disinformation, which many users share with faith that it is true."[52] In addition, neither the terminology of the DSA and the DMA, which will be discussed below, nor the definitions set in the ECD and the AVMS are fully harmonised.

An analysis of the negative aspects of the proposed regulation shows that, in terms of liability, it follows the path taken by national regulations (such as the German NetzDG,[53] the French Avia law[54] or the Austrian law against hate speech[55]), which force platforms to monitor users' content on a continuous basis in order to comply with the rules and avoid fines.[56] This can result in excessive measures—tending towards censorship—meaning that, as the ECtHR put it, "the entity in charge of filtering will err on the side of protecting its own liability, rather

[49] DSA, Article 52(3).

[50] DSA, Article 70(1).

[51] See Sect. 4.4.4.

[52] Yar et al. (2020).

[53] Gesetz zur Verbesserung der Rechtsdurchsetzung in sozialen Netzwerken (Netzwerkdurchsetzungsgesetz, NetzDG), BGBl. I S. 3352; Kéringer (2023), pp. 413–418.

[54] Although the French Constitutional Court declared it unconstitutional on 18 June 2020. Psychogiopoulou and de la Sierra (2022), p. 1.

[55] Bundesgesetz über Maßnahmen zum Schutz der Nutzer auf Kommunikationsplattformen (Kommunikationsplattformen-Gesetz, KoPl-G), BGBl. I Nr. 151/2020. Cf. Mchangama and Fiss (2019).

[56] Golunova (2021).

than protecting freedom of expression." [57] In relation to the new NAM legislation, it should be pointed out that the first point of the four-element notification requires the whistleblower to provide "a sufficiently substantiated explanation of the reasons why the individual or entity alleges the information in question to be illegal content."[58] As we have seen above, "illegal content as a broad category may present very diverse typologies",[59] so the necessity and proportionality tests may not be satisfied by the mere fact that a service provider must act on the basis of a notification alleging unlawfulness.[60] According to Geert Bourgeois, a Belgian MEP, "the consequence will be overly politically correct censorship."[61]

In addition, Joan Barata argued that the extraterritorial scope would "violate the international law principles of comity and reciprocity and open the door to the possibility that other countries with a more restrictive conception of the right to freedom of expression may be able to legitimately extend to the territory of the European Union (and globally) similar remedies based on their national law."[62] In Ruth Janal's view, the expected 45 million active users will prove to be too many in relation to the population of EU Member States.[63] Alexander Peukert also highlighted the risk of bureaucratisation for the digital services coordinator.[64] Some also noted that the necessary rules are already in place, so the EU should concentrate on enforcing them rather than adopting new legislation.[65]

6.2 Regulation on Digital Markets

Another element of the new European digital package regulates digital markets, and European Commission President Ursula von der Leyen told the Web Summit 2020[66] that the EU leadership elected in 2019 will seek to control the power of the big tech players much more firmly. In this context, she stressed that they want to regulate these giants not only in terms of content but also in terms of technology, and that the proposed regulation on Digital Markets serves this purpose.

---

[57] *Delfi AS v Estonia* App no. 64569/09 (ECtHR, 16 June 2015), Joint dissenting opinion of Judges Sajó and Tsotsoria, 2.

[58] DSA, Article 16(2) a).

[59] Barata (2021), p. 15.

[60] Moreover, this can be compared with the trend for service providers to take action on certain content within one hour. Regulation (EU) 2021/784 of the European Parliament and of the Council of 29 April 2021 on addressing the dissemination of terrorist content online, PE/19/2021/INIT, OJ L 172, 17.5.2021, pp 79–109.

[61] European Parliament News (2021).

[62] Barata (2021), p. 15.

[63] Janal (2021).

[64] Peukert (2021).

[65] Mussard (2020).

[66] European Commission (2020).

The key concept in the Digital Markets Act (DMA)[67] is the gatekeeper platform,[68] which covers service providers that have a significant impact on the internal market, enjoy a stable and lasting position and also operate at least one core platform service. Such core platform services may include:

- online intermediary services (including, for example, marketplaces, job exchanges and online intermediary services in other sectors such as mobility, transport or energy);
- online search engine;
- online social networking service;
- video-sharing platform service;
- number-independent interpersonal communications services;
- operating system;
- web browsers;
- virtual assistants;
- cloud computing services;
- online advertising services (including advertising networks, advertising marketplaces and any other advertising intermediary services provided by any of the above).[69]

As the legislator puts it in the Proposal, "a small number of large providers of core platform services have emerged with considerable economic power. (. . .) it is likely to lead in many cases to serious imbalances in bargaining power and, consequently, to unfair practices and conditions for business users as well as end users of core platform services provided by gatekeepers, to the detriment of prices, quality, choice and innovation therein."[70] On this basis, to ensure conditions of fair competition, these giant providers will be singled out and subject to a much stricter set of conditions and sanctions.[71] Moreover, as we have seen above in the case of the DSA, these operators are by their very nature international, so national regulations can only achieve partial results against them.[72] Under the envisaged procedure, the Commission will designate a provider as a gatekeeper if it meets three criteria: number of users reached, amount of annual traffic and duration of operation.[73] By

---

[67] Regulation (EU) 2022/1925 of the European Parliament and of the Council of 14 September 2022 on contestable and fair markets in the digital sector and amending Directives (EU) 2019/1937 and (EU) 2020/1828 (Digital Markets Act), PE/17/2022/REV/1, OJ L 265, 12.10.2022, pp 1–66.

[68] DMA, Article 3(1).

[69] DMA, Article 2(2).

[70] Proposal for a Regulation of the European Parliament and of the Council on contestable and fair markets in the digital sector, COM/2020/842 final (DMA Proposal), 3–4.

[71] Capello (2021), pp. 86–90.

[72] See DMA Proposal, Explanatory Memorandum, 2: "Almost 24% of total online trade in Europe is cross-border."

[73] Bálint (2023).

examining the three conditions in detail, it is proposed that there should be a presumption of compliance if the platform:

- achieves an annual Union turnover equal to or above EUR 7.5 billion in each of the last 3 financial years, or where its average market capitalisation or its equivalent fair market value amounted to at least EUR 75 billion in the last financial year, and it provides the same core platform service in at least three Member States;
- it provides a core platform service that in the last financial year has at least 45 million monthly active end users established or located in the Union and at least 10,000 yearly active business users established in the Union; and
- where the above thresholds were met in each of the last 3 financial years.[74]

It is clear from the setting of each of these thresholds that the European Union is genuinely seeking to limit the anti-competitive practices of the largest players and is in no way seeking to impose any unjustified restrictions on Internet services of a smaller size and reach.[75]

The new regulation entered into force on 1 November 2022, and all DSA provisions will apply 15 months after its entry into force, in March 2024. Most of the act's provisions will apply as of 2 May 2023, when the gatekeeper designation procedure will start. That designation follows notification by the respective platforms to the Commission.[76] Operators designated as gatekeepers will have to comply with a range of obligations and prohibitions within 6 months of their designation as gatekeepers. The Commission may adopt implementing or delegating acts or guidelines to frame the application of the DMA.[77]

6.2.1 *Benefits of the Proposed Regulation*

Among the benefits, the most important one to start with is the definition of the gatekeeper platform. Speaking at the Web Summit 2020, Ursula von der Leyen said that with more power comes more responsibility.[78] The key sentence on all these technological restrictions is to be found in the explanatory memorandum of the Proposal, which states that "the conduct of combining end user data from different sources or signing in users to different services of gatekeepers gives them potential

[74]DMA, Article 3(2).

[75]"The purpose of the DMA is to prevent the distortion of competition" Domokos and Belyakova (2022), p. 5.

[76]The first list of gatekeepers was published in September 2023 and "Microsoft and Apple are reportedly pushing to keep Bing and iMessage, respectively, off the list". Robertson (2023).

[77]European Parliament (2022b).

[78]European Commission (2020).

advantages in terms of accumulation of data, thereby raising barriers to entry."[79] In other words, on the one hand, the regulation aims to strengthen market entry for new service providers and services, and, on the other hand, it aims to protect end users' data and opportunities.[80] Such technological barriers, as set out in DMA Article 6, include:

- refraining from aggregating personal data from multiple locations;
- refraining from allowing end users to access other services of the gatekeeper for the purpose of aggregating personal data;[81]
- allowing business users to offer the same products or services to end users through third party online intermediary services at prices or conditions that differ from those offered through the gatekeeper's online intermediary service;
- refraining from preventing or restricting business users from contacting any relevant authority regarding any practices of gatekeepers;
- refraining from requiring business users to use the gatekeeper identification service *(lock-in)*;
- refraining from requiring business users or end-users to subscribe or register for (...) any other core platform service in order to access, subscribe or register for any of (...)'s core platform services.[82]

In particular, gatekeepers shall ensure the effective portability of data generated by business and end user activities, and in particular provide end users with the tools to facilitate the exercise of portability, including through continuous and real-time access.[83] Violators of the main rules may be subject to strict sanctions, similar to the DSA rules: the Commission may impose a fine of up to 10% of the total worldwide turnover in the preceding financial year.[84] Of course, the use of so-called *interim measures* is also included in this proposal for a Regulation.[85]

6.2.2 Disadvantages of the Proposed Regulation

The most serious criticisms, in addition to the conceptual inconsistency[86] mentioned above, have been expressed by many in relation to the classification as a gatekeeper in Article 3 of the DMA. Indeed, under the provisions of the DMA, the Commission may designate a service provider as a gatekeeper, even if the criteria discussed above

[79] DMA Proposal, 36.

[80] Fasquelle and Inacio (2021), pp. 4–11.

[81] For example, signing in to Gmail mailbox does not automatically sign into the YouTube account.

[82] For example, allowing non-Apple devices to use the Apple App Store.

[83] DMA, Article 6(9).

[84] DMA, Article 30(1).

[85] DMA, Article 24.

[86] See Sect. 6.1.2.

are not met. According to Teresa Rodríguez de las Heras Ballell, the use of "the list-based definition of core platform services is not optimal for guaranteeing a technology-neutral, structure-agnostic adaptability of the DMA to future challenges."[87] The methodology for the designation of the DMA as a gatekeeper is still to be worked out, just as it is not clear to what extent and in what proportions the criteria set out in Article 3(6), which the Commission must take into account, will be considered in the assessment. It is also unclear whether there is any order of priority between the three main criteria, and the burden of proving non-compliance is, according to the procedure, placed on the service provider. Similarly, there are no precise rules on the transfer of data for businesses and end users, so it is technically unclear at this stage whether the implementation will provide any real help and solutions to the practical problems encountered.

6.3 Conclusion

Whether David Cicilline is right and Facebook (and its tech giant counterparts) are incompatible with democracy is highly questionable at the very least. Nevertheless, that stricter regulation than the current—almost *laissez-faire*—regime is needed does not seem in doubt, and on this, all the regulators in our politically polarised world—right or left—seem to agree. The internet as such is nothing more than a vast ecosystem.[88] And like all of them, complex, ever-changing and diverse. The intention to put the regulation of this vast ecosystem on a new footing is welcome, but the devil is always in the detail.

Although the legislation seems to be in line with the political desires and regulatory directions of the Member States, much will depend on the implications and the detailed rules.[89] What is certain is that the new digital package has many advantages and, fortunately, there seems to be a consensus that incorporating the experience of the last 20 years should be a priority. In addition, it is envisaged that the Regulation will be kept under review, so it is possible that we will not have to wait another two decades[90] if we come to another Internet evolution or a problem that needs to be addressed at global level. In other words, regulation will be much better able to keep pace with changes in market practice than it is at present.

Whatever their fate will be in practice, the digital package sets the direction the European Union intends to follow in the near future. However, despite their positive aspects, it is clear that only the first steps on the road have been taken.

---

[87] Rodríguez de las Heras Ballell (2021).

[88] Ma et al. (2015), pp. 85–98.

[89] Clément Perarnaud's study on EU Member States' preferences and coalitions for the Digital Single Market between 2016 and 2019 could be a sign of things to come. Perarnaud (2021).

[90] Podszun et al. (2021).

References

Bálint J (2023) The Digital Markets Act: the future of competition law in the digital market. Versenytükör 19(2)

Barata J (2021) The Digital Services Act and its impact on the right to freedom of expression: special focus on risk mitigation obligations. Plataforma en Defensa de la Libertad de Información, 22 June. https://libertadinformacion.cc/wp-content/uploads/2021/06/DSA-AND-ITS-IMPACT-ON-FREEDOM-OF-EXPRESSION-JOAN-BARATA-PDLI.pdf

Bobák Á (2020) Bemutatták a törvényjavaslatot, ami jelentősen megtépázhatja a nagy technológiai cégek hatalmát Európában (A bill has been presented that could significantly erode the power of big technology companies in Europe). Raketa.hu, 16 December. https://raketa.hu/digitalis-szolgaltatasok-torveny-europai-bizottsag/

Broughton Micova S (2021) What is the harm in size? Very large online platforms in the Digital Services Act. Centre on Regulation in Europe, Brussels

Bundesgesetz über Maßnahmen zum Schutz der Nutzer auf Kommunikationsplattformen (Kommunikationsplattformen-Gesetz, KoPl-G), BGBl. I Nr. 151/2020

Capello M (ed) (2021) Unravelling the Digital Services Act package. European Audiovisual Observatory, Strasbourg

Cauffman C, Goanta C (2021) A new order: the Digital Services Act and Consumer Protection. Eur J Risk Regul 12(4)

Cunningham F (2020) European Commission publishes landmark package to regulate digital platforms and services. Bird & Bird News Centre, December. https://www.twobirds.com/en/news/articles/2020/global/european-commission-publishes-landmark-package-to-regulate-digital-platforms-and-services/

De Witte B (2008) Legal instruments and law-making in the Lisbon Treaty. In: Griller S, Ziller J (eds) The Lisbon Treaty. Schriftenreihe der Österreichischen Gesellschaft für Europaforschung (ECSA Austria)/European Community Studies Association of Austria Publication Series, Springer, Vienna

Detrekői Z (2023) Who are the tech giants who will soon face the EU's new digital regulations? Medium, 6 June. https://medium.com/journalism-trends/who-are-the-tech-giants-who-will-soon-face-the-eus-new-digital-regulations-923886125eac/

Domokos M, Belyakova O (2022) Digital Markets Act. In: CMS: digital horizons. A series of reports exploring CEE's digital future. CMS. https://cms.law/en/media/local/cms-cmno/files/publications/publications/cee-digital-horizon-report-data-centres

Easton A (2021) Poland proposes social media 'free speech' law. BBC News, 15 January. https://www.bbc.com/news/technology-55678502/

European Commission (2020) Web Summit 2020 – a Europe for everybody with EC president. 2 December. https://www.youtube.com/watch?v=jgOBZv2nHjA/

European Parliament (2022a) Digital Services Act: Application timeline. https://www.europarl.europa.eu/RegData/etudes/ATAG/2022/739227/EPRS-AaG-739227-DSA-Application-timeline-FINAL.pdf

European Parliament (2022b) Digital Markets Act: Application timeline. https://www.europarl.europa.eu/RegData/etudes/ATAG/2022/739226/EPRS-AaG-739226-DMA-Application-timeline-FINAL.pdf

European Parliament News (2021) Social media and democracy: we need laws, not platform guidelines. European Parliament News, 10 February. https://www.europarl.europa.eu/news/en/headlines/society/20210204STO97129/social-media-and-democracy-we-need-laws-not-platform-guidelines/

Fasquelle D, Inacio E (2021) DMA/DSA: Une nouvelle et importante étape dans la régulation européenne des acteurs du numérique (DMA/DSA: A new and important step in the European regulation of digital players). Europe: Actualité du droit de l'Union européenne 2021(5)

Favro K, Zolynski C (2021) DSA, DMA: L'Europe encore au milieu du gué (DSA, DMA: Europe still in the middle of the road). Dalloz IP/IT 2021(4)

Gesetz zur Verbesserung der Rechtsdurchsetzung in sozialen Netzwerken (Netzwerkdurchsetzungsgesetz, NetzDG), BGBl. I S. 3352
Golunova V (2021) The Digital Services Act and freedom of expression: triumph or failure? Maastricht University Blog, 8 March. https://www.maastrichtuniversity.nl/blog/2021/03/digital-services-act-and-freedom-expression-triumph-or-failure/
Huszák D (2021) Bejelentették: szabályozza Magyarország a Facebookot és a nagy techcégeket (It has been announced that Hungary will regulate Facebook and big tech companies). Portfolio.hu, 26 January. https://www.portfolio.hu/uzlet/20210126/bejelentettek-szabalyozza-magyarorszag-a-facebookot-es-a-nagy-techcegeket-466858/
Janal R (2021) Eyes wide open. Adapting the Digital Services Act to the realities of intermediary service provision. VerfBlog, 7 September. https://verfassungsblog.de/power-dsa-dma-15/
Kéringer S (2023) NetzDG, avagy gyakorlati példa a platformszabályozás megvalósítására (NetzDG, or a practical example of how to implement platform regulation). In: Török B, Ződi Z (eds) Digitalizálódó társadalom. Tanulmányok az új technológiák társadalmi-jogi hatásairól (A digital society. Studies on the socio-legal implications of new technologies). Ludovika Egyetemi Kiadó, Budapest
Kim NS, Telman DA (2015) Jeremy: Internet giants as quasi-governmental actors and the limits of contractual consent. Missouri Law Rev 80(3)
Kirton D, Moore L, Casey L, Jones S (2023) Amazon joins Zalando in challenging its designation under the Digital Services Act. Lexology, 20 July. https://www.lexology.com/library/detail.aspx?g=8a4e6ab4-d53c-410e-9299-715d4c705fea/
Klein T (2023) Az újmédia szabályozásának új iránya? – A Digital Services Act alapjogvédelmi mechanizmusa (A new direction for new media regulation? – The basic rights protection mechanism of the Digital Services Act). In: Török B, Ződi Z (eds) Digitalizálódó társadalom. Tanulmányok az új technológiák társadalmi-jogi hatásairól (A digital society. Studies on the socio-legal implications of new technologies). Ludovika Egyetemi Kiadó, Budapest
Kuczerawy A (2018) Intermediary liability and freedom of expression in the EU: from concepts to safeguards. Intersentia, Cambridge
Kuczerawy A (2023) Remedying overremoval. In: van Hoboken J, Quintais JP, Appelman N, Fahy R, Buri I, Straub M (eds) Putting the Digital Services Act into practice. Enforcement, access to justice, and global implications. Verfassungsblog gGmbH, Berlin
Libor C (2021) EU-Kommission: Entwürfe zum Digital Services Act und Digital Markets Act. AfP 52(1)
Ma RTB, Lui JCS, Misra V (2015) Evolution of the internet economic ecosystem. IEEE/ACM Tran Netw 23(1)
Mchangama J, Fiss J (2019) The Digital Berlin Wall: how Germany (accidentally) created a prototype for Global Online Censorship. Justitia, Copenhagen
Meyer C (2021) Canada looks at Australia's experience regulating social media. Canada's National Observer, 1 February. https://www.nationalobserver.com/2021/02/01/news/canada-looking-australias-experience-regulating-social-media/
Moravec O, Smieško I, Galewska E, Gosztonyi G, Zolea S, Schneiders P (2021) Digital Services Act proposal (social media regulation). Studia Politica Slovaca 14(2–3)
Mussard H (2020) Digital advertising industry warns against misguided EU regulation. IAB Europe, 29 September. https://iabeurope.eu/all-news/digital-advertising-industry-warns-against-misguided-eu-regulation/
Perarnaud C (2021) A step back to look ahead: mapping coalitions on data flows and platform regulation in the Council of the EU (2016–2019). Internet Policy Rev 10(2)
Petrányi D (2022) Digital Services Act. In: CMS: digital horizons. A series of reports exploring CEE's digital future. CMS. https://cms.law/en/media/local/cms-cmno/files/publications/publications/cee-digital-horizon-report-data-centres/
Peukert A (2021) Five reasons to be skeptical about the DSA. VerfBlog, 31 August. https://verfassungsblog.de/power-dsa-dma-04/

Podszun R, Bongartz P, Langenstein S (2021) Proposals on how to improve the Digital Markets Act. SSRN Electronic Journal. https://papers.ssrn.com/sol3/papers.cfm?abstract_id=3788571/
Proposal for a Regulation of the European Parliament and of the Council on a Single Market For Digital Services (Digital Services Act) and amending Directive 2000/31/EC, COM/2020/825 final
Proposal for a Regulation of the European Parliament and of the Council on contestable and fair markets in the digital sector (Digital Markets Act), COM/2020/842 final
Psychogiopoulou E, de la Sierra S (2022) European supranational courts and judicial decision-making in the era of digitalisation. In: Psychogiopoulou E, de la Sierra S (eds) Digital media governance and supranational courts. Selected issues and insights from the European judiciary. Edward Elgar, Cheltenham
Regulation (EU) 2021/784 of the European Parliament and of the Council of 29 April 2021 on addressing the dissemination of terrorist content online, PE/19/2021/INIT, OJ L 172, 17.5.2021, pp 79–109
Regulation (EU) 2022/1925 of the European Parliament and of the Council of 14 September 2022 on contestable and fair markets in the digital sector and amending Directives (EU) 2019/1937 and (EU) 2020/1828 (Digital Markets Act), PE/17/2022/REV/1, OJ L 265, 12.10.2022, pp 1–66
Regulation (EU) 2022/2065 of the European Parliament and of the Council of 19 October 2022 on a Single Market For Digital Services and amending Directive 2000/31/EC (Digital Services Act), PE/30/2022/REV/1, OJ L 277, 27.10.2022, pp 1–102
Robertson A (2023) Apple and Microsoft reportedly want iMessage and Bing off the EU's tech 'gatekeeper' list. The Verge, 5 Sep. https://www.theverge.com/2023/9/4/23858948/eu-microsoft-apple-bing-imessage-dma-gatekeeperslist-dispute/
Rodríguez de las Heras Ballell T (2021) The scope of the DMA. Pivotal for success, critically assessed. VerfBlog, 30 August. https://verfassungsblog.de/power-dsa-dma-02/
Stelter B (2021) What Australia's new law might mean for the news you see in the future. CNN, 1 March. https://edition.cnn.com/2021/02/27/media/australia-facebook/index.html/
Toor A (2017) Germany passes controversial law to fine Facebook over hate speech. The Verge, 30 June. https://www.theverge.com/2017/6/30/15898386/germany-facebook-hate-speech-law-passed/
Török D (2020) Félrement uniós szabályozásra figyelmeztet a digitális piac (Digital market warns of misguided EU regulation). IAB Hungary Blog, 14 October. https://blog.iab.hu/2020/10/14/digital-services-act-iab-europe/
Török B (2021) Platforms and fundamental rights. Hungarian Conserv 1(2)
Van Canneyt T (2021) The proposed DSA – part 1 – transforming the delivery of online services through EU regulation. fieldfisher, 12 January, https://www.fieldfisher.com/en/services/technology-outsourcing-and-privacy/technology-and-outsourcing-blog/the-digital-services-act/
Wilman F (2023) Between preservation and clarification: the evolution of the DSA's liability rules in light of the CJEU's case law. In: van Hoboken J, Quintais JP, Appelman N, Fahy R, Buri I, Straub M (eds) Putting the digital services act into practice. Enforcement, access to justice, and global implications. Verfassungsblog gGmbH, Berlin
Yar L, Hendrych L, Strzałkowski M, Szicherle P (2020) Visegrad Four want to distinguish between 'illegal' and 'harmful' content in Digital Services Act. Euractiv, 2 November. https://www.euractiv.com/section/digital/news/visegrad-four-want-to-distinguish-between-illegal-and-harmful-content-in-digital-services-act/
Ződi Z (2023) Platformjog (Platform law). Ludovika Egyetemi Kiadó, Budapest

Chapter 7
The Chinese Model

Although it is less talked about, and many people look the other way, there is a third way to regulate the internet, content moderation and censorship, in addition to the US' *immunity model* and the European *safe harbour model*, and that is the Chinese (or Asian) model. Obviously, it is not possible to put all Asian countries in one basket and one regulatory model in terms of social, social or even political situation, but it is clear that, despite the differences, they have chosen a much stricter path than Europe or the United States of America when it comes to responsibility for Internet regulation and content governance. The Chinese solution is based on Internet sovereignty,[1] namely the (near) perfection of the idea that countries around the world have the right to choose how they develop and regulate their Internet. To examine and understand the details, it is necessary to travel back in time a few years.

7.1 The Origins of Chinese Content Regulation

Without delving into the history of press and media regulation in China,[2] it is worth pointing out that the Kuomintang, the leadership of the Chinese Communist Party, knew from the very beginning that influencing people's minds and public opinion would play an important role in its success and in maintaining its power. "Having ruled China for more than half a century by means of political violence, ideological education, and propaganda, the Communist regime has succeeded in making many Chinese people reject universal human values, such as human rights, freedom, democracy, and respect for life as bourgeois principles."[3] As a result, until 1978, the Chinese press was characterised by severe political repression, including the

[1] Schmitt (2017), pp. 11–13.

[2] For details, see He (2008), pp. 2–41.

[3] Ibid., pp. 4–5.

G. Gosztonyi, *Censorship from Plato to Social Media*, Law, Governance and Technology Series 61, https://doi.org/10.1007/978-3-031-46529-1_7

censorship of published content for political reasons, both before and after the fact.[4] In the early 1980s, the changing international political and economic environment prompted the Chinese state to make concessions on media regulation,[5] but these were effectively withdrawn in 1989 (the events in Tiananmen Square in China and the collapse of the Soviet bloc in the world following events in the Soviet Union). "The Central Committee's Propaganda Department and General Office sent a 48-article set of top-secret instructions to lower-level officials, explaining which issues could be discussed and under what specifications. Anyone who failed to follow these secret instructions risked various legal sanctions."[6] In the early 2000s, it seemed that general reforms could be introduced, not only in the economic but also in the political arena, but in practice this proved to be a pipe dream: the detailed list of rules issued in August 2003 already introduced measures such as

- requiring all media to follow the "right political line";
- a single state news agency that provides news for all media;
- strengthening the political nature of press control.[7]

7.2 Chinese Internet Regulation

All this information has also become important in the context of the emergence of the internet in China. In China, the Internet became available for public use in 1995; as elsewhere, the number of users grew exponentially in the 2000s.

	Number of users (June 2000)	Number of users (June 2022)	Population (June 2022)	Users as % of population (June 2022)	% of Asian users (June 2022)
China[8]	22,500,000	1,010,740,000	1,448,314,408	69.8%	34.4%

It is clear to see that, while in 2000, roughly 1.7% of the Chinese population at the time (1,267,430,000[9]) used the internet, today, 20 years later, almost 70% of the population are internet users.[10] However, it should be noted that there is a wide variation in internet penetration between regions.[11] This was already a mass of

[4]Tai (2014), pp. 185–209.

[5]Roberts (2018), pp. 98–101.

[6]He (2008), p. 14.

[7]Ibid., pp. 18–20.

[8]Chinese data exclude residents and users in special administrative regions (such as Hong Kong, Macau and Taiwan). https://www.internetworldstats.com/stats3.htm.

[9]https://www.statista.com/statistics/263765/total-population-of-china/.

[10]The big jump in numbers was seen between 2006 and 2012, when more than 40% of the population used it, up from 10%.

people who the Chinese Communist Party leadership could not allow to exercise their right to freedom of expression, so even before the big jump in numbers, in 1998, a new Cyber Police was set up[12] to carry out the 'traditional' tasks of restricting the exchange of opinions on the Internet, using a wide range of content control and censorship tools.[13] This is where the first manifestations of the state's subsequently developed content regulation tools can be observed: for domestic content, the repertoire ranged from intimidation to banning, while for foreign content, blocking access to Chinese users was the rule. The forerunners of the closed internet can thus be seen here, at the end of the 1990s, when 'only' 22 million—one might say privileged—Chinese citizens had access to this new communication technology.

Legal regulation started to be more focused from 2000, the same year that the State Council of the People's Republic of China issued Decree No 292,[14] which already required ISPs to register certain domain names and IP addresses. Two years later, in 2002, the government issued the Provisional Regulations on the Administration of Internet Content,[15] which mainly targeted websites displaying political content, but the rules also applied to websites offering other content. The regulations stated, among other things, that:

- operating as an information service provider may only be with prior authorisation (for commercial purposes) or registration (for non-commercial purposes);
- service providers are required to report any content they display that may be associated with state security or social discontent;
- in this context, they must make and keep a copy of the content uploaded by the third party;
- they are obliged to adopt a system of editorial responsibility, whereby editorial staff monitor compliance with the law for all content published on the internet.

So, if a service provider wants to obtain a business licence, it is expected to "prevent the appearance of politically objectionable content through automated means, or to police content being uploaded by users for unacceptable material, which is then taken down manually by company employees."[16] It is therefore clear that the Chinese model has from the outset opted for clear editorial responsibility, backed up by sanctions (ranging from warnings, suspension and confiscation to fines).[17] In 2005, the system was further tightened up with the adoption of the

[11] Petley (2009), p. 90.

[12] However, according to Harwit and Clark, it was not until the end of 2000 that the organisation really began to operate—first in Anhui province and then in 20 others. Harwit and Clark (2001), p. 394.

[13] He (2008), p. 168.

[14] Zhu Rongji (2010), pp. 30–35.

[15] Boas (2004), pp. 438–443.

[16] MacKinnon (2006), p. 12.

[17] He (2008), p. 170.

Provisions on News Information Services, which in its Article 19 lists in detail the items that constitute prohibited online content in the PRC:[18]

- violation of the principles enshrined in the Constitution;
- endangering national security, revealing state secrets, subverting the national system or threatening the unity of the nation;
- harm to the honour or interests of the nation;
- incitement to hatred against peoples, racism against peoples or disruption of solidarity between peoples;
- disrupting national religious policy, spreading evil cults and feudal superstitions;
- spreading rumours, disturbing social order or upsetting social stability;
- obscenity, pornography, gambling, violence, spreading terror or incitement to commit a crime;
- insulting or defaming third parties, violating the legal rights and interests of third parties;
- incitement to unlawful meetings, associations, processions, demonstrations or assemblies which disturb social order;
- acting on behalf of an unlawful NGO; and
- any other content prohibited by law or regulation.

These concepts are ambiguous enough to give the state considerable leeway as to the "types of people they can punish for online behaviour."[19] In addition, since 2001, all Internet service providers operating in China have been required to "voluntarily" sign the "Public Pledge on Self-discipline for the Chinese Internet Industry", in which they vow to refrain from "producing, posting, or disseminating pernicious information that may jeopardise state security and disrupt social stability."[20] The pledge was initiated by the China Internet Society, which is designated as an NGO but reports to the Ministry of Information Industry. The main aim of the legislation is of course political: to prevent the spread of ideas in the online world that could potentially provoke political opposition in real life. As Nicolas P. Suzor put it, the content that is censored most consistently is that which "tries to organise any form of physical meeting or protest."[21] Moreover, this task is not only carried out by service providers and cyber police: in 2013, Chinese state media revealed that there were two million people tasked with monitoring online content.[22] In 2018, the state surveillance system was simplified: instead of the myriad of ministries and state agencies, two bodies now bear most responsibility for control and censorship, the Cyberspace Affairs Commissions and the Network Security Bureau within the Public Security Bureau.[23] The annual cost of this system is enormous: some

[18] MacKinnon (2006), pp. 18–19.
[19] Roberts (2018), p. 117.
[20] MacKinnon (2006), p. 12.
[21] Suzor (2019), p. 80.
[22] Hunt and Xu (2013).
[23] Fedasiuk (2021).

estimates suggest that in 2020 alone, US $6.6 billion would be spent to maintain the system.[24]

7.3 "Old Style Censorship Is Being Replaced with a Massive, Ubiquitous Architecture of Surveillance: The Golden Shield"[25]

"What is better? Big brother Internet? Or no Internet at all?"[26] This was the question posed to Michael Robinson, a young American computer engineer who, after 1996, became disillusioned with Chinese solutions while midwifing the development of the Chinese internet. The Golden Shield project has provided the answer: the internet can be used by millions of Chinese, but only if someone is always watching.[27] After the Great Wall of China, the Great Firewall of China,[28] which is part of the Golden Shield project, was built before our eyes. According to Greg Walton,[29] the contradiction surrounding its creation is that, on the one hand, the Chinese government understands that information technology and the internet is what makes the world economy work today and that if they want to be part of it they have to use these tools, and on the other hand, that the Chinese state is a one-party system with an authoritarian structure and as such cannot allow anyone to challenge its authority.

"The Great Firewall, as it is called by foreigners, which is a system of limiting access to foreign websites which started in the late 1990s,[30] and the Golden Shield, a system for domestic surveillance set up in 1998 by the Ministry of Public Security."[31] At the time of their design, although we saw an active Cyber Police force overseeing the implementation of editorial responsibility and unwanted content being hidden from the eyes of Chinese citizens, there was still a technical possibility to hide from Big Brother's watchful eye. It did not need a corner of the room—like Winston Smith hiding from the teletype in George Orwell's *1984*—but a virtual

---

[24] RSF (2021).

[25] Walton (2001), p. 5.

[26] Cited by Gutmann (2002).

[27] Ironically, the introduction of Internet censorship in China was abetted by major US tech companies, most notably Cisco, "which began supplying filtering and surveillance equipment to Chinese censors in the early 1990s." Griffiths (2019), p. 33.

[28] Taneja and Xiao Wu (2014), pp. 297–309.

[29] Walton (2001), p. 5.

[30] Unsurprisingly, there is not even agreement on when the project started: Sonali Chandel and his colleagues say it started in 1996, adding that (after several intermediate stages) it was not fully implemented until 2008. Chandel et al. (2019), p. 112.

[31] E. H. (2013).

private network (VPN).[32] However, the construction and operation of the Golden Shield[33] brought a degree of total control of internet communications that few thought possible.[34] The main aim is, of course, political; to prevent the spread of ideas in the online world that could potentially provoke political opposition in real life. However, the surveillance system is characterised by uncertainty and unpredictability: it is not known exactly why content has and has not slipped through the filter, nor why certain content is available in some parts of the country but not in others, nor why certain content is hidden from the eyes of certain social groups.[35] The Golden Shield project is therefore seen by some as akin to Jeremy Bentham's Panopticon, which envisaged a prison where prisoners do not know when they are being watched by guards, or if they are being watched at all. As Barna Mezey said about the Panopticon, "In this structure, it was practically impossible to talk to each other, to communicate. The construction eliminated the danger of any possible conspiracy, it also prevented riots or outbreaks."[36] The same is true of the current state of Chinese Internet governance: it has been described by Bobbie Johnson as "hit-and-miss technology",[37] by János Boris as "adaptive authoritarianism" because of the deliberately built-in "safety valves" and of errors and omissions,[38] while Séverine Arséne[39] and Margaret E. Roberts[40] have called it "porous censorship". The deliberate imprecision and ambiguity of this technology and regulation means that, in the case of third-party content, the provider is more likely to remove or censor the content in order to minimise liability risks. "Companies generate their 'block-lists' based on educated guesswork plus trial-and-error; what they know to be politically sensitive, what they are told in meetings with Chinese officials and complaints they may receive from Chinese authorities in response to the appearance of politically objectionable search results."[41] Moreover, the Golden Shield is constantly refining and learning, both from humans (i.e. cyber police and moderators) and from artificial intelligence.[42]

---

[32] In 2017, there were conflicting reports about the use of VPN applications in China. According to the Guardian, the Chinese government ordered the country's three largest state-owned telecoms operators (China Mobile, China Unicom, China Telecom) to block VPN use altogether, while the Diplomat, citing Chinese statements, reported that only illegal VPN use would be banned in the country from 2018. The author of the article also saw the irony in this, as it is for the Chinese state to decide what constitutes illegal VPN use. Haas (2017) and Gao (2017).

[33] Chandel et al. (2019), p. 114.

[34] Weber (2019).

[35] "Chances of exposure to censorship vary a lot from user to user, depending on their news attention and who and what they follow online." Zhang et al. (2022), p. 809.

[36] Mezey (2018), p. 337.

[37] Johnson (2010).

[38] Boris (2016), p. 62.

[39] Arséne (2019), p. 961.

[40] Roberts (2018), p. 2.

[41] MacKinnon (2006), pp. 13–14.

[42] Qiufan (2019), pp. 89–95.

In 2020, Freedom House's annual report on the internet said, "China's surveillance systems remain the most advanced and pervasive in the world."[43] Indeed, the elements of the Golden Shield will no longer simply monitor online activity and censor it when necessary, but will form an interconnected system that will allow for easy political and social profiling. This includes, for example:

- "monitoring of information space;
- Big Data analysis;
- monitoring of public spaces;
- installing cameras in and around homes;[44]
- a bans on online activities;
- health status applications,
- thermal detection technology,
- applications that track online contacts, and
- use of facial recognition technology."[45]

This is how we have moved from the previous traditional threats to press freedom to an era where the use of traditional means of Internet access has led to a state capable of almost total surveillance.[46] The People's Republic of China takes a different view: for them, the issue is about internet sovereignty,[47] based on a speech delivered by Xi Jinping, President of the People's Republic of China, at the Second World Internet Conference in 2015[48] in which he called on countries around the world to respect each other's *cybersovereignty* and different models of internet governance. He stressed that countries around the world have the right to choose how to develop and regulate their internet and, in an obvious reference to the United States, rejected the idea of any country acquiring internet hegemony in this non-legislative space, cyberspace. As James Griffiths summed up Xi Jinping's words with his own, "We have border controls and import duties in the physical world, so why should the digital sphere be any different? The doctrine of *cybersovereignty* is a vision of total internet control, and emanates from a stance of deep suspicion about the web and its potential risk to state power."[49] All this leads to the question; is there, can there be a 'Chinese internet'? 'American internet', 'Egyptian internet' or even a 'Hungarian internet'? The intention here is to compare

---

[43] FH (2020), p. 21.

[44] Cf. "Privacy and freedom of expression are interlinked and mutually dependent; an infringement upon one can be both the cause and consequence of an infringement upon the other. Without adequate legislation and legal standards to ensure the privacy, security and anonymity of communications, journalists, human rights defenders and whistleblowers, for example, cannot be assured that their communications will not be subject to States' scrutiny." UNHRC (2013), p. 79.

[45] FH (2020), p. 21.

[46] It should be pointed out that the increase in the volume of surveillance of users has also been observed in several other states. On US practice, see Cook and Delrossi (2021).

[47] Denyer (2016).

[48] BBC News (2015).

[49] Griffiths (2019), p. 17.

internet regulation with early press regulation or broadcasting regulation, whereby states make their own rules and then, if necessary—ideally but not necessarily—consult with the leaders of the surrounding countries concerned.[50] We must not forget that this was the regulatory method that was completely transformed by the development of technology, by the emergence of cross-border television and radio signals and then by the Internet.

In addition to restrictions on civil and political rights, we are of course also talking about economic issues. In 2008, YouTube was made inaccessible because of the situation in Tibet, while the same fate befell Facebook (2008) and Twitter (2009), and then Wikipedia (2019), because of the events in the Xinjiang Uyghur Autonomous Region. What can be done? Lose hundreds of millions of users on the altar of democratic principles, or join the queue by applying economic or self-censorship? Google has chosen the latter,[51] as it has made certain search content inaccessible to searches on google.cn in the People's Republic of China by various means since the beginning of its presence on the Chinese market in 2006.[52] However, this was unacceptable to US politicians and the general public,[53] and the numerous attacks led Google to cease its activities in China.[54] At the same time, as Ryan Gallagher revealed in 2018,[55] in a project codenamed *Dragonfly,* in order to get back into the Chinese market, Google would develop a censored search engine that would ban websites and search terms related to human rights, democracy, religion and peaceful protest, among others. The *Dragonfly* project was officially shut down in 2019.

The question that the Chinese leaders running the Golden Shield are seeking to answer is whether there can be a solution in the twenty-first century that ensures both economic openness and development, while at the same time ensuring informational closure. The answer will probably not be known for several years, but it is already clear that, for both conditions to work together, "the country has the largest and most sophisticated online censorship[56] operation in the world."[57] In addition to the American system based on immunity and the European safe harbour, a third way has been built: a system based on total surveillance, which, as a rule, does not allow millions of private users to make mistakes by cutting them off from information. If information does get through, whether by deliberate 'safety valves' or by other means, the ISPs and platforms are clearly held accountable, without immunity or

[50] Goldsmith and Wu (2006a, b).

[51] Stevenson (2007), p. 543.

[52] Microsoft has chosen the same path. Ibid., p. 544.

[53] Griffiths (2019), p. 96.

[54] The official explanation is that the withdrawal from the Chinese market was due to an attack by Chinese hackers. Griffiths (2019), pp. 137–138.

[55] Gallagher (2018).

[56] It is an interesting thought, as Margaret E. Roberts notes in her book *Censorship*, that "the thirty billion pieces of information generated each day by Chinese citizens quite simply cannot be censored", so that perfect control can never be achieved. Roberts (2018), p. 1.

[57] Economy (2018).

exemption.[58] This is complemented by a continuous monitoring obligation on the part of the operators, i.e. free opinions would have to pass through three "gates" to reach the public:

- user self-censorship;
- economic censorship (service provider monitoring);
- state censorship (Golden Shield).

Is this the way of the future? Systems such as the Golden Shield, based on a complex and constantly changing and expanding legal and technological background, which ensure *cybersovereignty* under the watchful eye of millions of people? China, North Korea, Russia, Iran and Myanmar have already embarked on this path. Some are ahead, some are behind, but they are heading in the same direction. Tim-Berners Lee—known only as one of the fathers of the internet[59]—predicted in a 2013 interview that "the Berlin Wall tumbled down, the great firewall of China – I don't think it will tumble down, I think it will be released."[60] Ten years have passed and on this point he has been proved wrong. In fact, with ever-evolving technology, the Golden Shield is bigger, smarter and more accurate than ever.

References

Arséne S (2019) La Chine et le contrôle d'Internet. Une cybersouveraineté ambivalente (China and the control of the Internet. Ambivalent cyber sovereignty). Annuaire Français de Relations Internationales 2019(20)

BBC News (2015) China internet: Xi Jinping calls for 'cyber sovereignty'. BBC News, 16 December. https://www.bbc.com/news/world-asia-china-35109453/

Boas TC (2004) Weaving the authoritarian web. Curr Hist 103(677)

Boris J (2016) A Nagy tűzfal és a SZORM, avagy a zárt internet orwelli világa (The Great Firewall and SZORM, or the Orwellian world of the closed internet). Athenaeum 2(1)

Chandel S, Jingji Z, Yunnan Y, Jingyao S, Zhipeng Z (2019) The Golden Shield Project of China: a decade later – an in-depth study of the Great Firewall. International conference on cyber-enabled distributed computing and knowledge discovery. https://www.researchgate.net/profile/Sonali-Chandel/publication/338361425TheGoldenShieldProjectofChinaADecadeLater-Anin-DepthStudyoftheGreatFirewall/links/5e136bce299bf10bc392fc09/The-Golden-Shield-Project-of-China-A-Decade-Later-An-in-Depth-Study-of-the-Great-Firewall.pdf

Cook S, Delrossi M (2021) The worrying expansion of the social media surveillance-industrial complex. Knight First Amendment Institute, 6 December. https://knightcolumbia.org/blog/the-worrying-expansion-of-the-social-media-surveillance-industrial-complex/

Denyer S (2016) China's scary lesson to the world: censoring the Internet works. The Washington Post, 23 May. https://www.washingtonpost.com/world/asia_pacific/chinas-scary-lesson-to-the-world-censoring-the-internet-works/2016/05/23/413afe78-fff3-11e5-8bb1-f124a43f84dc_story.html/

[58] For slightly different cases of copyright and trademark infringement, see Friedmann (2020), pp. 277–294.

[59] Inmesol (2014).

[60] Faulconbridge (2013).

E. H. (2013) How does China censor the internet? The Economist, 22 April. https://www.economist.com/the-economist-explains/2013/04/21/how-does-china-censor-the-internet/
Economy EC (2018) The great firewall of China: Xi Jinping's internet shutdown. The Guardian, 29 June. https://www.theguardian.com/news/2018/jun/29/the-great-firewall-of-china-xi-jinpings-internet-shutdown/
Faulconbridge G (2013) Father of Web says China will dismantle 'great firewall'. Reuters, 22 November. https://www.reuters.com/article/uk-china-internet-berners-lee-idUKBRE9AL00120131122/
Fedasiuk R (2021) Buying silence: the price of Internet Censorship in China. China Brief 21(1)
Freedom House (FH) (2020) Freedom on the Net 2020. The Pandemic's Digital Shadow. 21 October. https://freedomhouse.org/sites/default/files/2020-10/10122020_FOTN2020_Complete_Report_FINAL.pdf
Friedmann D (2020) Oscillating from safe harbor to liability: China's IP regulation and omniscient intermediaries. In: Frosio G (ed) Oxford handbook of online intermediary liability. Oxford University Press, Oxford
Gallagher R (2018) Google plans to launch censored search engine in China. The Intercept, 1 August. https://theintercept.com/2018/08/01/google-china-search-engine-censorship/
Gao C (2017) China clarifies reports of VPN Ban. The Diplomat, 13 July. https://thediplomat.com/2017/07/china-clarifies-reports-of-vpn-ban/
Goldsmith JL, Wu T (2006a) Who controls the Internet? Illusions of a borderless world. Oxford University Press, Oxford
Goldsmith JL, Wu T (2006b) Digital borders: national boundaries have survived in the virtual world and allowed national laws to exert control over the internet. Leg Aff 40
Griffiths J (2019) The Great Firewall of China: how to build and control an alternative version of the Internet. Zed Books, London
Gutmann E (2002) Who lost China's Internet? The Weekly Standard, 15 February. https://ethan-gutmann.com/who-lost-chinas-internet/
Haas B (2017) China moves to block internet VPNs from 2018. The Guardian, 11 July. https://www.theguardian.com/world/2017/jul/11/china-moves-to-block-internet-vpns-from-2018/
Harwit E, Clark D (2001) Shaping the Internet in China. Evolution of political control over network infrastructure and content. Asian Survey 41(3)
He Q (2008) The fog of censorship: media control in China. Human Rights in China, New York
Hunt K, Xu C (2013) China 'employs 2 million to police internet'. CNN, 7 October. https://edition.cnn.com/2013/10/07/world/asia/china-internet-monitors/index.html/
Inmesol (2014) The fathers of the Internet. Inmesol, 16 March. http://www.inmesol.com/blog/fathers-internet/
Johnson B (2010) How Google censors its results in China. The Guardian, 13 January. https://www.theguardian.com/technology/2010/jan/13/how-google-censors-china/
MacKinnon R (2006) Race to the bottom. Corporate complicity in Chinese Internet Censorship. Hum Rights Watch 18(8)
Mezey B (2018) A börtönügy a 17–19. században. A börtön európai útja (The prison system in the 17th–19th centuries. The European Road of the Prison). Gondolat Kiadó, Budapest
Petley J (2009) Censorship. A beginner's guide. Oneworld Publications, Oxford
Qiufan C (2019) The reunion: a new science-fiction story about surveillance in China. MIT Technol Rev 122(1)
Reporters Without Borders (RSF) (2021) China's cyber censorship figures. rsf.org, 12 March. https://rsf.org/en/news/chinas-cyber-censorship-figures/
Roberts ME (2018) Censored. Distraction and diversion inside China's Great Firewall. Princeton University Press, Princeton
Schmitt MN (ed) (2017) Tallinn Manual 2.0 on the international law applicable to cyber operations. Cambridge University Press, Cambridge
Stevenson C (2007) Breaching the Great Firewall: China's Internet Censorship and the quest for freedom of expression in a connected world. Boston Coll Int Comp Law Rev 30(2)

Suzor NP (2019) Lawless. The secret rules that govern our digital lives. Cambridge University Press, Cambridge

Tai Q (2014) China's Media Censorship: a dynamic and diversified regime. J East Asian Stud 14(2)

Taneja H, Xiao Wu A (2014) Does the Great Firewall really isolate the Chinese? Integrating access blockage with cultural factors to explain web user behavior. Inf Soc 30(5)

UNHRC (2013) Report of the Special Rapporteur on the promotion and protection of the right to freedom of opinion and expression. UN Doc A/HRC/23/40

Walton G (2001) China's Golden Shield: corporations and the development of surveillance technology in the People's Republic of China. Rights & Democracy, Montreal

Weber V (2019) The worldwide web of Chinese and Russian information controls. University of Oxford Centre for Technology and Global. Affairs Working Paper Series 2019(11)

Zhang L, Tandoc EC Jr, Han S (2022) Rage or rationality: exposure to Internet censorship and the impact on individual information behaviors in China. Policy Internet 14(4)

Zhu Rongji P (2010) Measures for the management of internet information services. Chin Law Gov 43(5)

Chapter 8
Human and Technical Aspect of Content Management

Between 1612 and 1614, the world-famous Flemish painter Peter Paul Rubens painted his painting of *The Descent from the Cross*, and around 1614–1615 he painted *Venus in front of the Mirror*. It was probably not only because of his social media obscurity at the time that he never imagined that his painting—or, more precisely, the events surrounding it—would make a company a subject of public notoriety a few centuries later. In 2018, the state-run Flemish Tourist Office launched an advertising campaign on Facebook using these two paintings, but Facebook removed both paintings on the grounds that they contained gratuitous nudity.[1] In a letter to the company, the Flemish Tourist Office wrote: "Even though we secretly have to laugh about it (. . .) censorship is making life rather difficult for us."[2] Rubens' work has previously met a similar fate to Gustave Courbet's 1866 painting *The Origin of the World*[3] (which was the subject of an 8-year court case in France[4]) or the photo of Venus de Willendorf,[5] as explicit depictions of nude body parts were deemed pornography by the company's Community Standards (*CS*) moderation guidelines.[6] However, it's not just paintings that have faced a similar situation: the iconic statue of the Danish capital Copenhagen, the Little Mermaid, was also removed because it contained "too much bare skin or sexual overtones", according to Facebook.[7] A painting of Santa Claus kneeling in front of the baby Jesus in a manger has also been removed because of its violent content. But it's also

---

[1] Frieze (2018).

[2] Ibid.; It should be added, however, that the events saw a fortunate increase in traffic at Flemish museums during the period, and the agency produced a video mocking Facebook's policy: Visitflanders (2018).

[3] Stapley-Brown (2018).

[4] For the interesting case that ended in a settlement between the parties, see Gosztonyi (2022).

[5] Dawson (2018).

[6] Facebook Community Standards, III.14. Adult nudity and sexual activity.

[7] BBC News (2016).

G. Gosztonyi, *Censorship from Plato to Social Media*, Law, Governance and Technology Series 61, https://doi.org/10.1007/978-3-031-46529-1_8

easy to imagine being banned for a photo of a cat: one user had his account blocked in 2016 for sharing a picture of a cat in a suit. Or a company may have deleted content—at the request of the US police—in which a black woman made a video of white police officers. The list could go on and on.

For all these reasons—and as a result of the campaign by the US NGO National Coalition Against Censorship—Facebook has agreed that CS needs to be reviewed,[8] but the process takes time.[9] As they put it in the Daily Mail, "After all, a butt is a butt and a nipple is a nipple. But deciding when a nipple is art, porn or protest gets murky even when humans are doing the deciding. Teaching AI software about human sexual desire is a whole other ballgame."[10]

But why is this interesting? Facebook had 2.8 billion users in 2020, and the company "generates 4 petabytes of data per day – that's a million gigabytes. All those data are stored in what is known as the Hive, which contains about 300 petabytes of data."[11] Or put another way, "60 seconds on the web in 2021 consist of more than 500 hours of content uploaded on YouTube, 695,000 stories shared on Instagram and nearly 70 million messages sent via WhatsApp and Facebook Messenger."[12] Much of this huge amount of data is obviously legitimate content, but even the small amount that should not be uploaded is huge. The scrutiny of this content, as we saw above, has been 'privatised' by the state.

8.1 Facebook Moderation Policy or the Content in Question

In the preamble to the moderation policy, the company states, "The goal of our Community Standards is to create a place for expression and give people a voice. Meta wants people to be able to talk openly about the issues that matter to them, even if some may disagree or find them objectionable. In some cases, we allow content – which would otherwise go against our standards – if it's newsworthy and in the public interest. We do this only after weighing the public interest value against the risk of harm, and we look to international human rights standards to make these judgments."[13] CS identifies four core values that it follows and expects all its users to adhere to: authenticity, security, privacy and dignity.

---

[8]NCAC (2019).

[9]And Angelo Stagnaro probably misunderstands the process when writing: "Facebook has had a long history of censoring Christian organizations and individuals, flagging our beliefs as being 'hateful' or otherwise inappropriate, but it is their actions and inaction that is most accurately branded as hateful." Stagnaro (2018).

[10]Daily Mail Online (2020).

[11]Roy (2020).

[12]Jenik (2021).

[13]https://transparency.fb.com/policies/community-standards/.

CS has five categories for the types of content it does not wish to host on its own platform:

1. Violence and criminal behavior
   (a) Violence and Incitement
   (b) Dangerous Individuals and Organizations
   (c) Coordinating Harm and Promoting Crime
   (d) Restricted Goods and Services
   (e) Fraud and Deception
2. Safety
   (a) Suicide and Self-Injury
   (b) Child Sexual Exploitation, Abuse and Nudity
   (c) Adult Sexual Exploitation
   (d) Bullying and Harassment
   (e) Human Exploitation
   (f) Privacy Violations
3. Objectionable content
   (a) Hate Speech
   (b) Violent and Graphic Content
   (c) Adult Nudity and Sexual Activity
   (d) Sexual Solicitation
4. Integrity and authenticity
   (a) Account Integrity and Authentic Identity
   (b) Spam
   (c) Cybersecurity
   (d) Inauthentic Behavior
   (e) Misinformation
   (f) Memorialization
5. Respecting intellectual property
   (a) Intellectual property

It can be seen that these are the types of content where the legislator often encounters difficulties. However, it should be pointed out that, in the era of 'privatisation' of content regulation, these issues were the sole responsibility of the service providers, so it is not particularly surprising that CS is constantly changing. In 2018, after a long time and many complaints, the company made these moderation policies public: as Mónika Pintér put it so eloquently, "if Facebook is a country, here is its new constitution."[14] The big change was not just the publicity, but also the fact

[14] Pintér (2018); Cf. Rebecca MacKinnon's term 'Facebookistan'. MacKinnon (2013).

that the internal guidelines that govern the company's content regulation practices were made public. This means that content is classified using a combination of artificial intelligence and human intervention: together, they are the first line of defence in the war against unsolicited content. But why only the first line of defence, you may ask. Tarleton Gillespie, in his book, compared the actors involved in moderation to a pyramid, each with their own role to play.[15]

8.2 Moderation Using Artificial Intelligence[16]

Artificial intelligence in its current form[17] still has many difficulties to overcome: context, irony, slang, etc. "It is very good (better than humans[18]) at identifying porn, spam and fake accounts, but it's still not great at identifying hate speech."[19] Users create content in more than a hundred languages, and in its current form AI is not yet capable of interpreting more complex content. However, its need is not in question: there are not enough employable people to handle the volume of data in these days. "Facebook says its AI tools – many of which are trained with data from its human moderation team – detect nearly 100 percent of spam, and that 99.5 percent of terrorist-related removals, 98.5 percent of fake accounts, 96 percent of adult nudity and sexual activity, and 86 percent of graphic violence-related removals are detected by AI, not users."[20] In contrast to all these figures, AI was only able to correctly detect, interpret and manage 36% of content related to hate speech as a social, human consensus-based concept.[21]

In relation to the process, Thiago Dias Oliva also points out that "whilst traditional law enforcement encompasses detection, prosecution, adjudication and punishment performed by different actors, algorithmic content policing does that all at once, focusing on early detection and prevention in a less transparent fashion."[22] The FTC warned in a statement in April 2021 that there may be worrying racial and gender biases associated with AI.[23] Kinga Sorbán also draws attention to the dangers of automated filtering systems and freedom of expression.[24] In addition to this, Jack

---

[15] Gillespie (2018), p. 116.

[16] It should be stressed that although the term artificial intelligence is used in public discourse, it "can refer to the use of a variety of automated processes at different phases of content moderation." Llansó et al. (2020), p. 3.

[17] Huszár (2022).

[18] Interpretative insertion by the author.

[19] Koebler and Cox (2018).

[20] Ibid., 2018.

[21] Joaquin Quiñonero Candela, the company's Head of Artificial Intelligence, was interviewed about the shortcomings of Facebook and its use of artificial intelligence. Hao (2021).

[22] Dias Oliva (2020), p. 612.

[23] Jillson (2021).

[24] Sorbán (2021), pp. 72–73.

M. Balkin—ironically—points out the economic rationality: "algorithmic employees cost even less than human employees: they do not have families, they do not take coffee breaks."[25]

Emma Llansó and her colleagues summarised the legislative dilemmas related to the use of AI as follows:[26]

- In the public discourse, moderation by artificial intelligence should be replaced by something else that goes into more detail about the technology, which is more indicative of automatism.
- Automatic moderation should not be made mandatory by law, because the current state of the technology is neither sufficiently reliable nor sufficiently effective.
- Tech companies using automatic moderation should provide more transparency on their procedures.
- Not everything can be solved by automatic moderation.
- As automatic moderation can also lead to conflicts with fundamental rights—most notably the freedom of expression—it is important to be careful not to *over* remove.
- There is no 'neutral' automatic moderation.
- Developing media literacy is crucial to this issue.

8.3 Moderation by Humans

If AI cannot handle the exponentially growing volume of content and users, then giant tech companies have responded by hiring more and more people. The change in 10 years is almost unimaginable. "They tried to make fair decisions on content and conflicts of law posted by the then one hundred and twenty million users."[27] These private individuals were Justicia's scales. Compare the 2009 figure with the 2018 figure: "Facebook employs a total of 7,500 moderators worldwide, a position in which the company now employs 40 percent more than it did this time last year."[28] The workers, called *Community Operations (CO),* are the ones who review signals from users 24 h a day, and in the vast majority of cases manage to process reports within 24 h. Very little is known about their work, which companies say is in their own defence against users. The leaked information is generally horrific (post-traumatic reactions to the content viewed, terrible working conditions, low wages, outsourced workers, constant stress and emotional pressure, mental health problems, and all of this leading to unimaginable levels of staff turnover[29]), to which Mark

[25] Balkin (2018), p. 2024.

[26] Llansó et al. (2020), pp. 2–3.

[27] Huszár (2021), p. 34.

[28] Nlc.hu (2018).

[29] Newton (2019a); Cf. Buni and Chemaly (2016).

Zuckerberg said: "The public things, I think, tend to be a little more dramatic."[30] On the positive side, however, the company has "a team of four clinical psychologists in three regions to help moderators who regularly encounter violent, abusive content."[31]

And there are times when it may be needed: based on the reports and the amount of data, it takes about 30 s to decide on an entry, and around 400 cases a day—how to assess and interpret the context of the text in that time is questionable, to say the least. In this way, according to Ruckenstein and Turunen,[32] human moderators are increasingly being treated as machines by tech companies, which will obviously not be profitable in the long term in terms of the working environment.

As moderators are not experts in a particular area, Facebook provides them with a guide, with yes/no answers to a series of questions, at the end of which they can decide whether or not to remove content. Context, languages, dialects and user intent can further complicate the issue. In addition, legislation can vary considerably from country to country, so this 'world guide' is not always useful. This brings us back to Kyle Langvardt's suggestion above, the basic question of which is: are we sure that 'privatising' the decision to regulate content is the right way forward?

8.4 Solution for Moderation: Sharing

The solution is therefore unlikely to be a choice between human moderation or moderation by artificial intelligence, but rather a combination of the two in the future. In 2020, during the COVID-19 pandemic—while big tech companies were also making their employees work from home and giving artificial intelligence more tasks[33]—"Facebook and Google roughly doubled the amount of potentially harmful material they removed in the second quarter of this year compared with the three months through March",[34] and there were many more complaints about the decisions as a result, making it clear that human content scrutiny will not be unnecessary for some time. YouTube has also reported the "excessive censorship" of its own artificial intelligence tools.[35]

The United Nations (UN) Special Rapporteur on Freedom of Expression has issued a report calling for "radical transparency"[36] from social media providers in the way they create and enforce their rules, and sharing can filter out one of the most dangerous problems: bias. And although you might think that this is only true for

[30]Newton (2019b).

[31]Hvg.hu (2019).

[32]Ruckenstein and Turunen (2020), pp. 1026–1042.

[33]Gillespie (2020), p. 2.

[34]Scott and Kayali (2020).

[35]Barker and Murphy (2020).

[36]UNHRC (2018), p. 64.

human moderators, there is also the concept of the so-called "discriminatory algorithm",[37] which is caused by insufficient data and which, as a consequence, mainly affects minority groups underrepresented in social media.

The ideal flowchart of moderation[38] was summarised in a report prepared for Ofcom, the UK media regulator. According to the study, the use of AI can perfectly complement human moderation in three ways:

- "AI can be used to improve the pre-moderation stage and flag content for review by humans, increasing moderation accuracy.
- AI can be implemented to synthesise training data to improve pre-moderation performance.
- AI can assist human moderators by increasing their productivity and reducing the potentially harmful effects of content moderation on individual moderators."[39]

References

Balkin JM (2018) Free speech is a triangle. Columbia Law Rev 118(7)

Barker A, Murphy H (2020) YouTube reverts to human moderators in fight against misinformation. Financial Times, 20 September. https://www.ft.com/content/e54737c5-8488-4e66-b087-d1ad426ac9fa/

BBC News (2016) Denmark: Facebook blocks Little Mermaid over 'bare skin'. BBC News, 4 January. https://www.bbc.com/news/blogs-news-from-elsewhere-35221329/

Buni C, Chemaly S (2016) The secret rules of the internet. The murky history of moderation, and how it's shaping the future of free speech. The Verge, 13 April. https://www.theverge.com/2016/4/13/11387934/internet-moderator-history-youtube-facebook-reddit-censorship-free-speech/

Cambridge Consultants (2019) Use of AI in online content moderation. Ofcom, 18 July. https://www.ofcom.org.uk/__data/assets/pdf_file/0028/157249/cambridge-consultants-ai-content-moderation.pdf

Daily Mail Online (2020) Do naked bodies belong on Facebook? Tech giant struggles with changing 'vague and unevenly enforced' rules over nudity and body art without suppressing freedom of speech. Daily Mail Online, 15 January. https://www.dailymail.co.uk/sciencetech/article-7890913/Does-naked-body-belong-Facebook-It-s-complicated.html/

Dawson A (2018) Facebook censors 30,000 year-old Venus of Willendorf as 'pornographic'. The Art Newspaper, 27 February. https://www.theartnewspaper.com/news/facebook-censors-famous-30-000-year-old-nude-statue-as-pornographic/

Dias Oliva T (2020) Content moderation technologies: applying human rights standards to protect freedom of expression. Hum Rights Law Rev 20(4)

Facebook Community Standards, https://transparency.fb.com/policies/community-standards/

Frieze (2018) Facebook censors Rubens Paintings for nudity. Frieze, 24 July. https://www.frieze.com/article/facebook-censors-rubens-paintings-nudity/

Gillespie T (2018) Custodians of the internet: platforms, content moderation, and the hidden decisions that shape social media. Yale University Press, New Haven

Gillespie T (2020) Content moderation, AI, and the question of scale. Big Data Soc 7(2)

37 Turner Lee et al. (2019).

38 Cambridge Consultants (2019), p. 5.

39 Ibid., pp. 6–8.

Gosztonyi G (2022) Nyolc évnyi pereskedés egy női nemiszervért, avagy Facebook, cenzúra, meztelenség, művészet (Eight years of litigation over a female genital organ – Facebook, censorship, nudity, art). JOG.történet. 2 May. https://mtajogtortenet.elte.hu/blog/gosztonyi-gergely-facebook-meztelenseg

Hao K (2021) How Facebook got addicted to spreading misinformation. MIT Technology Review, 11 March. https://www.technologyreview.com/2021/03/11/1020600/facebook-responsible-ai-misinformation/

Huszár D (2021) A véleménynyilvánítás és kifejezés szabadsága a közösségi média platformjain (Freedom of opinion and expression on social media platforms). Média Kábel Műhold 25(4)

Huszár D (2022) Az algoritmusalapú tartalommoderálás kezdete, jelene és jövője (The beginnings, present and future of algorithm-based content management). Joghistória 27(2)

Hvg.hu (2019) Mégis megszólalt a Facebook: így dolgoznak a bejegyzéseinket átnéző moderátorok (Facebook has spoken: this is how moderators reviewing our posts work). hvg.hu, 29 July. https://hvg.hu/tudomany/20180728_facebook_moderator_bejegyzesek_ellenorzese/

Jenik C (2021) A minute on the internet in 2021. statista.com, 30 July. https://www.statista.com/chart/25443/estimated-amount-of-data-created-on-the-internet-in-one-minute/

Jillson E (2021) Aiming for truth, fairness, and equity in your company's use of AI. ftc.gov, 19 Apr. https://www.ftc.gov/news-events/blogs/business-blog/2021/04/aiming-truth-fairness-equity-your-companys-use-ai/

Koebler J, Cox J (2018) The impossible job: inside Facebook's struggle to moderate two billion people. Vice, 23 August. https://www.vice.com/en/article/xwk9zd/how-facebook-content-moderation-works/

Llansó E, van Hoboken J, Leerssen P, Harambam J (2020) Artificial intelligence, content moderation, and freedom of expression. Working paper of the Transatlantic Working Group on content moderation online and freedom of expression, 26 February. https://www.ivir.nl/publicaties/download/AI-Llanso-Van-Hoboken-Feb-2020.pdf

MacKinnon R (2013) Consent of the networked. The worldwide struggle for internet freedom. Basic Books, New York

NCAC (2019) Facebook agrees to reconsider artistic nudity policies. NCAC, 5 June. https://ncac.org/news/facebook-agrees-to-reconsider-artistic-nudity-policies/

Newton C (2019a) The trauma floor. The secret lives of Facebook moderators in America. The Verge, 25 February. https://www.theverge.com/2019/2/25/18229714/cognizant-facebook-content-moderator-interviews-trauma-working-conditions-arizona/

Newton C (2019b) Read the full transcript of Mark Zuckerberg's leaked internal Facebook meetings. The Verge, 1 October. https://www.theverge.com/2019/10/1/20892354/mark-zuckerberg-full-transcript-leaked-facebook-meetings/

Nlc.hu (2018) Nyilvánosak a Facebook moderálási alapelvei (Facebook's moderation policy is public). nlc.hu, 24 April. https://nlc.hu/szabadido/20180424/facebook-moderalasi-alapelvek-nyilvanos-fellebbezes/

Pintér M (2018) Ha a Facebook egy ország, itt az új alkotmánya (If Facebook is a country, here is its new constitution). 24.hu, 24 April. https://24.hu/tech/2018/04/24/facebook-uj-szabalyzat-community-standard/

Roy AS (2020) How does Facebook handle the 4+ petabyte of data generated per day? Cambridge Analytica – Facebook data scandal. Medium, 16 September. https://medium.com/@srank2000/how-facebook-handles-the-4-petabyte-of-data-generated-per-day-ab86877956f4/

Ruckenstein M, Turunen LLM (2020) Re-humanizing the platform: content moderators and the logic of care. N Media Soc 22(6)

Scott M, Kayali L (2020) What happened when humans stopped managing social media content. Politico, 21 October. https://www.politico.eu/article/facebook-content-moderation-automation/

Sorbán K (2021) Ethical and legal implications of using AI-powered recommendation systems in streaming services. Információs Társadalom 21(2)

Stagnaro A (2018) Facebook censors image of Santa Kneeling before our Lord. National Catholic Register, 26 December. https://www.ncregister.com/blog/facebook-censors-image-of-santa-kneeling-before-our-lord/

Stapley-Brown V (2018) Paris court hears arguments in Facebook censorship case centering on Courbet's origin of the world. The Art Newspaper, 2 February. https://www.theartnewspaper.com/news/paris-court-hears-arguments-in-facebook-censorship-case-centering-on-courbet-s-origin-of-the-world/

Turner Lee N, Resnick P, Barton G (2019) Algorithmic bias detection and mitigation: best practices and policies to reduce consumer harms. Brookings Institution, 22 May. https://www.brookings.edu/research/algorithmic-bias-detection-and-mitigation-best-practices-and-policies-to-reduce-consumer-harms/

UNHRC (2018) Report of the Special Rapporteur on the promotion and protection of the right to freedom of opinion and expression. UN Doc A/HRC/38/35

Visitflanders (2018) Social media doesn't want you to see Rubens' paintings. 21 July. https://www.youtube.com/watch?v=UZq3cVgU5AI/

Chapter 9
The Case Law of the European Court of Human Rights and the Court of Justice of the European Union for a Better Understanding of Liability Issues

The two most important international courts for our topic are the CJEU in Luxembourg and the ECtHR in Strasbourg. The difference between the two courts is that "the CJEU can be seen as an integrative agent, striving for further EU harmonisation, the ECtHR's mandate is that of providing a minimum human rights standards protection, beyond which wider scope is left for pluralism and national sovereignty within the EU."[1] In fact, the CJEU mediates in disputes between the EU institutions and between the EU institutions and the Member States, and also "ensures compliance with EU Treaty at the national level, and by the Treaty of Maastricht has the right to impose fines for legal entities and Member States that violated EU law."[2] On the other hand, "ECtHR ruling will result in a "more gradual (and perhaps less politically costly) implementation" of the decision than in the case of an adverse ECJ ruling."[3] These courts take into account each other's judgments in which human rights violations are invoked,[4] but it is important to underline that "the case law of the ECJ shows that where fundamental rights come into conflict with the economic Treaty freedoms, the economic freedoms may sometimes prevail over fundamental rights."[5] At the same time, "through judicial law development, the CJEU has developed robust theories of fundamental rights protection, despite the fact that formally the CJEU is not a human rights court, and thus fundamental rights protection is a mere secondary corollary of the CJEU's work."[6] This is all the more important because, as Oreste Pollicino notes, "The ECtHR and the ECJ have protected freedom of speech in a very different manner. Whereas the former does actually work as a constitutional court of fundamental rights, the latter has been more

[1] Imbarlina (2013).

[2] Bardarova (2013).

[3] Imbarlina (2013).

[4] Gless and Jeannine (2013), pp. 36–52.

[5] De Vries (2013), pp. 78–79.

[6] Daka (2020), p. 72.

G. Gosztonyi, *Censorship from Plato to Social Media*, Law, Governance and Technology Series 61, https://doi.org/10.1007/978-3-031-46529-1_9

influenced by the original economic nature of the European Community."[7] These differences are also evident in the practice of the two courts on content regulation issues for platform providers.

9.1 Landmark Cases Before the European Court of Human Rights

As we have seen above, since the adoption of the ECD, the legislator has not been sufficiently careful and precise in the way it has formulated its intentions on a number of issues. The examination of these problematic points is crucial for the practice of platform providers, as without them it is not possible to determine whether content is lawfully removed or whether censorship effects are being seen. In other words, we are talking about the applicability framework of the immunity issue described above, so that the questions raised (for example, when can it be said that the provider's knowledge is actual; what is the meaning of manifestly illegal content; what is the time limit within which the provider must act; and are we talking about an active or passive type of provider; but several have suggested that there should be more than one type of procedure for different types of content) are left to case law rather than the legislator, and the ECtHR has made key decisions on this.

9.1.1 *Delfi AS v Estonia (2015)* [8]

The first landmark case concerned the Estonian online news portal Delfi, which allowed users to comment anonymously.[9] Some of these comments proved controversial, sometimes offensive and even defamatory.[10] While the portal had a built-in content filter that would delete comments if a certain kind of language was reached, the only other way to remove comments was for another reader to mark them as inappropriate and wait for Delfi to decide. Importantly, Delfi removed some comments based on its own review, but it did so only very rarely. In 2006, there were about twenty[11] comments under one article that were considered threatening or offensive by the people concerned. After being notified, the portal deleted the content but refused to pay the compensation requested, and, after a long court procedure[12] the case was referred to the ECtHR, which had to deal with the possible

[7] Pollicino (2019), p. 168.

[8] *Delfi AS v Estonia* App no. 64569/09 (ECtHR, 16 June 2015).

[9] Deák (2015), pp. 56–59.

[10] Derieux (2015), pp. 26–29.

[11] From the one hundred and eighty-five that came with this article. *The author.*

[12] Nádori (2013), pp. 131–140.

liability of the platform provider for content uploaded by a third party. The ECtHR ruled that Estonia had not breached Article 10 of the European Convention on Human Rights (ECHR) by holding Delfi liable on the basis of comments posted alongside its articles. In the case, both the Chamber and the Grand Chamber examined four aspects: [13]

- the context of the comments;
- the measures taken by the portal to "prevent or remove" the comments in question;
- the possibility of holding the actual author(s) liable as an alternative to the portal's liability; and
- the consequences of the national judgment for the portal.[14]

At the end of the proceedings, the ECtHR considered it clearly established that the unlawful comments had reached the level of hate speech[15] and did not consider it necessary to carry out a specific linguistic or legal verification to support this.[16] It is important to note that the ECtHR agreed with the Estonian court that Delfi was a publisher—of an economic nature—in relation to the comments, in other words, that it was not acting as a mere passive technical service provider. However, in the present case, the ECtHR did not examine the liability of the original commentator, but found that the aggrieved party could have sued either the service provider or the author of the original comment—in this case an anonymous author—on the basis of his own decision. The ECtHR also stated in paragraph 109 that the "established law in the European Union and other countries envisaged the notice-and-take-down system as a legal and practical framework for Internet content hosting. This balance of responsibilities between users and hosts allowed platforms to identify and remove defamatory or other unlawful speech, whilst at the same time enabling robust

[13] *Delfi AS v Estonia* App no. 64569/09 (ECtHR, 16 June 2015), [144.]-[161.].

[14] It is interesting to compare this with the criteria examined by the ECtHR in the traditional media cases Axel Springer AG v Germany and Von Hannover v Germany:

- the level of contribution to a public debate of public interest;
- the public profile of the person in question;
- the prior conduct of the person concerned;
- the way the information is obtained and its veracity;
- the content, form and implications of the publication, and
- the severity of the penalty imposed.

Axel Springer AG v Germany App no. 39954/08 (ECtHR, 7 February 2012), [89.]-[95.]; *Von Hannover v Germany (No. 2)* App nos. 40660/08 and 60641/08 (ECtHR, 7 February 2012), [108.]-[113.].

[15] For an inadmissible case, where the online statements did not amount to hate speech but was an opinion or a value judgment, see: Włodzimierz Kucharczyk v Poland App no. 72966/13 (ECtHR, 17 December 2015).

[16] Krenc and van Drooghenroeck (2015), p. 821.

discussion of controversial topics of public debate." [17] In other words, in the view of the ECtHR, the NTDS can "function in many cases as an appropriate tool for balancing the rights and interests of all those involved." [18] This therefore means that the ECtHR took the view in 2015 that, where content posted by a third party on an ISP reaches the level of hate speech, Member States may hold ISPs liable if they fail to use means to remove clearly offensive comments without delay, regardless of whether they have been notified of them.[19]

One of the sharpest criticisms of the decision was made by judges András Sajó and Nona Tsotsoria in a joint opinion: "The consequences are easy to foresee. For the sake of preventing defamation of all kinds, and perhaps all "illegal" activities, all comments will have to be monitored from the moment they are posted. As a consequence, active intermediaries and blog operators will have considerable incentives to discontinue offering a comments feature, and the fear of liability may lead to additional self-censorship by operators. This is an invitation to self-censorship at its worst."[20] Neville Cox stresses[21] that the judgment in no way takes into account the national legislation in force at the time and does not seek (or fail) to set a precedent for future cases.[22] In addition, Nádori raises as an important criticism, that "the Grand Chamber saw the comments area of the portal as distinct not only from the hosting services, but also from '*other Internet fora*' for user content. It is interesting to ask on what basis, as the strong statement lacks any reasoning behind it. The Grand Chamber stressed that the judgment is not applicable to so-called social networking sites, but it is not easy to see what is the essential characteristic that would make a news portal and a social networking site different in the relevant respect."[23]

---

[17] *Delfi AS v Estonia* App no. 64569/09 (ECtHR, 16 June 2015), [109.]. Cf. "If major web platforms such as YouTube, Facebook and Twitter are now accused of censorship, it is because they have taken a leading role in democratic debate, becoming a privileged space for discussion and mobilisation on a daily basis." Badouard (2020), p. 13.

[18] *Delfi AS v Estonia* App no. 64569/09 (ECtHR, 16 June 2015), [159.]. See also Sepsi (2015), p. 108.

[19] Ibid., [159.].

[20] Ibid., Joint dissenting opinion of Judges Sajó and Tsotsoria, I. 1.

[21] Cox (2014), pp. 619–629.

[22] Challenging this argument, Roberto Spano argues that the relevant ECtHR judgments can only be considered as a starting point, with limited precedent value. Spano (2017), pp. 665–679.

[23] Nádori (2019), p. 362.

9.1.2 *Magyar Tartalomszolgáltatók Egyesülete and Index.hu Zrt. v Hungary (2016)* [24]

About six months later, in another landmark case, the ECtHR took a slightly different approach.[25] In the then leading Hungarian online media, *Index.hu,* some comments were offensive to a third party company ("sly, rubbish, mug company"[26]). The third party criticised in the comments brought a civil action against the Magyar Tartalomszolgáltatók Egyesülete and Index.hu Zrt. After being informed of the court proceedings, *Index.hu* removed the incriminated comment. The Hungarian courts concluded that *Index.hu* had an objective responsibility for the unlawful comments of readers, but the ECtHR later ruled that such an explanation was unjustified, stating that "this amounts to requiring excessive and impracticable forethought capable of undermining freedom of the right to impart information on the Internet."[27] The ECtHR ruled that Hungary had violated Article 10 ECHR when it held *Index.hu* liable on the basis of the comments posted alongside its articles. The ECtHR, citing the Delphi case, held that internet news portals must assume obligations and responsibilities for comments and third-party content posted on their platforms, but stated that the present case differed from the Delfi case, in that while the Delphi case involved clearly unlawful content that rose to the level of hate speech, the *Index.hu* case involved (only) offensive and vulgar speech. The ECtHR considered that the "test of liability"[28] established in Delfi—namely the context in which the comments were read, the measures taken by the company to prevent or remove the defamatory comments, the liability of the actual authors of the comments and the consequences of the national judgment—could be used in the present case, despite the absence of hate speech.[29] In addition to all these conditions, it introduced two further points of inquiry:

- the victim's behaviour and
- the consequences of the comments for the victim.[30]

As regards the victim's behaviour, the ECtHR considered it a negative aspect that the party did not ask *Index.hu* to remove the comments but immediately went to court. As to the consequences of the comments for the victim, the ECtHR found that

---

[24] *Magyar Tartalomszolgáltatók Egyesülete and Index.hu Zrt. v Hungary* App no. 22947/13 (ECtHR, 2 February 2016).

[25] For a detailed comparison of the two cases, see Sidlauskiene and Jurkevičius (2017), pp. 46–75; Papp (2017), pp. 315–326.

[26] *Magyar Tartalomszolgáltatók Egyesülete and Index.hu Zrt. v Hungary* App no. 22947/13 (ECtHR, 2 February 2016), [12.].

[27] Ibid., [82.].

[28] Gosztonyi et al. (2023).

[29] *Magyar Tartalomszolgáltatók Egyesülete and Index.hu Zrt. v Hungary* App no. 22947/13 (ECtHR, 2 February 2016), [70.].

[30] Ibid., [80.]-[85.].

the national court had not examined this at all, but there was little chance that these comments would have had any negative effect on the third party. With the addition of the two new aspects to be examined, the ECtHR has taken a step towards formulating "the universal criteria for internet news portal managers' liability" instead of examining all "*ad hoc* in each case."[31] Although the literature is not uniform on the issue, Tamás Szigeti and Éva Simon argue that the present case "can be seen as a correction of the previous unfortunate decision."[32]

9.1.3 *Pihl v Sweden (2017)* [33]

Unlike in previous cases, the applicant in Pihl v Sweden was a private individual who brought a claim for violation of his right to privacy and reputation,[34] as the authorities refused to prosecute the operator of a blog on which a defamatory blog post and an anonymous comment about Rolf Anders Daniel Pihl had appeared. Here, the ECtHR clearly applied the "liability test" outlined above as a precedent.[35] An exciting element in the analysis of the above test was that the ECtHR attached particular importance to the fact that the blog was run by a small non-profit enterprise, unknown to the wider public, and that the blog post and comment seemed unlikely to attract a large number of comments or wide readership. [36] As Attila Tatár put this dichotomy: "while in the MTE case the Strasbourg court, in finding no liability, did not attach much importance to the fact that one of the applicants was the owner of one of Hungary's largest news portals, in the Pihl case, in finding no liability, it already explicitly emphasised that the small blog was run by a non-profit association."[37] In any event, in the present case, the ECtHR held that Sweden had not violated the ECHR.

9.1.4 *Tamiz v United Kingdom (2017)* [38]

British local politician Payam Tamiz was preparing for a local election when a blog post about him and his photo was published on Blogger.com, a blog service run by Google, at the end of April 2011, which attracted a number of anonymous

---

[31] Sidlauskiene and Jurkevičius (2017), p. 49.

[32] Szigeti and Simon (2016), p. 113.

[33] *Pihl v Sweden* App no. 74742/14 (ECtHR, 9 March 2017).

[34] Popović (2023).

[35] Voorhoof (2020a).

[36] *Pihl v Sweden* App no. 74742/14 (ECtHR, 9 March 2017), [31.].

[37] Tatár (2019), p. 11.

[38] *Tamiz v United Kingdom* App no. 3877/14 (ECtHR, 19 September 2017).

comments. Payam Tamiz considered several of these anonymous comments to be defamatory and reported them to the company using the reporting platform provided by the blogging service. He also reported his complaint in writing, and Google requested clarifications in writing. After a few months, in August 2011, Google sent the notification letter to the author of the blog, who removed both the blog post and the comments. However, Payam Tamiz had already also filed a lawsuit against the company, asking the national court to find Google liable. The national court found only five of the offending posts to be vulgar, while three were found to be arguably defamatory.[39] On the question of whether Google is a distributor or a publisher, the national court[40] said that "It is no doubt often true that the owner of a wall which has been festooned, overnight, with defamatory graffiti could acquire scaffolding and have it all deleted with whitewash. That is not necessarily to say, however, that the unfortunate owner must, unless and until this has been accomplished, be classified as a publisher." [41] However, the national court said that even if Google did qualify as a publisher, it had done its best to have the disputed content removed. An important new element is that the national court also examined [42] the notification sent to Google, as the legal validity of the notification is necessary for the service provider to have actual knowledge of the illegal content.[43] The national court recorded that "a notification whose sender merely states that the challenged content is defamatory is not accurate and well founded, because the service provider cannot be expected to take such a statement granted".[44]

Tamiz later argued before the ECtHR, among other things, that the NTDS was not function properly as it required four months for removal of the said contents. [45] He also argues that the comments were clearly defamatory so they did not contribute to the public debate in the public interest. [46] The ECtHR stressed that content deemed defamatory must reach "a certain level of seriousness", [47] as millions of users post on the internet every day and most of the content is insignificant or low in content and therefore cannot cause significant harm to someone's reputation. Moreover, as a politician, Payam Tamiz has an extra duty of tolerance compared to the average

[39] Ibid., [25.].

[40] For more on the relevant UK case law, see McGoldrick (2013), pp. 125–151.

[41] *Tamiz v United Kingdom* App no. 3877/14 (ECtHR, 19 September 2017), [29.].

[42] *Tamiz v Google Inc Google UK Ltd* [2013] EWCA Civ 68.

[43] On this point, see also *Bunt v Tilley & Others* [2006] EWHC 407 (QB); [2007] 1 WLR 1243; [2006] 3 All ER 336; [2006] EMLR 523; *Davison v Habeeb & Others* [2011] EWHC 3031 (QB); *Kaschke v Gray & Hilton (No 2)* [2010] EWHC 1907 (QB); *Jameel (Yousef) v Dow Jones & Co. Inc.* [2005] EWCA Civ 75; [2005] QB 946; [2005] 2 WLR 1614; [2005] EMLR 353.

[44] Tatár (2019), p. 9; Ullrich (2021), pp. 184–186.

[45] *Tamiz v United Kingdom* App no. 3877/14 (ECtHR, 19 September 2017), [69.].

[46] *Axel Springer AG v Germany* App no. 39954/08 (ECtHR, 7 February 2012), [90.]; *Von Hannover v Germany (No. 2)* App nos. 40660/08 and 60641/08 (ECtHR, 7 February 2012), [109.].

[47] *Tamiz v United Kingdom* App no. 3877/14 (ECtHR, 19 September 2017), [80.].

user.[48] The ECtHR examined the "real and substantial harm" test[49] used in national law and found that the national court had struck the right balance between the platform provider's freedom of expression and the individual's right to a good reputation.[50]

The ECtHR rejected Tamiz's argument that the test used in the Delfi case should be applied in the present case, because while Delfi is a professional business news portal that produces content and (for economic reasons) explicitly asks and encourages its users to comment, [51] Google does not produce its own content and has no editorial responsibility for a blog post. Moreover, as shown above, in Delfi, the Grand Chamber expressly held—even if not supported by actual content—that platform providers are distinguished from *other fora* for user content and are, therefore, not governed by the Delfi judgment. In light of this, it is not surprising that the ECtHR held that the UK had not breached the ECHR in the present case.

9.1.5 Magyar Jeti Zrt. v Hungary (2018) [52]

A slightly different question arose in 2013 concerning a *hyperlinked* content. An article appeared on 444.hu, an online news portal run by Magyar Jeti Zrt., which included a link to a YouTube video where a Roma leader said that football fans singing racist songs were members of Jobbik, a Hungarian far-right party known for its anti-Roma actions. The party sued both the Roma leader and Magyar Jeti Zrt. for defamation. The Hungarian courts found the joint stock company liable for disseminating content containing false information. Years later, the ECtHR confirmed—contrary to the decisions of national courts[53]—that the strict liability of the media company for the content hyperlinked in their articles violated the right to freedom of expression under Article 10 ECHR.[54] This is because, in the ECtHR's view, hyperlinking has a navigational role on the internet, the hyperlink provider has no control over the hyperlinked content and the hyperlink does not create new content. [55] The ECtHR also introduced a new criterion in the case, namely the need to examine the following questions:[56]

---

[48] In this context, see Koltay (2019).

[49] Little (2019).

[50] Milkaite (2017).

[51] *Tamiz v United Kingdom* App no. 3877/14 (ECtHR, 19 September 2017), [85.].

[52] *Magyar Jeti Zrt. v Hungary* App no. 11257/16 (ECtHR, 4 December 2018).

[53] Vander Maelen (2019).

[54] Surrel (2019), p. 2376.

[55] *Magyar Jeti Zrt. v Hungary* App no. 11257/16 (ECtHR, 4 December 2018), [73.]-[75.].

[56] Ibid., [77.].

- Did the journalist endorse or approve the content?
- Did the journalist merely repeat the content (without endorsing or approving it)?
- Did the journalist merely hyperlink to the content in question (without endorsing, approving or repeating it)?
- Did the journalist know, or could the journalist reasonably have known, that the challenged content was defamatory or otherwise unlawful?
- Has the journalist acted in good faith, respected journalistic ethics and exercised the due diligence expected in responsible journalism?

According to the ECtHR's summary opinion, the objective liability for hyperlinking established by a national court may have foreseeable negative consequences for the flow of information on the internet, "impelling article authors and publishers to refrain altogether from hyperlinking to material over whose changeable content they have no control. This may have, directly or indirectly, a chilling effect[57] on freedom of expression on the Internet." [58]

9.1.6 *Høiness v Norway (2019)* [59]

In the Høiness case, the ECtHR found that there was no violation of the ECHR when the domestic courts refused to find the operator of an internet portal liable after vulgar comments were posted on it. The private applicant, Mona Høiness, is a Norwegian national and she considered that three anonymous comments constituted sexual harassment against her. The *Hegnar Online* portal removed the content as soon as it became aware of it. Although the case before the ECtHR deals with issues of content regulation on the internet, it was not Article 10 ECHR that was examined, but Article 8 ECHR.[60] The ECtHR found, in line with the national court, that the comments, while vulgar, did not rise to the level of hate speech, nor did they amount to an incitement to violence.[61] However, the ECtHR also found that there was no need to examine the nature of the comments in depth. [62] As in its previous practice, in examining this case it considered that the NTDS in operation was capable of precluding a finding of liability.

---

[57] *Fatullayev v Azerbaijan* App no 40984/07 (ECtHR, 22 April 2010), [100.]-[103.]; *Belpietro v Italy* App no 43612/10 (ECtHR, 24 September 2013), [61.]; *Magyar Tartalomszolgáltatók Egyesülete and Index.hu Zrt. v Hungary* App no. 22947/13 (ECtHR, 2 February 2016), [86.]; *Khadija Ismayilova v* Azerbaijan App no 30778/15 (ECtHR, 27 February 2020), [83.].

[58] *Magyar Jeti Zrt. v Hungary* App no. 11257/16 (ECtHR, 4 December 2018), [83.].

[59] *Høiness v Norway* App no. 43624/14 (ECtHR, 19 March 2019).

[60] A&M (2019), p. 380.

[61] Voorhoof (2020b), pp. 11–46.

[62] *Høiness v Norway* App no. 43624/14 (ECtHR, 19 March 2019), [69.].

9.1.7 *Sanchez v France (2023)* [63]

In the most recent case in the area, the ECtHR found that there was no violation of the ECHR when the domestic courts found Franck Sanchez guilty for not removing comments from his Facebook-wall. In October 2011, Sanchez was the Front National candidate in the French parliamentary elections in the Nîmes constituency. At the time of the events, F.P., then a Member of the European Parliament and first deputy to the mayor of Nîmes, was one of Sanchez's political opponents and both wanted to launch a new website. Sanchez succeeded in doing so, while F.P. did not, a fact that Sanchez noted in a post to his followers on his Facebook (FB) page. The post received around fifteen comments, which both in their wording and content clearly blamed Muslims for the difficulties of the city and its white population.[64] A few days later, L.T., who was F.P.'s partner, noticed the post and the comments and felt that they were racist and directly and personally offensive to her. L.T. filed a complaint against Sanchez as the owner of the given Facebook-wall and against S.B. and L.R. for offensive comments posted on Sanchez's public FB wall. A day later, Sanchez asked the users of his Facebook-wall to "be careful with the content of [their] comments", but he left the comments already posted intact, without moderating or removing them.[65] The French courts decided against Sanchez and he has exhausted the national remedies available to him, so he submitted an application to the ECtHR, alleging a violation of Article 10 of the ECHR.[66]

The main issue in the case was whether Sanchez, as an individual, was responsible for the hateful and exclusionary comments posted by third parties on his social networking site. The ECtHR clearly found that the content of the comments constituted unlawful and hate speech, and it was also clear that the comments were anti-Muslim.[67] The Court also stressed the responsibility of politicians in the fight against hate speech. The Court found that Sanchez, as the "publisher" of the site, was aware that there were hate posts on the site, yet he did not act to remove them, and in fact made his Facebook-wall public, and therefore his liability was established.[68]

Although in the judgment itself the ECtHR has repeatedly underlined the narrow scope for restricting political communication and political discourse, the present

[63] *Sanchez v France App no. 45581/15 (15 May 2023).*

[64] Lemmens (2022).

[65] Ibid., [19.].

[66] Voorhoof (2021).

[67] Korpisaari (2022).

[68] In the case, Judge Mouru-Vikström dissented, referring to the ECtHR's previous judgment in the Delphi case, and pointing out that, when it comes to determining liability for third-party online comments, a distinction must be made between commercially run, professionally operated news portals and platform providers and platforms of individuals registered on social media platforms. Ibid., [98.]–[99.].

decision is a clear contrast to the consistent practice to date.[69] "In practice, this judgment means that certain prominent individuals on social media would have the same obligations as the platforms."[70] Such an extension of—even criminal—responsibility for online content carries with it a number of dangers: it can expose certain prominent users (influencers, politicians, public figures etc.) to attacks—by e.g. bots[71]—that are almost impossible to defend against.[72]

9.2 Landmark Cases Before the Court of Justice of the European Union

Regarding the Delfi case, Estonia noted that the CJEU "had never adjudicated a case similar to Delfi." [73] In response, the ECtHR referred to the L'Oréal case but, in fact, it had already dealt with the issue a year earlier.[74] Before examining the cases concerned in relation to the practice of the CJEU,[75] it is worth referring to Oreste Pollicino's study, in which he writes that the CJEU "delivers its decisions in the context of preliminary proceedings. In this case, a crucial role is played by domestic courts, which refer questions to the CJEU. Such a difference leads the Luxembourg Court to play *de facto* a role as the fundamental rights adjudicator."[76]

---

[69] Cf. Wingrove v the United Kingdom App no. 17419/90 (25 November 1996), [58.]; Stoll v Switzerland App no. 69698/01 (10 December 2007), [106.].

[70] Article-19 (2023).

[71] Kovács (2022).

[72] Media Defence – Electronic Frontier Foundation (2022), pp. 1–2.

[73] *Delfi AS v Estonia* App no. 64569/09 (ECtHR, 16 June 2015), [85.].

[74] See Sect. 9.2.1.

[75] This book only analyses directly related judgments: for cases indirectly related to liability see Filatova-Bilous (2021).

[76] Pollicino (2019), p. 161; For more details see de Burca (2013), pp. 168–184.

9.2.1 *Google France SARL and Google Inc. v Louis Vuitton Malletier SA, Google France SARL v Viaticum SA and Luteciel SARL, Google France SARL v Centre national de recherche en relations humaines (CNRRH) SARL and Others (2010)* [77]

In the first major case on the subject, several different trademark owners sued Google's French subsidiary and the cases were consolidated. In each case, the lawsuits concerned the use of their trademarks by the Google search engine as part of a paid referencing service called 'AdWords', with the results leading to pages of counterfeit products. All parties concerned asked the national court to hold Google liable for the infringement. Google argued that it had no control over the linked sites and therefore could not be held liable. The case was referred to the CJEU, which, in view of the complexity and importance of the case, ruled in a Grand Chamber and took the view that, first, search engine services are clearly an information society service under the ECD[78] and, second, Google is not a passive, technical service provider, since it is the company's criteria that determine the order of the results and, third, it can change the order of the results on the basis of the paid service.[79] In this case, the CJEU therefore indicated to the national court that a general exemption from liability was not conceivable in the case in question, but that it is for the national court to examine whether the service provider has an active role in the services in question.[80]

9.2.2 *L'Oréal SA and Others v eBay International AG and Others (2011)* [81]

In the second high-profile case, the French cosmetics company L'Oréal reported to the online marketplace eBay that counterfeit versions of its products were being sold under the L'Oréal brand name on several occasions, while the marketplace prohibits

[77] *Google France SARL and Google Inc. v Louis Vuitton Malletier SA* (C-236/08), *Google France SARL v Viaticum SA and Luteciel SARL* (C-237/08) and *Google France SARL v Centre national de recherche en relations humaines (CNRRH) SARL and Others* (C-238/08). ECLI:EU:C:2010:159.

[78] Ibid., [110.].

[79] Ibid., [115.].

[80] However, it is worth highlighting what the *Harvard Law Review* has written about the case and Advocate General Poiares Maduro's more logical reasoning than the CJEU's: "The Advocate General's opinion demonstrates, however, that a more traditional analysis could have avoided the flaws in the court's reasoning while still achieving the same result. (...) Traditional doctrine would have served the CJEU well in Google France, even in the age of the internet." Harward Law Review (2010), p. 655.

[81] *L'Oréal SA and Others v eBay International AG and Others* (C-324/09) ECLI:EU:C:2011:474.

the sale of counterfeit goods in contracts signed by its users. In addition, L'Oréal products intended for testing (and not for sale) had also been put up for sale on the website. The cosmetics company held eBay (and in particular the European subsidiary that operates eBay.co.uk in this case) liable, while it also sued Google, which displayed search results for the name of the cosmetic products and for eBay ads for these counterfeit products that should not be for sale.

In the case, Judge Arnold raised a number of possibilities that eBay could use to detect or minimise problems without having to monitor the content uploaded to it across the board, but noted that just because all of these things are possible does not mean that it is legally required to do them. "I am in no doubt that it would be possible for eBay Europe to do more than they currently do. For example, it would appear to be possible for eBay Europe to take some or all of the following steps, although some would be more technically challenging and costly than others:

(i) filter listings before they are posted on the Site;
(ii) use additional filters, including filters to detect listings of testers and other not-for-sale products and unboxed products;
(iii) filter descriptions as well as titles;
(iv) require sellers to disclose their names and addresses when listing items, at least when listing items in a manner which suggests that they are selling in the course of trade;
(v) impose additional restrictions on the volumes of high risk products, such as fragrances and cosmetics, that can be listed at any one time;
(vi) be more consistent in their policies, for example regarding sales of unboxed products;
(vii) adopt policies to combat types of infringement which are not presently addressed, and in particular the sale of non-EEA goods without the consent of the trade mark owners;
(viii) take greater account of negative feedback, particularly feedback concerning counterfeits;
(ix) apply sanctions more rigorously; and
(x) be more rigorous in suspending accounts linked to those of users whose accounts have been suspended (although it is fair to say that the evidence is that eBay Europe have recently improved their performance in this regard)." [82]

On the basis of all these observations, the English court referred the matter to the CJEU, *inter alia*, as to whether and under what conditions Article 14 of the ECD applies to the operator of an online marketplace. The CJEU took the clear view that the answer was in the affirmative, i.e. that the relevant legal position applies to

[82] *L'Oréal SA v eBay International AG* [2009] RPC 21, [2009] ETMR 53, [2009] EWHC 1094 (Ch), [277.].

operators of online marketplaces.[83] As regards liability, the Court indicated, as in the Google France case, that a neutral, passive type of service provider may be exempt from liability, but in the present case eBay actively contributed to the success of the sales (for example, in some cases it helped to optimise prices or was able to advertise certain products[84]), so. it did not qualify for exemption from liability. The CJEU therefore indicated to the national court in this case that a general exemption could not be envisaged in this particular case, but that it was for the national court to assess whether there was an active role for the service provider in it in relation to L'Oréal's products. If the answer to that question was in the affirmative, liability could be established. It is worth noting that the CJEU judgment led some (e.g. Christine Riefa[85]) to conclude that service providers would, from then on, have a general duty to monitor, but the CJEU did not take such a view in the formal documents in the case.[86]

9.2.3 *UPC Telekabel Wien GmbH v Constantin Film Verleih GmbH and Wega Filmproduktionsgesellschaft mbH (2014)*[87]

As a background to the case, two German film distribution companies informed UPC Telekabel in Austria that some of their copyrighted films were being downloaded without their permission from the kino.to website, which uses UPC's internet service. The two companies demanded that the kino.to website be completely shut down or made inaccessible. UPC denied responsibility, claiming that it had not been involved in the transmission of the copyrighted content. The case was referred to the CJEU, which, although it did not refer to the ECD but to the EU's Directive on Copyright in the Digital Single Market, held that an ISP that (also) transmits protected content to the public is an intermediary service provider and that there is no need for a contractual relationship between the ISP and the rightholder of the protected content to establish this. The CJEU stated that the choice of how and by what technical means the service provider protects intellectual property is left to its discretion[88]—and that it is for the national courts to determine whether this is lawful. However, the solution must take account of two conjunctive conditions:

---

[83] *L'Oréal SA and Others v eBay International AG and Others* (C-324/09) ECLI:EU:C:2011:474, [109.].

[84] Ibid., [114.].

[85] Riefa (2012), pp. 104–111.

[86] Gilbert (2011).

[87] *UPC Telekabel Wien GmbH v Constantin Film Verleih GmbH and Wega Filmproduktionsgesellschaft mbH* (C-314/12) ECLI:EU:C:2014:192.

[88] Wang (2014), p. 2.

(i) the measures taken must not unnecessarily deprive Internet users of their right to access the information available; and
(ii) these measures prevent unauthorised access to the protected subject matter, or at least make it difficult and seriously discourage Internet users from accessing content made available to them in violation of intellectual property rights. [89]

9.2.4 *Sotiris Papasavvas v O Fileleftheros Dimosia Etaireia Ltd and Others (2014)* [90]

In the case, which was referred to the CJEU by a Cypriot court in a preliminary ruling, Sotiris Papasavvas sued a newspaper publishing company, its editor-in-chief and two journalists over online content he felt was defamatory. The national court referred the case to the CJEU on, among other things, whether the information society services regime of the EU Directive:

- precludes the establishment of civil liability;
- applies to the online presence of a printed newspaper; and
- it makes a difference whether the online platform is available for free or for a fee.

On the basis of Article 3(1) of the ECD, the CJEU made it clear that Cyprus may lay down rules (in this case concerning defamation) in relation to information society services, which are in no way excluded by the ECD. Before answering the second question, the CJEU answered the third: the relevant element for exemption from liability is not whether the content is paid or free, but whether the provider plays an active or passive role in relation to the content in question.[91] The CJEU clearly stated that, since the content in question was the online publication of content produced by the publisher of a printed newspaper, the active role could not be called into question. However, the online interface of the printed newspaper was not considered by the CJEU to be an 'information society service', so the second question was not answered.[92]

[89] *UPC Telekabel Wien GmbH v Constantin Film Verleih GmbH and Wega Filmproduktionsgesellschaft mbH* (C-314/12) ECLI:EU:C:2014:192, [64.].

[90] *Sotiris Papasavvas v O Fileleftheros Dimosia Etaireia Ltd and Others* (C-291/13) ECLI:EU: C:2014:2209.

[91] Ibid., [46.].

[92] Ibid., [48.].

9.2.5 *Tobias Mc Fadden v Sony Music Entertainment Germany GmbH (2016)*[93]

Tobias Mc Fadden ran a shop in Germany selling light and sound equipment and, in order to serve his customers better, he also offered them access to a free Wi-Fi network, which was not password protected. In 2010, Sony Music officially notified him that a copyrighted track was available on the shop's network. Mc Fadden went to court, seeking a negative declaration *(negative Feststellungsklage),*[94] *as* known in German law, confirming that he was not liable for the infringement committed by providing the network, as he had no right to control the content. Sony Music filed a counterclaim, seeking a declaration that Mc Fadden was directly liable, in addition to claiming damages. As Mc Fadden did not appear before the national court, the terms of Sony Music's counterclaim were accepted. Mc Fadden appealed, and the national court referred the case to the CJEU, questioning whether, inter alia:

- the provision of a wifi network is an information society service;
- this service falls within the scope of simple transmission and whether Article 12 of the EU Directive applies;
- it is relevant that the provider offered access to the wifi network as an additional service to its original market profile;
- the national court can oblige the provider to ensure that the wifi network is only provided with some form of protection.

The CJEU made it clear that the provision of a wifi network is an information society service. It reached this conclusion using a negative inference, since nothing in the definition of the term excludes it—so the present case is significant for extending the scope of the legislation. Moreover, it noted that it is sufficient that the service provider offers the service in order to promote the service according to its original market profile;[95] it is not necessary for the service provider to establish separate remuneration for it,[96] nor that there is a separate contractual relationship with the users of the network.[97]

As regards liability, the CJEU maintained its previous position and pointed out that the exemption applies if the conditions of Article 12 of the ECD are fulfilled.[98] In particular, the CJEU emphasised that the fulfilment of the conditions for exemption in Article 14 of the ECD does not apply *mutatis mutandis* in a case involving a

---

[93] *Tobias Mc Fadden v Sony Music Entertainment Germany GmbH* (C-484/14), ECLI:EU:C:2016:689.

[94] Kellner and Liebel (2020), pp. 510–511.

[95] Ibid., [43.].

[96] Ibid., [41.].

[97] Ibid., [50.].

[98] However, as István Harkai accurately notes in his analysis of the decision, "It is possible to claim damages even if the intermediary service provider has discharged its civil liability." Harkai (2021), p. 222.

simple transmission service within the meaning of Article 12 of the ECD. [99] Of particular interest to our topic is the issue of the protection of the national court's access to the network, where the CJEU (by majority) accepted Advocate General Szpunar's Opinion. [100] The CJEU stated that although the national court has a judicial role under national and EU law, of the three technical solutions hypothetically proposed by the national court (termination of the service, [101] password protection[102] or general traffic monitoring obligation[103]), only password protection could pass the test of legality,[104] but only if the national court sufficiently balanced the three fundamental rights at stake in the present case were by, namely freedom of expression, freedom to operate a business, and intellectual property rights were upheld.[105] The difficulty of all this in the context of continuous technological development was described by Ciarán Burke and Alexandra Molitorisová as like a game of "catch me if you can."[106] Martin Husovec went even further, arguing that the CJEU, due to its own framing problem, thus drilled another hole in the safe harbour protection paradigm.[107]

9.2.6 *Eva Glawischnig-Piesczek v Facebook Ireland Limited (2019* [108]

In the Glawischnig-Piesczek case, the CJEU had to take a position on Article 15 of ECD. Whereas primarily in the above L'Oréal case , but also in the two SABAM cases [109] the CJEU concluded that general monitoring is not an obligation for service providers, there seems to be a slight change of direction on this issue. In this case, defamatory text about the Austrian MEP Eva Glawischnig-Piesczek was posted on Facebook with a photo of her. She asked the service provider not only to remove the content in question, but also to remove all similar content. The national court ordered

---

[99] *Tobias Mc Fadden v Sony Music Entertainment Germany GmbH* (C-484/14), ECLI:EU:C:2016:689, [65.].

[100] *Tobias Mc Fadden v Sony Music Entertainment Germany GmbH* (C-484/14), ECLI:EU:C:2016:170, Opinion of Advocate General Szpunar, [125th]-[150th].

[101] *Tobias Mc Fadden v Sony Music Entertainment Germany GmbH* (C-484/14), ECLI:EU:C:2016:689, [89.].

[102] Ibid., [99.].

[103] Ibid., [87.].

[104] Advocate General Szpunar questioned the legality of all three methods in his submission.

[105] Jütte (2016).

[106] Burke and Molitorisová (2017), p. 241.

[107] Husovec (2017), p. 125.

[108] *Eva Glawischnig-Piesczek v Facebook Ireland Limited* (C-18/18). ECLI:EU:C:2019:821.

[109] *Scarlet Extended SA v Société belge des auteurs, compositeurs et éditeurs SCRL (SABAM)* (C-70/10), ECLI:EU:C:2011:771; *Belgische Vereniging van Auteurs, Componisten en Uitgevers CVBA (SABAM) v Netlog NV* (C-360/10), ECLI:EU:C:2012:85.

the service provider to remove not only the content of the incriminated content, but also all similar content brought to the defendant's attention by the plaintiff. However, the national court referred the matter to the CJEU, inter alia, asking that

- whether Article 15 allows the application of NTDS not only to the content in question, but also to any similar content that may be shared;
- if the answer is yes, what are the conditions for finding similarity;
- if it allows national legislation or courts to impose such a requirement only on the provider not within the country; or
- these obligations do not conflict with the prohibition of the "general monitoring obligation".

In its decision, the CJEU pointed out that "information society services are characterised both by their rapidity and by their geographical extent", [110] and that "there is a genuine risk that information which was held to be illegal is subsequently reproduced and shared by another user of that network."[111] On this basis, the CJEU concluded that Member States not only have the possibility to require the removal of the content in question, but also to impose such requirements on any similar content that may be shared.[112] The reasoning behind this decision is that if the ban were to apply only to a particular piece of content, its effects "could easily be circumvented by the storing of messages which are scarcely different from those which were previously declared to be illegal" [113] and thus the aggrieved party would have to bring new and additional proceedings in each case.

However, the CJEU stressed that, contrary to the national court's finding, the removal of such content should not only be done at the request of the aggrieved party, as this would impose an undue burden on the legislator or the enforcer. In order to establish if the contents are indentical, it is necessary to compare the content as a whole and not merely the words. CJE also pointed out that this can only be achieved if the provider is not required "to carry out an independent assessment",[114] in which case an undue burden would be imposed on him. As these above can be achieved by automated means, the CJEU also considered it appropriate to balance the conflicting fundamental rights,[115] and, on the other hand, summarised, with reference to Article 47 of the ECD, that the requirement of *ad hoc* monitoring does not conflict with the prohibition in Article 15 of the ECD. [116] With regard to

[110] *Eva Glawischnig-Piesczek v Facebook Ireland Limited* (C-18/18) ECLI: EU:C:2019:821, [3.].

[111] Ibid., [36.].

[112] This is what the literature calls the 'notice and blocking' (NSD) procedure.

[113] *Eva Glawischnig-Piesczek v Facebook Ireland Limited* (C-18/18) ECLI:EU:C:2019:821, [41.].

[114] Ibid., [46.].

[115] The complexity of the issue is illustrated by the fact that some commentators have predicted the legal 'death' of active/passive discrimination in the context of the above decision. Andolina and Tuninetti Ferrari (2020).

[116] *Eva Glawischnig-Piesczek v Facebook Ireland Limited* (C-18/18) ECLI:EU:C:2019:821, [34.].

extraterritorial scope,[117] the CJEU stated that the ECD does not contain a prohibition in this respect, so national legislation may oblige service providers to apply a prohibition beyond national borders "within the framework of the relevant international law." [118] Joan Barata sums up the legitimate question: "which international legal standards permit the identification and global banning of content, on the basis of the adjudication made by one single State?"[119]

All of this, however much the CJEU refers to Article 47 of the ECD, seems to be general monitoring rather than a specific case.[120] It is notable that the CJEU has not found a clear dividing line between prohibited general monitoring and ad hoc monitoring measures.[121] As Dorina Gyetván concludes in her study, "the arguments put forward in the judgments as a whole paint a rather worrying picture as regards the interpretation and enforcement of the prohibition of general monitoring."[122]

9.2.7 *Frank Peterson v Google LLC and Others and Elsevier Inc. v Cyando AG (2021)* [123]

In the present case, copyright-infringing content was uploaded to YouTube (owned by Google) and Uploaded (owned by Elsevier) and the CJEU had to answer questions from the German court in a preliminary procedure. The CJEU's view, confirming its previous decisions, is that the following questions should be examined in relation to the service providers:

- whether the service provider has put in place appropriate technological measures that can be expected to counter copyright infringements on its platform credibly and effectively;
- whether the service provider is involved in the selection of protected content illegally disclosed to the public;
- whether the provider explicitly provides means for the illegal sharing of such content; and

[117] Sander (2021), p. 173.

[118] *Eva Glawischnig-Piesczek v Facebook Ireland Limited* (C-18/18) ECLI:EU:C:2019:821, [53.].

[119] Barata (2021), p. 14.

[120] Same was granted in front of lower courts in Germany: Künast v Facebook, Landgericht Frankfurt am Main, 2-03 O 188/21, 8 April 2022 and Blume v Twitter, Landgericht Frankfurt am Main, 2-03 O 325/22, 14 December 2022.

[121] De Streel et al. (2018), p. 20.

[122] Gyetván (2021), pp. 299–315.

[123] *Frank Peterson v Google LLC and Others and Elsevier Inc.v Cyando AG* (C-682/18 and C-683/18), ECLI:EU:C:2021:503.

- the operator knowingly encourages such sharing, for example by adopting a financial model that encourages users to illegally communicate protected content to the public through their platform.[124]

It is important to underline that the CJEU did not address Article 17 of the EU's Directive on Copyright in the Digital Single Market when examining the issue, although it did detect the links. [125] In the CJEU's view, neither the mere fact that illegal content is present on the service provider's platforms, nor the fact that it may have had "general knowledge" that the platform could be used to share illegal content, nor the fact that the service provider seeks to make a profit from its activities, does not in itself constitute a basis for liability. [126] In relation to actual knowledge, the CJEU confirmed that being "aware of facts or circumstances from which the illegal activity or information is apparent – refers to specific illegal information and activities."[127] In the CJEU's view, notifications must contain sufficient information to enable the platform operator to be satisfied, without detailed legal examination, that the content is illegal and that its removal is compatible with freedom of expression.[128] However, this statement is at odds with the ECtHR's decision in the above-analysed Tamiz v United Kingdom case, so ensuring consistency will certainly be left for the next period.

9.2.8 *Puls 4 TV GmbH & Co. KG v YouTube LLC and Google Austria GmbH (2021)*[129]

Of the four questions referred for a preliminary ruling in the case, the first and fourth could have been given priority, since they dealt with the liability of service providers, namely, in which cases the service provider is an active and in which cases it is a neutral actor. The answer could also have covered the additional activities of service providers (e.g. suggesting videos by topic; making it easier for visitors to search by title or content by means of an electronic directory where the user can enter the title or content; providing online guidance on the use of the service ('help'); linking videos uploaded by the user with advertising (but not the platform operator's own advertising), subject to the user's consent, on the basis of the target group's choice). In addition, the fourth question related to the question of actual knowledge of the unlawful activity or information and the possibilities for national courts to do

[124] Ibid., [84.].

[125] Ibid., [59.].

[126] Ibid., [86.].

[127] Ibid., [112.].

[128] Brady and Larkin (2021).

[129] Request for a preliminary ruling from the Oberster Gerichtshof (Austria) lodged on 1 July 2019 – *Puls 4 TV GmbH & Co. KG v YouTube LLC and Google Austria GmbH* (C-500/19), https://curia.europa.eu/juris/liste.jsf?num=C-500/19&language=en.

so. However, no answers could be provided in this case, as Austria withdrew the questions on 2 August 2021 and the President of the CJEU ordered the case to be withdrawn on 29 October 2021.

9.3 Summary of the Legal Development Activities of International Courts and Tribunals

As we have seen, the practice of the ECtHR and the CJEU covers a wide range of liability issues for platform providers. The jurisprudence of the two courts is complementary, as the ECtHR approaches the problems on human rights grounds, while the CJEU approaches them on economic grounds. As Evangelia Psychogiopoulou puts it: "The jurisprudence of the CJEU dealing with new technologies and digitalization shows that engagement with ECtHR case law is not 'cosmetic'."[130] Nevertheless, it is clear that these two approaches contribute to the protection of freedom of expression, so they are cleary related to the content moderation practices.[131]

On the one hand, the ECtHR has made important clarifying statements about the NTDS, which, as it said in Delfi, is in many cases an appropriate means of balancing the rights and interests of all concerned and can therefore be used to exclude liability. However, the ECtHR has recognised that different types of content would require different types of proceedings and, with particular emphasis on content that rises to the level of hate speech, it is clear that it also sees the case for broadening the scope of the uniform rules. In addition, the ECtHR has consistently maintained its position in its decisions on the active or passive role of service providers that only and exclusively neutral, passive service providers can be exempted from liability in the application of the rules.

Unlike the CJEU, the ECtHR's practice is particularly significant, in that it consciously seeks to establish more generally applicable tests that can assist parties as well as national enforcers. The ECtHR's test of liability follows this path and clarifies the test for determining whether the ECJ Directive and the ECHR are applicable. As such, it is necessary to examine:

- the context of the comments;
- the measures taken by the portal to 'prevent or remove' the comments in question;
- the possibility of holding the actual author(s) liable as an alternative to the portal's liability;
- the consequences of the national judgment for the portal;
- the conduct of the victim; and
- the consequences of the comments for the victim.

---

[130] Psychogiopoulou (2022), p. 158.

[131] Papp (2022), pp. 95–122.

On the other hand, the CJEU has clarified the concept of information society services, by stating that whether it is a search engine service, an online marketplace or the provision of a wifi network, it is covered by the concept and therefore by the Directive. Moreover, in the latter case, the CJEU used the negative inference, thus extending its scope.

It also includes the fact that the CJEU has clearly stated, on the basis of Article 3(1) of the ECD, that national legislation may decide on civil liability in relation to information society services, as this option is in no way excluded by the ECD. In addition, the CJEU has consistently maintained in its decisions that, in relation to the active or passive role of service providers, only a neutral, passive type of service provider can be exempted from liability in the application of the rules.

The last significant issue that the CJEU has addressed is the question of the general prohibition of the obligation to monitor in Article 15 of the ECD. However, it should be noted in this context that the CJEU seems to have made a minor policy change in the time between the L'Oréal case in 2011 and the Eva Glawischnig-Piesczek case in 2019, and although it referred to case-by-case monitoring, it seems to have shifted towards the adoption of general monitoring when analysing the case.

Although the ECtHR and the CJEU differ on certain issues, this is not surprising, as the two courts examine the same issues from different angles. At the same time, we can expect that "the courts will keep setting standards for national legislators and judiciaries, ensuring respect for both the freedom to receive and impart information whilst approaching new media actors with a due note of the specificities of the digital age and the opportunities opened by the Internet."[132] The complementary jurisprudence of the two international courts contributes significantly to ensuring that the liability of platform providers and the internet as a complex and constantly changing ecosystem is on a more solid footing in the practice of national courts.

References

A&M (2019) C.E.D.H., 19 mars 2019. Hoiness c. Norvège (ECtHR, 19 March 2019. Hoiness v Norway). Auteurs & média 2019(3)

Andolina A, Tuninetti Ferrari A (2020) Court of Rome and CJEU again on Internet Service Providers' liability: two days of ordinary (dis)harmonization. Lexology, 27 Jan. https://www.lexology.com/library/detail.aspx?g=f3bcbdbb-1689-46df-a126-100d0868a2b9/

Article-19 (2023) European Court of Human Rights: dangerous decision for free speech online. article19.org, 15 May. www.article19.org/resources/european-court-of-human-rights-dangerous-decision-for-free-speech-online/

Badouard R (2020) Les nouvelles lois du web. Modération et censure (The new laws of the web. Moderation and censorship). Le Seuil, Paris

Barata J (2021) The digital services act and its impact on the right to freedom of expression: special focus on risk mitigation obligations. Plataforma en Defensa de la Libertad de Información,

[132] Cendic and Gosztonyi (2022), p. 155.

22 June. https://libertadinformacion.cc/wp-content/uploads/2021/06/DSA-AND-ITS-IMPACT-ON-FREEDOM-OF-EXPRESSION-JOAN-BARATA-PDLI.pdf

Bardarova S (2013) Comparison Between the European Court of Justice and European Court of Human Rights. SSRN Paper. https://ssrn.com/abstract=2281215/

Brady C, Larkin D (2021) CJEU rules on liability of internet platforms for user uploads. William Fry, 15 July. https://www.williamfry.com/newsandinsights/news-article/2021/07/15/cjeu-rules-on-liability-of-internet-platforms-for-user-uploads/

Burke C, Molitorisová A (2017) What does it matter who is browsing? ISP liability and the right to anonymity. J Intellect Prop Inf Technol E-Commerce Law 8(3)

Cendic K, Gosztonyi G (2022) New technologies and public watchdogs before the European Court of Human Rights: reflections on European supranational litigation. In: Psychogiopoulou E, de la Sierra S (eds) Digital media governance and supranational courts. Selected issues and insights from the European Judiciary. Edward Elgar Publishing, Cheltenham

Cox N (2014) Delfi AS v Estonia: the liability of secondary internet publishers for violation of reputational rights under the European Convention on Human Rights. Mod Law Rev 77(4)

Daka M (2020) Az Emberi Jogok Európai Egyezménye és az Európai Unió alapjogvédelmi rendszerének összefüggései – konvergencia és divergencia az európai jogi térben (The European Convention on Human Rights and the European Union's system of fundamental rights protection – convergence and divergence in the European legal space). Doctoral thesis. https://ajk.pte.hu/sites/ajk.pte.hu/files/file/doktori-iskola/daka-marija/daka-marija-muhelyvita-ertekezes.pdf

De Burca G (2013) After the EU Charter of Fundamental Rights: The Court of Justice as a Human Rights Adjudicator? Maastricht J Eur Compet Law 20(2)

De Streel A, Buiten M, Peitz M (2018) Liability of online hosting platforms. Should exceptionalism end? Centre on Regulation in Europe, Brussels

De Vries SA (2013) Editorial EU and ECHR: conflict or harmony? Utrecht Law Rev 9(1)

Deák I (2015) Ki felel a kommentekért? A Delfi AS kontra Észtország ügy (Who is responsible for the comments? The Delfi AS v Estonia case). Közjogi Szemle 8(3)

Derieux E (2015) Responsabilité d'un portail d'actualités du fait de commentaires diffamatoires postés par des internautes (Liability of a news portal for defamatory comments posted by Internet users). Revue Lamy droit de l'immatériel 2015(118)

Filatova-Bilous N (2021) Once again platform liability: on the edge of the 'Uber' and 'Airbnb' cases. Internet Policy Rev 10(2)

Gilbert K (2011) L'Oréal v eBay: ECJ Judgment. SCL, 12 July. https://www.scl.org/news/2165-l-or-al-v-ebay-ecj-judgment/

Gless S, Jeannine M (2013) The comparative method in European Courts: a comparison between the CJEU and ECtHR? Bergen J Crim Law Crim Justice 1(1)

Gosztonyi G, Huszár D, Lendvai GF (2023) Hungarian Digital Media Cases Before Supranational European Courts. In: Szabó M, Gyeney L, Láncos PL (eds) Hungarian yearbook of international law and European law 2022. Eleven International Publishing, The Hague

Gyetván D (2021) Az általános nyomon követési kötelezettség mint a közvetítő szolgáltatók felelősségének jövője? (A general monitoring obligation as the future of intermediary service providers' liability?). In: Fazekas M (ed) Jogi Tanulmányok 2021 (Legal Studies 2021). Eötvös Loránd Tudományegyetem Állam- és Jogtudományi Kar Állam- és Jogtudományi Doktori Iskola, Budapest

Harkai I (2021) Az internet hatása a többszörözési és a nyilvánossághoz közvetítési jogra (The impact of the internet on reproduction and communication rights). Iurispertius Kiadó, Szeged

Harward Law Review (2010) Joined Cases C-236/08, C-237/08 & C-238/08, Google France SARL v Louis Vuitton Malletier SA. Harward Law Rev 124(648)

Husovec M (2017) Holey Cap! CJEU drills (yet) another hole in the E-Commerce Directive's Safe Harbors. J Intellect Prop Law Pract 12(2)

Imbarlina E (2013) The roles and relationship between the two European Courts in Post-Lisbon EU Human Rights Protection. Jurist, 12 Sep. https://www.jurist.org/commentary/2013/09/elena-butti-lisbon-treaty/

Jütte BJ (2016) CJEU sheds light on liability for operators of open Wi-Fi networks. European Law Blog, 28 Sep. https://europeanlawblog.eu/2016/09/28/cjeu-sheds-light-on-liability-for-operators-of-open-wi-fi-networks-case-c-48414-mc-fadden-v-sony-music/

Kellner M, Liebel F (2020) Negative Feststellungsklage wegen Klagsdrohung. BankArchiv 64(7)

Koltay A (2019) A közügyek vitáinak szabadsága és a személyiségi jogok védelme (Freedom of debate on public affairs and protection of individual rights). Pázmány Law Working Papers 2019(4)

Korpisaari P (2022) From Delfi to Sanchez – when can an online communication platform be responsible for third-party comments? An analysis of the practice of the ECtHR and some reflections on the Digital Services Act. J Media Law 14(2)

Kovács A (2022) Botok, automatizált fiókok a közösségi médiában (Bots, automated accounts on social media). In: Nagy M, Fazekas M (eds) Jogi Tanulmányok 2022 (Legals Studies 2022). Eötvös Loránd Tudományegyetem Állam- és Jogtudományi Kar Állam- és Jogtudományi Doktori Iskola, Budapest

Krenc F, van Drooghenroeck S (2015) Chronique de jurisprudence de la Cour européenne des droits de l'homme (Case-law of the European Court of Human Rights). Journal des tribunaux 134(39)

Lemmens K (2022) Freedom of expression on the internet after Sanchez v France: how the European Court of Human Rights Accepts Third-Party 'Censorship'. Eur Conv Hum Rights Law Rev 3(3)

Little A (2019) Defamation – test of serious harm. Hill Dickinson, 2 Oct. https://www.hilldickinson.com/insights/articles/defamation-test-serious-harm/

McGoldrick D (2013) The limits of freedom of expression on Facebook and social networking sites: a UK perspective. Hum Rights Law Rev 13(1)

Media Defence – Electronic Frontier Foundation (2022) Intervention in Sanchez v France. mediadefence.org, 8 Apr. https://www.mediadefence.org/wp-content/uploads/2022/05/20220408-FINAL-Sanchez-v-France-MD-EFF-Written-Comments-1.pdf

Milkaite I (2017) Tamiz v UK: Google's blog-publishing service is not liable for offensive comments. Strasbourg Observers, 23 Nov. https://strasbourgobservers.com/2017/11/23/tamiz-v-uk-googles-blog-publishing-service-is-not-liable-for-offensive-comments/

Nádori P (2013) Delfi AS v Észtország: strasbourgi döntés a névtelen kommentekért viselt szolgáltatói felelősségről (Delfi AS v Estonia: Strasbourg ruling on service provider liability for anonymous comments). Infokommunikáció és Jog 10(56)

Nádori P (2019) Úton a tömeges internetes szólás jogi megítélésének új megközelítése felé. A strasbourgi Nagykamara ítélete a Delfi-ügyben (Towards a new approach to the legal treatment of mass internet speech. Judgment of the Strasbourg Grand Chamber in the Delphi case). In Medias Res 8(2)

Papp JT (2017) Liability for third-party comments before the European Court of Human Rights – comparing the Estonian Delfi and the Hungarian Index-MTE decisions. In: Szabó M, Láncos PL, Varga R (eds) Hungarian Yearbook of International and European Law 2016. Eleven International Publishing, The Hague

Papp JT (2022) A közösségi média szabályozása a demokratikus nyilvánosság védelmében (Social media regulation to protect the democratic public sphere). Wolters Kluwer, Budapest

Pollicino O (2019) Judicial protection of fundamental rights in the transition from the world of atoms to the word of bits: the case of freedom of speech. Eur Law J 25(2)

Popović I (2023) Online privacy and freedom of expression – the ECtHR's approach. Institute of Justice in Warsaw, Warsaw

Psychogiopoulou E (2022) Judicial dialogue and digitalization. CJEU engagement with ECtHR case law and fundamental rights standards in the EU. JIPITEC 13(2)

Riefa C (2012) The end of Internet Service Providers liability as we know it – uncovering the consumer interest in CJEU Case C-324/09 (L'Oréal/eBay). J Eur Consum Market Law 1(2)

Sander B (2021) Democratic disruption in the age of social media: between marketized and structural conceptions of human rights law. Eur J Int Law 32(1)

Sepsi T (2015) No comment? Az internetes hozzászólásokért való jogi felelősség (No comment? Legal liability for comments on the internet). Fundamentum 19(4)

Sidlauskiene J, Jurkevičius V (2017) Website operators' liability for offensive comments: a comparative analysis of Delfi as v Estonia and MTE & Index v Hungary. Baltic J Law Polit 10(2)

Spano R (2017) Intermediary liability for online user comments under the European Convention on Human Rights. Hum Rights Law Rev 17(4)

Surrel H (2019) Responsabilité d'un portail d'actualité en raison de l'affichage d'un hyperlien: CEDH, 4 décembre 2018. Magyar Jeti Zrt c/Hongrie (Liability of a news portal for posting a hyperlink: ECtHR, 4 December 2018. Magyar Jeti Zrt v Hungary). La Semaine Juridique: Édition Générale 2019(52)

Szigeti T, Simon É (2016) A hozzászólás szabadsága: a közvetítő szolgáltatói felelősség aktuális kérdéseiről (Freedom to comment: on current issues of intermediary service provider liability). Fundamentum 20(2–4)

Tatár A (2019) A tárhelyszolgáltatók körében felmerülő felelősségi kérdésekről (On liability issues for hosting providers). Infokommunikáció és Jog 16(72)

Ullrich C (2021) Unlawful content online. Towards a new regulatory framework for online platforms. Nomos, Baden-Baden

Vander Maelen C (2019) Magyar Jeti Zrt v Hungary: the Court provides legal certainty for journalists that use hyperlinks. Strasbourg Observers, 19 Jan. https://strasbourgobservers.com/2019/01/18/magyar-jeti-zrt-v-hungary-the-court-provides-legal-certainty-for-journalists-that-use-hyperlinks/

Voorhoof D (2020a) The Court's subtle approach of online media platforms' liability for user-generated content since the 'Delfi Oracle'. Strasbourg Observers, 10 Apr. https://strasbourgobservers.com/2020/04/10/the-courts-subtle-approach-of-online-media-platforms-liability-for-user-generated-content-since-the-delfi-oracle/

Voorhoof D (2020b) Same standards, different tools? The ECtHR and the protection and limitations of freedom of expression in the digital environment. In: O'Boyle M (ed) Human rights challenges in the digital age: judicial perspectives. Council of Europe, Strasbourg

Voorhoof D (2021) European Court of Human Rights: Sanchez v France. IRIS 9(1)

Wang FF (2014) Site-blocking orders in the EU: justifications and feasibility. In: 14th Annual Intellectual Property Scholars Conference (IPSC), Boalt Hall School of Law, University of California, Berkeley, 7–8 Aug

Chapter 10
The Practice of Restricting Internet Access Before the European Court of Human Rights or New Tools of Political Censorship

In recent years, compared to the Muižnieks' Declaration of 2017, the situation of internet restrictions imposed by states has noticeably deteriorated further, so it is worth examining the extent to which freedom of access to the internet can be enjoyed as a means of receiving and transmitting information and ideas. It is also worth looking at the legal avenues of resistance to the increasingly common phenomenon of states blocking their citizens' access to information. The latest report of the UN High Commissioner for Human Rights 2022 sets out the situations in which malfunctions in access to key information may occur: "Hospitals being unable to contact their doctors in cases of emergency, voters being deprived of information about candidates, handicraft makers being cut off from customers, and potentially facing imminent economic ruin, peaceful protesters who fall under violent attack being unable to call for help, students missing entrance exams for academic programmes and refugees being unable to access information on the risks that they face owing to the coronavirus disease (COVID-19) pandemic are just some of the situations confronted when an Internet and telecommunications services shutdown occurs."[1]

10.1 "Filtering, Blocking and Hacking Replaced Scissors and Black Ink"[2]

In 2011, the UN Special Rapporteur on Freedom of Expression spoke about the promotion and protection of freedom of expression and opinion; "some of the ways in which States are increasingly censoring information online, namely through: arbitrary blocking or filtering of content; criminalisation of legitimate expression;

[1] UNHRC (2022), p. 1.

[2] Bennett and Naim (2015).

G. Gosztonyi, *Censorship from Plato to Social Media*, Law, Governance and Technology Series 61, https://doi.org/10.1007/978-3-031-46529-1_10

imposition of intermediary liability; disconnecting users from Internet access,[3] including on the basis of intellectual property rights law; cyber- attacks; and inadequate protection of the right to privacy and data protection."[4] The report cites various measures and attempts by states to prevent content from reaching the end user, including:

- denying users access to certain websites, IP addresses and domain name extensions;
- removing websites from the host server;
- use filtering technologies to exclude pages containing certain keywords or to prevent certain content from loading.

Perhaps the most pressing question is what is the reality behind the 'Potemkin's village' that certain countries have erected. The #KeepItOn report on internet shutdowns in 2019[5] is a cause for concern. "From Bolivia to Malawi, India, Sudan, and beyond, 2019 was a difficult year, online and off. The #KeepItOn coalition has documented an increase in internet shutdowns in 2019,[6] as well as a trend toward sustained and prolonged shutdowns, and targeted internet shutdowns."[7] There were at least 213 documented shutdowns worldwide in 2019, and the number of countries affected increased from 25 in 2018 to 33. This number represents 17% of the world's countries,[8] so the question arises: how many countries in the world today can be said to have a government that has used this measure against its own citizens? The three countries at the top of the list are India, Venezuela and Yemen, but it is not only authoritarian regimes and countries in transition that have restricted the internet: in 2019, there were at least five internet shutdowns across Europe.[9] It is also noteworthy that almost 20% of all shutdowns lasted more than a week. Moreover, the situation did not get any rosier for 2020: although the report[10] highlights that the number of internet shutdowns has decreased compared to 2018 and 2019, it notes that a "smaller number of shutdowns is not an indication of the lessened impact of a shutdown or an overall increase in digital rights."[11]

Even when a state has not been able to shut down the internet within its own geographical borders, it has achieved much the same thing, just by different means.

---

[3] The first known internet shutdown occurred in 2007 in the Republic of Guinea. Carpenter (2021).

[4] UNHRC (2011), Summary.

[5] AccessNow (2020).

[6] It is worth noting that the document monitors a wide range of shutdowns, including both mobile and internet network blockages, whether total or partial. The document thus includes issues involving the blocking of IP addresses and government actions involving only the slowing down of traffic.

[7] AccessNow (2020), p. 1.

[8] Worldometer (2022).

[9] AccessNow (2020), p. 3. Cf. "These shutdowns are not solely associated with authoritarian regimes. They also happen in "consolidated democracies"." Barata and Richter (2023), p. 9.

[10] AccessNow (2021b).

[11] Ibid., p. 2.

One method is *bandwidth throttling, which* effectively slows down internet traffic, while other methods have targeted social media sites only, but both methods interfere with the free flow of information. The actual number of shutdowns or slowdowns is almost impossible to quantify precisely. The governments discussed in this chapter acknowledged 116 shutdowns[12] in 2019, which was only 54% of the 213 observed. The governments' admitted legal objectives included "fighting fake news, hate speech, or content promoting violence, followed by precautionary measures, public safety, national security, third-party actions, school exams, and technical problems."[13] The states also cited the growing number of technical problems as an excuse, although observers and critics dispute this claim and believe the real causes lie elsewhere, mainly related to protests, violence, elections and political instability. As De Gregorio and Stremlau put it, shutting down the Internet "appears to be used by governments when they want to act quickly, particularly to quell perceived or potential civil unrest, and might have limited capacity for other mechanisms of online control."[14] According to the #KeepItOn report, in exceptional circumstances (e.g. elections, military actions, religious holidays, visits by government officials), states apparently tend to use extraordinary (non-statutory) measures to prevent open criticism of perceived or real problems. Preventive precautions, which sound somewhat bureaucratic, "are almost always used by the Indian government to justify shutting down the internet in situations of military action, such as in Jammu and Kashmir."[15]

10.2 Landmark Cases Before the European Court of Human Rights

Article 10 ECHR states that "everyone has the right to freedom of expression. This right shall include freedom to hold opinions and to receive and impart information and ideas without interference by public authority and regardless of frontiers." Article 10 then goes on to state that this right may be subject to formalities, conditions, restrictions or sanctions, but that these must meet the ECtHR's three-part test.[16] This means that the measures challenged must not be arbitrary: the interference must be "A) suitable to achieve the legitimate aim pursued (*suitability*); B) the least intrusive instrument amongst those which might achieve the legitimate aim (*necessity*); and C) strictly proportionate to the legitimate aim pursued (*proportionaility sensu stricto*)."[17] In other words, "the technique, level and

[12] AccessNow (2020), p. 12.

[13] Ibid., p. 13; AccessNow (2021b), p. 11.

[14] De Gregorio and Stremlau (2020), p. 4225.

[15] AccessNow (2020), p. 13.

[16] Bayer (2017), pp. 117–128.

[17] Oster (2015), pp. 123–124; Bychawska-Siniarska (2017), pp. 32–33; ICJ (2022).

ideology of the blocking must be chosen carefully so that fundamental rights are not infringed but the blocking achieves its objective."[18]

The landmark ECtHR cases on this particular issue involve two countries, Russia and Turkey. In each of these cases, the basic problem was blocking internet access, although the methods used by each state differed.[19] The cases varied from *collateral blocking* (the blocked IP address was shared by several sites, including the targeted site), *excessive blocking* (an entire website was blocked because of a single page or file deemed unacceptable) or *wholesale blocking* (all or part of the internet was blocked). In most cases, the ECtHR found that the measures taken violated Article 10 ECHR, as they did not pass the necessity or proportionality part of the test mentioned above.

10.2.1 Akdeniz v Turkey (2014) [20]

The case of Akdeniz v Turkey is somewhat different from the cases discussed below but, as it relates to *admissibility, it* is worth dealing with it first. In June 2009, the media division of the Turkish Public Prosecutor's Office ordered a total restriction of access to the myspace.com and last.fm websites on the grounds that these websites infringed copyright by distributing musical works. The applicant had applied as a user of the websites and the main question was who could be the 'victim' of the Internet blocking. In 2014, the ECtHR declared the application inadmissible (incompatible personal jurisdiction—*ratione personae*) on the grounds that the applicant was only indirectly affected by the restrictive measure and that there was insufficient evidence to establish whether he could be considered a 'victim'. The ECtHR held that "the fact that the applicant had been deprived of access to those websites had not prevented him from taking part in a debate on a matter of general interest",[21] which means that if the person concerned could have obtained the necessary information (in this case music) from other sources, this could justify the application of certain types of restrictions by the State.

---

[18] Pogácsás (2020), p. 168.

[19] Note that another angle from which the issue can be examined is the question of restrictions on detainees' access to the internet: *Kalda v* Estonia App no. 17429/10 (ECtHR, 19 January 2016); *Jankovskis v Lithuania* App no. 21575/08 (ECtHR, 17 January 2017); *Ramazan Demir v Turkey* App no. 68550/17 (ECtHR, 9 February 2021).

[20] *Akdeniz v Turkey* App no. 20877/10 (ECtHR, 11 March 2014).

[21] ECtHR (2014), p. 23.

10.2.2 *Ahmet Yıldırım v Turkey (2012)* [22]

The Criminal Court of First Instance in Denizli blocked all access to Google sites under Turkish law, an interim measure taken in the context of a single criminal case against a website. The problem was that this particular website was considered by the state to have insulted the memory of Mustafa Kemal Atatürk, who founded the modern Turkish state in 1923. A Turkish student, Ahmet Yıldırım, had uploaded his academic writings to a website created with Google Sites,[23] so the blocking mentioned above—and completely unrelated to him—also affected his domain. The ECtHR found that this constituted a violation of Article 10 ECHR, in particular because the measure applied by Turkey was not the least intrusive means and the State did not attempt to find a better way to achieve its objectives (e.g. limiting access to the relevant site rather than to all Google sites). The ECtHR also found that there was no strict legal framework in Turkish domestic law governing the scope of the blocking and the guarantee of judicial review. In Maya Hertig Randall's view, "Although the Court's reasoning was related to the principle of legality, considering that the Turkish legislation did not satisfy the foreseeability requirement under the Convention, it shows that wholesale blocking raises serious concerns in the light of the proportionality principle."[24] As the ECtHR put it, using other words, "in the Court's view, (the national authorities[25]) should have taken into consideration, among other elements, the fact that such a measure, by rendering large quantities of information inaccessible, substantially restricted the rights of Internet users and had a significant collateral effect." [26]

10.2.3 *Cengiz and Others v Turkey (2015)* [27]

In another case, Ankara's criminal court ruled that a post on YouTube violated the country's criminal laws, which prohibit insulting the memory of Atatürk. The court ordered the complete blocking of YouTube, which was opposed by law professor Serkan Cengiz and other professors from various Turkish law schools. In their application to the ECtHR, they claimed that they had been unable to use YouTube for an extended period of time, which violated their human rights. In this case, the ECtHR also found that the measures taken by Turkey violated Article 10 ECHR. At the same time, the ECtHR also held that YouTube was an important means for the

[22] *Ahmet Yıldırım v Turkey* App no. 3111/10 (ECtHR, 18 December 2012).

[23] The URL of the original site was http://sites.google.com/a/ahmetyildirim.com.tr/academic, but it is no longer available.

[24] Hertig Randall (2016), p. 238.

[25] Interpretative insert by the author.

[26] *Ahmet Yıldırım v Turkey* App no. 3111/10 (ECtHR, 18 December 2012), [66.].

[27] *Cengiz and Others v Turkey* App nos 48226/10 and 14027/11 (ECtHR, 1 December 2015).

applicants to exercise their right to receive and transmit information and ideas via the internet and that the violation could be found to have occurred despite the fact that both the harm suffered by the applicants and its effect were only incidental. [28] The Court also found the restriction to be disproportionate and, as above, questioned the legal framework governing the scope of the prohibition in Turkish national law. In addition, the court also found as an important circumstance—as a new factor to be taken into account compared to the previous ones—that the restriction had been maintained for a longer period of time.

10.2.4 *Kablis v Russia, Dmitriyeva v Russia (2019)* [29]

In one case, Grigory Kablis, a Russian activist, informed the municipality of the Komi capital, Siktivkar, of his intention to organise a protest. His request was rejected and, after Kablis criticised the decision on his social media blog Vkontakte, his account was blocked. The Russian authorities' decision was equally negative in the case of Russian citizen Elvira Dmitriyeva, who had also announced a protest in Russia. The Russian authorities have not issued any court orders in either case, so the measures taken by the Russian prosecutor's office were considered to be provisional. Moreover, Articles 10 and 11 ECHR were also examined in the Dmitriyeva case. In both cases, the ECtHR found that the Russian state had violated Article 10 of the ECHR: the court ruled that the Russian Information Act 'lacks the necessary guarantees against abuse required by the Court's case-law." [30] This requires a legal framework for all states that ensures both strict control of the scope of the prohibitions and effective judicial review to prevent abuse of power. [31]

10.2.5 *Wikimedia Foundation Inc. and Others v Turkey (2019)* [32]

The outcome of the third case where Turkey sought to apply a blocking order differs from the examples provided by Ahmet Yıldırım v Turkey and Cengiz and others v

[28] *Ibid., [64.].*

[29] *Elvira Dmitriyeva v Russia* App nos. 60921/17 and 7202/18 (ECtHR, 30 April 2019); *Kablis v Russia* App nos. 48310/16 and 59663/17 (ECtHR, 30 April 2019).

[30] *Kablis v Russia* App nos. 48310/16 and 59663/17 (ECtHR, 30 April 2019), [97.].

[31] *Ahmet Yıldırım v Turkey* App no. 3111/10 (ECtHR, 18 December 2012), [64.]. The ECtHR has also addressed the issue in *Association Ekin v France* App no. 39288/98 (ECtHR, 17 July 2001), [58]; *Editorial Board of Pravoye Delo and Shtekel v Ukraine* App no. 33014/05 (ECtHR, 5 May 2011), [55].

[32] *Wikimedia Foundation Inc. v Diğerleri Başvurusu* (Başvuru Numarasi: 2017/22355, Karar Tarihi: 26/12/2019).

Turkey, discussed above. In this case, the ECtHR did not find that Turkey had violated Article 10 ECHR. The background to the case is as follows: in 2017, the Turkish Information and Telecommunication Technology Authority blocked all language versions of Wikipedia, apart from Turkish, on the grounds that it had refused their request to remove content that identified Turkey as a supporter of the Islamic State and other terrorist organisations. At this point, it should be noted that in Turkey, by 2019, "more than 15 institutions and organizations are authorized to issue or request access-blocking orders under various regulations and most of these powers are exercised by submitting administrative blocking orders (. . .) without the need for judicial approval."[33] In relation to the above content, Turkey claimed that Wikipedia was engaged in a "smear campaign' against the country,[34] and the blocking was therefore maintained. As their attempts at conciliation failed, Wikipedia submitted an application to the ECtHR in 2019. Although there is no evidence that this had any effect, shortly afterwards the Turkish Constitutional Court ruled that the blanket restriction violated the right to freedom of expression guaranteed by Article 26 of the Turkish Constitution. It also ruled that the interpretation of the grounds for interference was too broad, making the potential grounds unpredictable and constituting a significant deterrent, in other words. a potential incentive for self-censorship. As the issue was settled within Turkey, the ECtHR did not rule on the application.

10.2.6 *Vladimir Kharitonov v Russia, OOO Flavus and Others v Russia, Bulgakov v Russia, Engels v Russia (2020)* [35]

Russia has been named as a defendant in recent cases concerning the blocking of websites. There are similarities in all of these cases and the ECtHR issued a consolidated judgment on the same date (23 June 2020) in all of them, although the applications were filed between 2013 and 2015. Vladimir Kharitonov noticed that the IP address of his website was blocked because the Russian Federal Drug Control Service wanted to block access to another website hosted by the same hosting provider and using the same IP address. In the OOO Flavus case, access to the website was blocked at the request of the Russian Prosecutor General without first obtaining a court order. Russia failed to inform the plaintiffs of which uploaded material it actually considered to be infringing content, so the plaintiff could not even

[33] Akdeniz and Güven (2020), p. 8; Akdeniz and Güven (2021), pp. 4–8.

[34] Atay Alam et al. (2017).

[35] *Bulgakov v Russia* App no. 20159/15 (ECtHR, 23 June 2020); *Engels v Russia* App no. 61919/16 (ECtHR, 23 June 2020); *OOO Flavus and Others v Russia* App nos 12468/15, 23489/15, and 19074/16 (ECtHR, 23 June 2020); *Vladimir Kharitonov v Russia* App no. 10795/14 (ECtHR, 23 June 2020).

remove it to regain access. Yevgeny Bulgakov's access was denied by court order because of an e-book stored on a section of his website containing extremist publications. The Russian court upheld the decision even after Mr Bulgakov deleted the book concerned, arguing that the restriction was comprehensive and did not apply only to the material itself. Grégory Engels found himself in a very similar situation because his website contained information on how to circumvent content filters. The blocking was ordered despite the fact that the information did not violate national law. The ECtHR unanimously found a violation of Article 10 ECHR in each of the court cases and clearly stated that the national procedures lacked the necessary legitimacy, as the provisions of Russia's Information Act used to block websites did not provide adequate safeguards against abuse. The court also stated that the "wholesale blocking of access to an entire website is an extreme measure which has been compared to banning a newspaper or television station." [36]

10.2.7 Akdeniz and Altiparmak v Turkey (2021) [37]

In the two cases concerned and related to the content, the Turkish authority unlawfully restricted access to more than 600 internet content providers (news portals, video portals, social media user accounts) in 2015 and 2016, according to the petitions, in violation of Articles 10 and 18 ECHR. No decision has been taken in the cases as of 2022, but the ECtHR has notified the Turkish government and addressed questions to the parties.[38]

10.3 The European Court of Human Rights' Law-Enforcement Activities

The ECtHR judgments show that restrictions on the internet may be acceptable in certain cases, but only if they meet certain requirements in order to be compatible with human rights. Careful attention must be paid to all three parts of the ECtHR's three-part test (legality, necessity and proportionality): however, the states examined in this article regularly fail to meet the necessity requirement of this test (e.g. there would be less intrusive methods) and the proportionality requirement (e.g. collateral

---

[36] *Vladimir Kharitonov v Russia* App no. 10795/14 (ECtHR, 23 June 2020), [38.].

[37] *Akdeniz and Altiparmak v Turkey* App no. 5568/20; *Akdeniz and Altiparmak v Turkey* App no. 35278/20.

[38] Which also means that Akdeniz in this case was not admitted for non-admission on the grounds of incompatible personal jurisdiction *(ratione personae)*, as we have seen in Sect. 10.2.1. The same happened with another of his petitions in 2021, *Akdeniz and Others v Turkey* App nos 41139/15 and 41146/15 (ECtHR, 4 May 2021).

damage is caused, such as when websites unrelated to the targeted material are taken down or restricted).

Given that the internet has become a tool for so many people to exercise and express human rights, to receive and transmit information and ideas, and to fight against the marginalisation of states and groups in different societies, the growing number of such cases is a clear warning. The landmark cases judged by the ECtHR have seen a variety of approaches to the way states try to restrict the internet and attempt to make certain content inaccessible to end users. International jurisprudence has—until now—prevented them from doing so, and the case law presented in this chapter confirms that any restriction on access to the Internet for lawful content is a drastic intervention that states around the world should only use as a last, highly justified measure. However, as the 2021 #KeepItOn report supplement[39] points out, there are four trends:

- increasingly longer Internet shutdowns;
- the use of this tool is intensified during elections;
- the use of this tool is intensified during demonstrations; and
- the use of this tool is intensified in active armed conflict zones.

What could be the future direction? Article-19, the international human rights organisation, details the requirements, following the ECtHR judgments, to achieve a legally reassuring resolution of the situation in the current legal environment. First, legislation should provide for measures that can be used to restrict, and should also set out in clear and predictable rules what content can be blocked and to what extent. In determining what content can be blocked, national legislation should follow the standards set by international human rights law. Second, blocking measures should be ordered by a court or an independent judicial body. Non-independent governmental bodies are likely to apply overly restrictive measures, as their primary objective is to protect interests that conflict with freedom of expression. Third, Internet users and ISPs should be able to challenge restrictive measures.[40] To this end, when they try to access a blocked site, they should be provided with sufficient information on how to challenge the measure. Finally, to avoid blocking legitimate content, blocking measures should be strictly targeted, so IP address technologies should only be used to target non-shared IP servers.[41]

In 2021, the UN Special Rapporteur on Freedom of Peaceful Assembly and of Association called on "States, international institutions, businesses, and other stakeholders to commit themselves to end internet shutdowns including in relation to peaceful protests and in the context of elections."[42] Let's hope it will have an impact.

[39] AccessNow (2021a).

[40] Barata and Richter (2023), p. 28.

[41] Article-19 (2020).

[42] UNHRC (2021), p. 69.

References

AccessNow (2020) Targeted, Cut off, and Left in the Dark, 24 Feb. https://www.accessnow.org/cms/assets/uploads/2020/02/KeepItOn-2019-report-1.pdf

AccessNow (2021a) #KeepItOn update: who is shutting down the internet in 2021? 7 June. https://www.accessnow.org/who-is-shutting-down-the-internet-in-2021/

AccessNow (2021b) Shattered dreams and lost opportunities – a year in the fight to. 3 March. https://www.accessnow.org/cms/assets/uploads/2021/03/KeepItOn-report-on-the-2020-data_Mar-2021_3.pdf

Akdeniz Y, Güven O (2020) An iceberg of unseen internet censorship in Turkey. İfade Özgürlüğü Derneği, Istambul

Akdeniz Y, Güven O (2021) Fahrenheit 5651: the scorching effect of censorship. İfade Özgürlüğü Derneği, Istambul

Article-19 (2020) Russia: European Court Judgment is Victory for Freedom of Expression. article19.org, 23 June. https://www.article19.org/resources/russia-european-court-judgment-is-victory-for-freedom-of-expression/

Atay Alam H, Arif M, Joe Sterling J (2017) Turkey Blocks Wikipedia over What it Calls Terror “Smear Campaign”. CNN, 29 Apr. https://edition.cnn.com/2017/04/29/europe/turkey-wikipedia/index.html/

Barata J, Richter A (2023) Internet shutdowns in international law. Columbia University, New York

Bayer J (2017) Az Emberi Jogok Európai Bíróságának 10. cikkel kapcsolatos joggyakorlatának egyes súlypontjai (Some key points in the case law of the European Court of Human Rights on Article 10). Állam- és Jogtudomány 58(4)

Bennett P, Naim M (2015) 21st-century censorship. Columbia Journal Rev 14(1)

Bychawska-Siniarska D (2017) Protecting the right to freedom of expression under the European Convention on Human Rights. A handbook for legal practitioners. Council of Europe, Strasbourg

Carpenter S (2021) The Internet Shutdowns Issue. The Current 2021(4). https://jigsaw.google.com/the-current/shutdown/

De Gregorio G, Stremlau N (2020) Internet shutdowns and the limits of law. Int J Commun 14(1)

European Court of Human Rights (ECtHR) (2014) Information Note on the Court’s case-law. 2014, 173. sz., Akdeniz v Turkey – 20877/10, Decision 11.3.2014 [Section II]. https://www.echr.coe.int/Documents/CLIN_2014_04_173_ENG.pdf

Hertig Randall M (2016) Freedom of expression in the internet. Swiss Rev Int Eur Law 26(2)

International Commission of Jurists (ICJ) (2022) Legal guidance on internet restrictions and shutdowns in Africa. International Commission of Jurists, Geneva

Oster J (2015) Media freedom as a fundamental right. Cambridge University Press, Cambridge

Pogácsás A (2020) Modern jogérvényesítés vagy modern cenzúra? A weboldalak blokkolásának újabb tanulságai (Modern law enforcement or modern censorship? Recent lessons on website blocking). In Medias Res 9(1)

UNHRC (2011) Report of the Special Rapporteur on the promotion and protection of the right to freedom of opinion and expression. UN Doc A/HRC/17/27

UNHRC (2021) Report of the Special Rapporteur on the rights to freedom of peaceful assembly and of association. UN Doc A/HRC/47/24/Add.2

UNHRC (2022) Internet shutdowns: trends, causes, legal implications and impacts on a range of human rights. UN Doc A/HRC/50/55

Worldometer (2022) How many countries are there in the world? https://www.worldometers.info/geography/how-many-countries-are-there-in-the-world/

Chapter 11
The Rise of Digital Authoritarianism Across the Globe

By 2022, it seems that few people today would regard audiovisual rules or internet regulation as "The Law of the Horse".[1] As David Bromel puts it: "the early years of the internet were a great party – wild and dangerous. But now the party is over, and all the guests have to help clean up."[2] What remains with us today of the basic ideas of *cyberlibertarianism* in decline[3] is the inherently liberating nature of technology and the internet, and their ongoing—seemingly hopeless—struggle for the decentralisation of communication, where everyone (privileged and disadvantaged alike) can have the space for communication that they deserve.[4] The practical impossibility of *cyberpaternalism*—or, to put it more simply, of regulating the Internet within the geographical and legal borders of the states themselves—seems remote, but not impossible. We have seen, and continue to see, the steps taken by China's *cybersovereignty* announced from 2015, and then by Russia, which joined in the late 2010s.

Over the past decade, almost every major media outlet has explicitly stated on its news pages on different occasions that "the UN declares access to the internet as a human right."[5] This can only be interpreted as a journalistic gimmick, since the none

---

[1] See Sect. 4.2.

[2] Bromel (2022), p. 217.

[3] Of course, the movement still has its representatives: perhaps the best known to the general public is Lawrence Lessig. Cyberlibertarianism is also discussed in one of the talks he gave at Politics and Prose bookstore (Washington, D.C.) in 2019 on his book *They Don't Represent Us:* https://youtu.be/9oA78WgIoO0?t=2311/.

[4] It is worth comparing this with the characteristics of the alternative type of traditional media, community media, which shows that the internet could have had an excellent early opportunity to play the role of a truly more democratic public space. Gosztonyi (2014), pp. 31–32; Hammer (2003), pp. 121–122; Lublinski et al. (2014), pp. 16–17.

[5] Kravets (2017); Velocci (2016); Jackson (2011).

G. Gosztonyi, *Censorship from Plato to Social Media*, Law, Governance and Technology Series 61, https://doi.org/10.1007/978-3-031-46529-1_11

of the specific texts of the UN Human Rights Council document does say so.[6] Although one stated that "for the Internet to remain global, open and interoperable, it is imperative that States address security concerns in accordance with their international human rights obligations, in particular with regard to freedom of expression, freedom of association and privacy",[7] this is not the same as recognising free access to the Internet as a human right.[8]

The threat of state intervention to block internet access remains. The UN Special Rapporteur on Freedom of Expression expressed concern in 2020 that "governments increasingly resort to shutting down the Internet, often for illegitimate purposes but in all cases having a disproportionate impact on the population."[9] In its July 2020 report,[10] the European Centre for Press and Media Freedom pointed out that a wide range of threats to media freedom persisted from March to June 2020; for example, "During this time, Turkish authorities continued to use media regulators to shut down outlets broadcasting critical or sensitive topics."[11]

Thus, politically motivated blocking of internet content will continue to be commonplace in many countries in the 2020s. Chinese internet sovereignty is the most widespread solution, but Russia had caught up by the summer of 2021: it experimented with the technology for a few years, and finally, between 15 June and 15 July 2021, it successfully[12] implemented a test run to physically disconnect its country from the international internet.[13] All this is based on the fact that Russia adopted and enacted in 2019, as an amendment to the 2013 Federal Law on Telecommunications,[14] the Sovereign Internet Law,[15] under which:

- Russian ISPs are required to install tools that enable deep content monitoring (DPI[16]) and allow ISPs and public authorities to find the original source of threatening content and block it if necessary;

---

[6]In fact, some countries have already recognized internet access as such, like Estonia, France, Finland, and Costa Rica. Barata and Richter (2023), p. 7.

[7]UNHRC (2016); Cf. The UN Human Rights Council "calls upon all States to promote and facilitate access to the Internet and international cooperation aimed at the development of media and information and communications facilities in all countries". UNHRC (2012), p. 3.

[8]On this point see also Szoszkiewicz (2020), pp. 49–62.

[9]UNHRC (2020), p. 25.

[10]EFJ – IPI – ECPMF (2020).

[11]Ibid., p. 19.

[12]Collman (2021).

[13]It should be pointed out that Insider was unable to confirm the information from two independent sources.

[14]On the process leading to the adoption of the law and the detailed rules of the law, see Tölgyesi (2020), pp. 113–132; Human Rights Watch (2020).

[15]Федеральный закон от 01.05.2019 № 90-ФЗ "О внесении изменений в Федеральный закон "О связи" и Федеральный закон "Об информации, информационных технологиях и о защите информации".

[16]For more details on the technology, see Fuchs (2012).

- ISPs must route the country's web traffic and information through government-controlled points;[17]
- the government has the right to physically disconnect the Russian internet from the international internet network in the event of an emergency.[18]

In addition, the vague legal definition of threatening content leaves it up to the authorities to decide which situations require monitoring, redirection or blocking, with the risk of arbitrariness. "The process is not transparent and opens the door to abuse", Human Rights Watch said, noting that the adoption of the law "is bad news for Russia and creates a dangerous precedent for other countries."[19] However, there were signs of things to come: in its 2019 report, the RSF puts the number of Russian laws that restrict press freedom or freedom of expression at 27.[20] Notable among these is the 2019 amendment to the 2006 Law on Information, Information Technologies and Information Protection,[21] which now includes a classic criminal sanction of imprisonment for those who share illegal content.[22] In addition, the report's addendum shows that, in a short two-year period (2020–2021), another 16 similar laws have been adopted in Russia.[23] The European Audiovisual Observatory 2021 highlighted that, as a result of the ECtHR cases analysed above,[24] Russia has moved away from blocking to imposing substantial fines:[25] personal data processing can now be fined between 1 and 6 million roubles for the first time, while the amount increases to 6–18 million roubles for repeat offences.[26]

After the brutal military aggression launched against Ukraine in 2022, the Russian situation has only worsened compared to before. The Russian government started blocking and declaring as extremist organisations those Western platforms (Twitter, Facebook, Instagram) that could provide the Russian population with real information other than propaganda news. These platforms have also been fined substantial sums of money in Russian courts for refusing to identify their users or remove "fake news" about the Russian-Ukrainian war, according to the Russian authorities. It is noteworthy that in February 2023, 1,331,276 sites were listed in the register of banned websites of an NGO, RoskomSvoboda.[27]

Giant-scale, constantly learning surveillance systems, making it difficult or impossible to use VPNs, monitoring and huge fines imposed on intermediary service

---

[17] This is compounded by the fact that, like in China, VPN use is subject to heavy and dissuasive fines. Meduza (2018).

[18] Ma (2019).

[19] Human Rights Watch (2019).

[20] RSF (2021), pp. 10–20.

[21] Federal Law No. 149-FZ.

[22] Richter (2021), p. 16.

[23] RSF (2021), pp. 9–18.

[24] See details in Sect. 10.2.6.

[25] Richter (2021), p. 10.

[26] Ibid., p. 11.

[27] https://reestr.rublacklist.net/ru/.

providers, unpredictable decisions by authorities and the judiciary following content deemed threatening—and all this in the world's most populous (China) and ninth most populous (Russia) state,[28] with an influence of over 20% of the world's total population.

In mid-September 2022, the Iranian Guidance Patrol, the religious morality police of the government, arrested Mahsa Amini for improperly wearing the hijab, who fell into a coma at the police station and died. There are two diametrically opposed readings of what happened, both by state officials and by Iranian citizens, but the fact is that it has triggered a wave of protests in the country on a scale not seen for three years. According to some sources, there have already been more than 200 deaths and thousands of injuries and arrests.[29] But that is not the only reason why the issue is of interest: according to Iranian Telecommunications Minister Eisa Zarepur, the Iranian government is "imposing certain restrictions for security reasons."[30] And although the minister denied making such a claim on the same day,[31] a cybersecurity and digital governance monitoring company that refers to itself only as an internet watchdog, NetBlocks, claims that "Iran has the tightest internet restrictions since the November 2019 massacre."[32] This has been coupled with the shutdown of most mobile networks, regionally observed internet access disruptions and restrictions on certain programs (Instagram, WhatsApp). Mahsa Amini's home province of Kurdistan has been completely cut off from international internet access.[33] What is happening in Iran reveals two fascinating and at the same time disturbing sets of ideas: on the one hand, more and more governments are using internet restrictions to temporarily solve problems by making it difficult for their citizens to communicate with each other, and on the other hand, they are doing so everywhere for the same hard-to-believe (and increasingly absurd and vague) reasons, which perhaps even governments do not believe.

The 2020 presidential elections in Belarus were not without Internet-related steps. While there is no consensus on whether a complete shutdown or near-complete restriction of the internet was the goal of President Alexander Lukashenko, who won the election on paper,[34] the post-election period saw an unprecedented wave of protests in Belarus, with hundreds of thousands of people protesting across the country daily and then weekly. The Internet disruption is illustrated by an image from Netblocks:

[28] Worldometer (2022).

[29] Fassihi and Engelbrecht (2022).

[30] Reuters (2022a).

[31] Reuters (2022b).

[32] https://twitter.com/netblocks/status/1572651793355603972.

[33] Moss (2022).

[34] The European Union does not recognise the results of the elections in Belarus: they were neither free nor fair. European Council (2020).

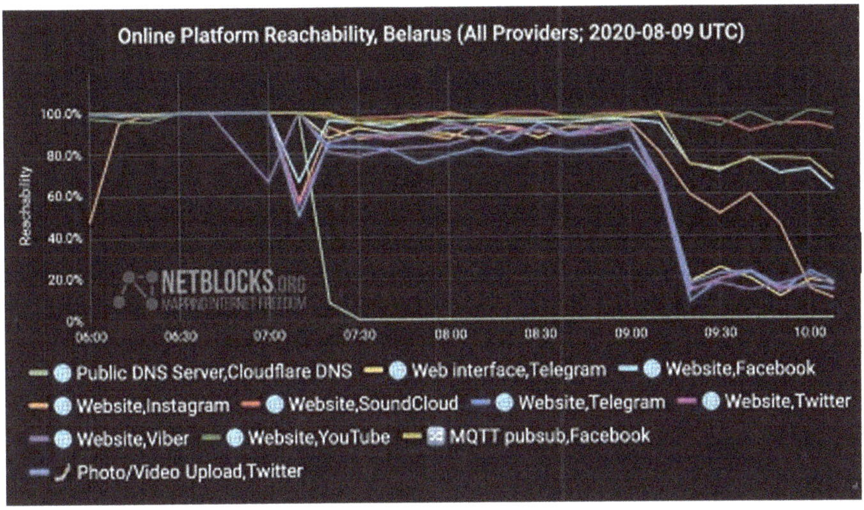

Access to online platforms in Belarus on 9 August 2020 (https://twitter.com/netblocks/status/1292407531046936577/photo/1/)

Internet traffic continuity was only restored on the fourth day. In addition, the use of DPI technology was observed to block international and Belarusian news sites and social media sites.[35] In addition, in 2021, because the Belarusian President said that "free access to the Internet poses a 'national security risk', (. . .) the Internet may be restricted and access may be denied in justified cases, and the government's Communications and Analytical Department will take full control of it."[36] We can see that arbitrary blocking of the Internet has now been subjected to the force of law.[37]

Moreover, very similar technologies, situations and rationales could be observed around the world in 2021 and 2022:

- The Taliban have shut down the internet in the Panjshir Valley, where the (last) resistance fighters still held out in Afghanistan;[38]
- Twitter restrictions in Nigeria after the President's tweet was deleted;[39]
- Mobile internet has been cut off in Iran amid protests for water in Khuzestan;[40]

[35] Alongside sites from providers such as Walmart, Samsung or Disney, which was probably intended to make the process look like a general technical problem. Gilbert (2020).

[36] Tóth (2021).

[37] Belsat (2021).

[38] Wani (2021).

[39] Campbell (2021).

[40] Gambrell (2021).

- Amid widespread anti-government protests, access to social media in Cuba is being restricted;[41]
- The internet has been cut off in Colombia amid anti-government protests;[42]
- Facebook has been restricted in Bangladesh amid protests against Indian Prime Minister Narendra Modi's visit;[43]
- Full internet shutdown in the Republic of Congo on Election Day;[44]
- In Senegal, social media and messaging apps were not available amid political unrest;[45]
- In Chad, the internet was cut off after a deadly incident at the house of an opposition candidate;[46]
- In Uganda, the government decided to make the internet unavailable on election night;[47]
- In Armenia, the internet has been cut off amid political unrest and an alleged coup attempt;[48]
- The internet was down in Myanmar amid the military uprising;[49]
- The 2022 protests shut down internet access to an entire region in Iran;[50]
- Since the beginning of the full-scale invasion of Ukraine, shutting down the internet has become part of the Russian military strategy;[51]
- In Cuba, internet crashes were detected in Los Palacios and Pinar del Rio amid anti-government protest[52]

In each case, the technical data supported the accusations against the given state,[53] the most expressive of which is the Congolese case:

---

[41] Marsh and Culliford (2021).

[42] Jackson (2021).

[43] CNA (2021).

[44] Digital Watch (2021b).

[45] Agbo (2021).

[46] Amnesty International (2021).

[47] Carpenter (2021).

[48] Digital Watch (2021a).

[49] AccessNow (2021).

[50] Abdolhoseinzadeh (2022).

[51] AccessNow (2021).

[52] Belson (2022).

[53] The NGO Witness Media Lab has produced a full guide on how to document internet shutdowns with offline techniques. http://lab.witness.org/projects/internet-shutdowns/.

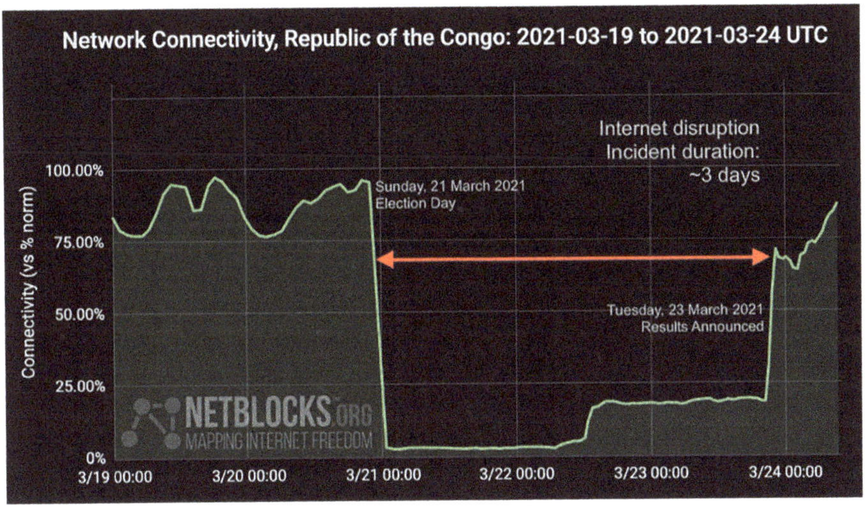

Network access in the Republic of Congo on 24 March 2021 (https://netblocks.org/wp-content/uploads/sites/8/2021/03/congo-republic-election-day-internet-shutdown-2021-03-21.png)

It is particularly interesting that governments are successfully trying not only to restrict access to foreign content and to deny citizens access to important information affecting their lives on the grounds of national security, but also to replace banned Western platforms with domestic platforms that they have reason to believe can be used to freely disseminate government views.[54] Such platforms in Russia are Vkontakte, which acts as an alternative to Facebook, Yandex instead of Google, RuTube instead of YouTube, or Yappi instead of TikTok. The same in China are Weibo as a substitute for Twitter or WeChat for WhatsApp, but Turkey has also launched its own messaging/VoIP app to replace WhatsApp, called BiP. With these alternatives, authoritarian governments can exercise a much tighter control over users' freedom of expression after internet shutdowns and app bans.[55]

The UN Special Rapporteur on Freedom of Expression highlighted in his 2020 report that "Internet shutdowns are an affront to the freedom of expression that every person is guaranteed under human rights law."[56] Moreover, as Bennett and Naim note, "One disturbing trend is the banding together of governments to create an internet that is easier to police. China has advised Iran on how to build a self-contained "Halal" internet. Beijing has also been sharing know-how with Zambia to block critical Web content."[57]

---

[54] Kelemen (2022).

[55] AccessNow (2022), p. 3.

[56] UNHRC (2020), p. 28.

[57] Bennett and Naim (2015). Cf. "Restrict the export of censorship and surveillance technology." FH (2021), p. 25.

Paul Bischoff came to the same remarkable conclusion in a research he published in early-2023.[58] His team used a six-factor analysis and looked at whether A) torrenting, B) pornography, C) news media, D) social media, E) VPNs and F) messaging/VoIP apps were being impaired in use and availability: for each factor, one point if services were available but restricted, and two points if they were completely blocked. The higher the overall score, the higher the degree of online censorship in the country. The research shows that the problem affects a significant number of countries around the world. And while we would sooner sit back in Europe, Bischoff and his team note that the situation in Europe is not perfect: 18 countries have partially or completely banned torrents, and several have created the legal framework to do so. In addition, four countries (Spain, Turkey, Ukraine, Belarus) restrict access to social media and two restrict VPN use. Vint Cerf, a US computer pioneer and one of the fathers of the internet, summed it up like this: "For some authoritarian governments, the freedom of the internet is a threat and the hazards of the online world provide an excuse for excessive monitoring of the users of the internet and censorship of content. Even in democratic countries, the risks of using online services have spurred efforts to impose content regulation on social media providers, web search services and even general internet access providers."[59]

In addition, we must not forget the economic impact of this practice: some authors estimate the cost of the COVID-19[60] shutdowns to the global economy at $8.05 billion, and the pandemic cost to the global economy at $4.01 billion in 2020 and $3.8 billion in 2021 (up to autumn 2021).[61] The estimated cost was $24 billion in 2022.[62]

At the same time, the regulation of tech giants is far from apolitical. "In response to the pandemic, many governments increased surveillance, in some cases introducing new technologies."[63] In the autumn of 2021, then Brazilian President Jair Bolsanaro signed a presidential decree—in defence of free speech, of course—aimed at limiting the right of tech companies to remove accounts and content. Under the regulation, companies must provide a "legitimate explanation and motivation" for removing an account or content. However, critics of the regulation say that the 'rubber stamps' it contains are more political than legal and technical, and do not help address situations such as when Bolsonaro promoted the use of hydroxychloroquine, an anti-malaria drug, and the anti-parasite drug Ivermectin as a treatment for coronavirus.[64]

[58]Bischoff (2023).

[59]Cerf (2022), p. 51.

[60]Lendvai (2023).

[61]Woodhams and Migliano (2021).

[62]Skelton (2023).

[63]Simon and Mahoney (2022), p. 10.

[64]BBC News (2021).

It is worth looking at Freedom House's report on the Internet in 2022, which states that, for almost 40% of the world's population, free and unrestricted access to the Internet, and therefore freedom of expression, is a pipe dream.[65]

In the autumn of 2021, Florian Zandt also produced country-by-country data, which included a ranking of internet freedom based on the strength of government control and censorship.[66] The article clearly shows the differentiation outlined above between countries around the world, and unfortunately we can expect the colours to darken in the coming years.

All of this means that, in 2023, there is still no consensus (even) on a solution that would enable the rule-makers to tread the fine line between content regulation and censorship. But "the pandemic allowed governments through censorship to consolidate and strengthen state power in nearly every corner of the globe."[67]

References

Abdolhoseinzadeh S (2022) International consequences of internet restrictions in Iran, Jurist, 24 Dec. https://www.jurist.org/commentary/2022/12/sharareh-abdolhoseinzadeh-iran-internet-censorship/

AccessNow (2021) Update: internet access, censorship, and the Myanmar coup. 15 Feb. https://www.accessnow.org/update-internet-access-censorship-myanmar/

AccessNow (2022) The return of digital authoritarianism. 24 May. https://www.accessnow.org/cms/assets/uploads/2022/05/2021-KIO-Report-May-24-2022.pdf

Agbo L (2021) #FreeSenegal: Senegal disables Facebook, other social media apps. Allnews Nigeria, 6 March. https://allnews.ng/news/freesenegal-senegal-disables-facebook-other-social-media-apps/

Amnesty International (2021) Chad: internet shutdowns impeding freedom of expression. Amnesty International, 9 Apr. https://www.amnesty.org/en/latest/news/2021/04/tchad-les-coupures-internet-une-entrave-la-liberte-dexpression/

Barata J, Richter A (2023) Internet shutdowns in international law. Columbia University, New York

BBC News (2021) Bolsonaro: new bill will limit tech giants' power to remove content. BBC News, 7 Sep. https://www.bbc.com/news/world-latin-america-58470093/

Belsat (2021) Lukashenka authorizes Internet blocking. Belsat TV, 25 May. https://belsat.eu/en/news/25-05-2021-lukashenka-authorizes-internet-blocking/

Belson D (2022) Internet disruptions overview for Q3 2022, The Cloudfare Blog, 18 Oct. https://blog.cloudflare.com/q3-2022-internet-disruption-summary/

Bennett P, Naim M (2015) 21st-century censorship. Columbia Journal Rev 14(1)

Bischoff P (2023) Internet Censorship 2023: a global map of internet restrictions. comparitech.com. https://www.comparitech.com/blog/vpn-privacy/internet-censorship-map/

Bromel D (2022) Regulating free speech in a digital age. Hate, harm and the limits of censorship. Springer International Publishing AG, Cham

Campbell J (2021) Nigerian President Buhari clashes with Twitter Chief Executive Dorsey. Council on Foreign Relations Blog, 8 July. https://www.cfr.org/blog/nigerian-president-buhari-clashes-twitter-chief-executive-dorsey/

---

[65] FH (2022), p. 5.

[66] Zandt (2021).

[67] Simon and Mahoney (2022), p. 155.

Carpenter S (2021) The internet shutdowns issue. The Current, 2021(4). https://jigsaw.google.com/the-current/shutdown/
Cerf V (2022) Censoring the net is not the answer, but... Index Censorship 51(1)
CNA (2021) Amid anti-Modi protests, Facebook says services restricted in Bangladesh. CNA, 27 March. https://www.channelnewsasia.com/news/asia/anti-modi-protests-bangladesh-facebook-restricted-14505020/
Collman A (2021) Russia disconnected itself from the rest of the internet, a test of its new defense from cyber warfare, report says. Insider, 23 July. https://www.businessinsider.com/russia-cuts-self-off-from-global-internet-tests-defenses-rbc-2021-7/
Digital Watch (2021a) Internet disrupted in Armenia amid political turmoil and alleged coup attempt. Digital Watch, 25 Feb. https://dig.watch/updates/internet-disrupted-armenia-amid-political-turmoil-and-alleged-coup-attempt/
Digital Watch (2021b) Internet shutdown in the Republic of the Congo on election day. Digital Watch, 21 March. https://dig.watch/updates/internet-shutdown-republic-congo-election-day/
European Council (2020) Restrictive measures following the 2020 Belarus presidential elections. 1 Oct. https://www.consilium.europa.eu/en/policies/sanctions/restrictive-measures-following-the-2020-belarus-presidential-elections/
European Federation of Journalists (EFJ) – International Press Institute (IPI) – European Centre for Press and Media Freedom (ECPMF) (2020) A four-month snapshot. https://www.mfrr.eu/wp-content/uploads/2020/07/MFRR-Monitoring-Report-FINAL.pdf
Fassihi F, Engelbrecht C (2022) Tens of thousands in Iran Mourn Mahsa Amini, whose death set off protests. The New York Times, 26 Oct. https://www.nytimes.com/2022/10/26/world/middleeast/iran-protests-40-days.html/
Federal Law No. 149-FZ of July 27, 2006 on Information, Information Technologies, and Information Protection
Freedom House (FH) (2021) Freedom on the Net 2021. The global drive to control big tech. 16 Sep. https://freedomhouse.org/sites/default/files/2021-09/FOTN_2021_Complete_Booklet_09162021_FINAL_UPDATED.pdf
Freedom House (FH) (2022) Freedom on the Net 2022. Countering an Authoritarian Overhaul of the Internet. 18 Oct. https://freedomhouse.org/sites/default/files/2022-10/FOTN2022Digital.pdf
Fuchs C (2012) Implications of Deep Packet Inspection (DPI) Internet Surveillance for Society. Uppsala University, Uppsala
Gambrell J (2021) Mobile internet disruptions seen in Iran amid water protests. AP, 22 July. https://apnews.com/article/technology-middle-east-business-health-iran-98b973da755a3ccf80428570bfdd3fb6/
Gilbert D (2020) Belarus cut off the internet and tried to make it look like an accident. Vice, 11 Aug. https://www.vice.com/en/article/z3e8v3/belarus-cut-off-the-internet-and-tried-to-make-it-look-like-an-accident/
Gosztonyi G (2014) Alternatív (?) Média (Alternative (?) Media). ELTE Eötvös Kiadó, Budapest
Hammer F (2003) Smells, sounds, walks like public service broadcaster. But then, why is it not? – Community media in Hungary. In: Gulyás Á, Hammer F (eds) Public service media in the digital age: international perspectives. Cambridge Scholars Publishing, Newcastle upon Tyne
Human Rights Watch (2019) Russia: new law expands government control online. Wider Internet Surveillance. 31 Oct. https://www.hrw.org/news/2019/10/31/russia-new-law-expands-government-control-online/
Human Rights Watch (2020) Russia: growing internet isolation, control, censorship. Authorities Regulate Infrastructure, Block Content. 18 June. https://www.hrw.org/news/2020/06/18/russia-growing-internet-isolation-control-censorship/
Jackson N (2011) United Nations declares internet access a basic human right. The Atlantic, 8 Aug. https://www.theatlantic.com/technology/archive/2011/06/united-nations-declares-internet-access-a-basic-human-right/239911/

Jackson J (2021) Internet disrupted in Colombia as protesters killed during rally against Iván Duque Márquez. Newsweek, 5 May. https://www.newsweek.com/internet-problems-colombia-protests-1588991/

Kelemen R (2022) Cyberfare state – Egy hibrid állammodell 21. századi születése (Cyberfare state – the 21st century birth of a hybrid state model). Military and Intelligence CyberSecurity Research Paper, 2(1)

Kravets D (2017) UN Report declares internet access a human right. Wired, 3 June. https://www.wired.com/2011/06/internet-a-human-right/

Lendvai GF (2023) "Of Covid, [say] nothing but the truth." – New scaremongering rules in the Hungarian Penal Code during the pandemic. In: Gosztonyi G, Lazar E (eds) Media regulation during the Covid-19 pandemic: a study from Central and Eastern Europe. Ethics International Press, Cambridge

Lublinski J, Wakili M, Berner P (2014) Introduction: a major challenge for media development. In: Lublinski J, Wakili M, Berner P (eds) In the service of the public. Functions and transformation of media in developing countries. DWAkademie, Bonn

Ma A (2019) Russia officially introduced a 'sovereign internet' law to let Putin cut off the entire country from the rest of the web. Insider, 1 Nov. https://www.businessinsider.com/russia-sovereign-internet-law-cut-web-access-censorship-2019-11/

Marsh S, Culliford E (2021) Faced with rare protests, Cuba curbs social media access, watchdog says. Reuters, 14 July. https://www.reuters.com/world/americas/cuba-curbs-access-facebook-messaging-apps-amid-protests-internet-watchdog-2021-07-13/

Meduza (2018) Госдума ввела штрафы за нарушение закона об анонимайзерах (The State Duma has introduced fines for violating the law on anonymizers). Meduza, 5 June. https://meduza.io/news/2018/06/05/gosduma-vvela-shtrafy-za-narushenie-zakona-ob-anonimayzerah/

Moss S (2022) Iran's Kurdish region hit by Internet blackout amid protests over death of Mahsa Amini. DCD, 20 Sep. https://www.datacenterdynamics.com/en/news/irans-kurdish-region-hit-by-internet-blackout-amid-protests-over-death-of-mahsa-amini/

Reporters Without Borders (RSF) (2021) Taking control? Internet censorship and surveillance in Russia. Updated. rsf.org, 31 Aug. https://www.reporter-ohne-grenzen.de/fileadmin/Redaktion/Downloads/Berichte/2021/russiareport-update.pdf

Reuters (2022a) Iran may disrupt internet for 'security reasons' as protests extend to day five. Reuters, 21 Sep. https://english.alarabiya.net/News/middle-east/2022/09/21/Iran-may-disrupt-internet-for-security-reasons-as-protests-extend-to-day-five/

Reuters (2022b) Iran minister says he was misquoted saying authorities might disrupt internet. Reuters, 21 Sep. https://www.reuters.com/world/middle-east/internet-may-be-disrupted-iran-security-reasons-2022-09-21/

Richter A (2021) Regulation of social media in Russia. European Audiovisual Observatory, Strasbourg

Simon J, Mahoney R (2022) The Infodemic. How censorship and lies made the world sicker and less free. Columbia Global Reports, New York

Skelton SK (2023) Internet shutdowns cost global economy $24bn in 2022. Computer Weekly, 11 Jan. https://www.computerweekly.com/news/252529078/Internet-shutdowns-cost-global-economy-24bn-in-2022/

Szoszkiewicz Ł (2020) Internet access as a new human right? State of the art on the threshold of 2020. Przegląd Prawniczy Uniwersytetu Im. Adama Mickiewicza 8(1)

Tölgyesi B (2020) Az orosz 'szuverén internet' törvényről (On the Russian 'sovereign internet' law). Nemzet és Biztonság: Biztonságpolitikai Szemle 13(2)

Tóth CT (2021) Lukasenka törvényben engedélyezte az internet azonnali korlátozását Belaruszban (Lukashenka passed a law to immediately restrict the internet in Belarus). azonnali.hu, 25 May. https://azonnali.hu/cikk/20210525lukasenka-torvenyben-engedelyezte-az-internet-azonnali-korlatozasat-belaruszban/

UNHRC (2012) The Promotion, Protection and Enjoyment of Human Rights on the Internet. UN Doc A/HRC/RES/20/80

UNHRC (2016) The Promotion, Protection and Enjoyment of Human Rights on the Internet. UN Doc A/HRC/32/L.20

UNHRC (2020) Disease pandemics and the freedom of opinion and expression. Report of the Special Rapporteur on the promotion and protection of the right to freedom of opinion and expression. UN Doc A/HRC/44/49

Velocci C (2016) Internet access is now a basic human right. Gizmodo, 4 July. https://gizmodo.com/internet-access-is-now-a-basic-human-right-1783081865/

Wani A (2021) Taliban shut down internet in Panjshir to prevent Amrullah Saleh from tweeting. India Today, 29 Aug. https://www.indiatoday.in/world/story/taliban-shut-down-internet-panjshir-amurullah-saleh-afghanistan-1846742-2021-08-29/

Woodhams S, Migliano S (2021) The global cost of internet shutdowns. Top10VPN, 4 Jan. https://www.top10vpn.com/cost-of-internet-shutdowns/

Worldometer (2022) Top 20 largest countries by population. https://www.worldometers.info/world-population/#top20

Zandt F (2021) Is free internet a myth? statista.com, 22 Sep. https://www.statista.com/chart/3942/internet-freedom-across-the-world-visualized/

Федеральный закон от 01.05.2019 № 90-ФЗ "О внесении изменений в Федеральный закон "О связи" и Федеральный закон "Об информации, информационных технологиях и о защите информации"

Chapter 12
Possible Directions for the Future

According to Martin Gurri, these are revolutionary times. Information revolutionary times, of which there have only been four in history, because "information has not grown incrementally over history, but has expanded in great pulses or waves."[1] The first of the five waves was the invention of writing, the second was the development of the alphabet, followed by the printing of books and the fourth was the advent of mass communication. And now, today, the internet and social media represent the fifth revolutionary wave of communication. "Welcome, friend" he writes, "to the Fifth Wave."[2]

12.1 The Problems—Splinternet?

We have seen how, for centuries, the state and the church regulated the various content to be published or published, sometimes in a religious, sometimes in a moral, sometimes in a political guise. As technology has made it increasingly possible for more and more people to access content, the legal and political tools have been refined considerably over time. The struggle for freedom of expression seemed to reach a turning point with the advent of the internet, which was seen in its early days as a means of communication offering complete freedom. However, the myth of a rights-free space soon began to dissipate, and the emergence of—to borrow Jack M. Balkin's phrase—the "new governors of digital expression",[3] the tech companies that grew to have unimaginable power in the area of speech and content publishing. All this against the backdrop of cautious attempts by states to regulate, either by granting them almost total immunity, as in the case of the United States, or by setting

[1]Gurri (2018), p. 27.
[2]Ibid.
[3]Balkin (2018), p. 1188.

G. Gosztonyi, *Censorship from Plato to Social Media*, Law, Governance and Technology Series 61, https://doi.org/10.1007/978-3-031-46529-1_12

up a system of rules as imprecise as those in the ECD. However, it should be remembered that these rules and the safe harbour provisions "were all drafted around the millennium at a time when electronic commerce was perceived as "embryonic and fragile", and internet auctions and social media were just a fledgling phenomenon."[4] Regarding Internet regulation, it might seem a little like the world has not progressed much in the last twenty-five years.

Regulation is often fragmented and characterised by low transparency and enforceability.[5] The cross-border nature of the internet is being addressed by specific solutions from increasingly closed nation states, but these have not yet produced long-term and legally sound solutions.[6] Moreover, "the internet's promise of open access to independent and diverse sources of information is a reality mostly for the minority of humanity living in mature democracies."[7] In the less democratic parts of the world, as we have seen, states are more likely to use axes than scalpels. "There are technological shortcomings, there are honest mistakes that are endlessly magnified and never forgotten, and there are also bad-faith attacks by sensationalist politicians and partisan media."[8] In early 2023, more and more governments seem to believe in the theory of internet sovereignty, which is increasingly working against the concept of a global, open and interoperable internet. In the contrast, we could find Splinternet where (A) more and more states are controlling the Internet infrastructure and using (often illegal) Internet shutdowns, (B) restricting the free flow of information, and (C) the cross-border transfer of user data. These states are clearly promoting the primacy of state news, which goes hand in hand with a deliberate downgrading of the importance of independent press, alternative media and civil society. All of this is part of a larger power game, the basic question of which is who will set the rules of the game in this communication space.

In addition, we have also seen that international courts have done their best to fill in the blanks in this ever-changing technological environment; they have "quite naturally extended and applied the traditional free speech framework to online communication whilst acknowledging that the specific features of the new technology may require adjustments. One characteristic of the internet is that it offers greatly enhanced communicative opportunities whilst magnifying the potential for harm. The burgeoning case law of the ECtHR (and other international courts[9]) shows that it

[4] Friedmann (2014), p. 13.

[5] Cf. "The ECD provisions, rather than aligning state-level policies, created differences in interpretation during the national implementation process." OSCE (2011), p. 32. "Under the DSA, the Internal Market will work in a unique and unified way, because up until now Member States have interpreted the e-Commerce Directive in very different ways." Horváth (2022), p. 12.

[6] Bayer (2021), pp. 25–45; Galewska (2021), pp. 105–136; Szőke (2021), pp. 105–120.

[7] Bennett and Naim (2015).

[8] Koebler and Cox (2018).

[9] Interpretative insert by the author.

is not easy to draw the line between justified and unjustified restrictions of the right to communicate online."[10]

The way forward is influenced not only by political actors but also by the vision of big tech companies. We have also seen Facebook's local problem-solving and Twitter's more global proposal. Depending on the attitude towards a particular company, these proposals can be seen as window dressing or as a positive vision for tech. And Mark Zuckerberg is not stopping there: in 2021 he announced that he would develop Facebook from a social media network into a 'metaverse company'[11] in the next five years,[12] where people use virtual reality (VR) tools to communicate with other people's holograms with VR headsets on their heads, rather than in front of a screen.[13] Ultimately, these solutions are not far from the collection of new types of data that underpin 'data capitalism'.[14] Which is no better, but serves a different purpose than the Chinese and Russian Big Brother-like surveillance state.[15]

Lawrence Lessig writes that "four modalities regulate cyberspace: the law, social norms, the market, and architecture."[16] The law, which is constituted by politics in a constitutional or dispositive way, the civil sector and the social cooperation of users, and tech companies are the three most important actors, but technological changes, which are referred to as the physical environment, constantly influence the actions of these actors. The problem, however, is that actors are often trying to solve content regulation and censorship issues on their own, rather than working together. As Robert Gorwa notes, "there have been very few (. . .) initiatives that bring together all three types of actors."[17] Above, we have seen the moves by the states and the market. The civil sector and users, however, seem to be left out of everything, or if they are there, they seem to be there only for the purpose of legitimacy. "There is a need to develop new frameworks that also consider the multiple and overlapping forms of governance."[18]

---

[10] Hertig Randall (2016), p. 253.

[11] For details on the metaverse concept, see Ball (2021).

[12] Newton (2021).

[13] This follows the acquisition of Oculus, a VR games company, by Facebook in 2014 for $2 billion. Solomon (2014).

[14] For more on data capitalism, see West (2019), pp. 20–41; Mayer-Schönberger and Ramge (2018).

[15] Tusikov (2017), pp. 400–402.

[16] The latter is what he calls the 'Code'. For details, see Lessig (1999), pp. 87–89 and an updated version: Lessig (2006).

[17] Gorwa (2019), p. 14.

[18] Ibid., p. 15.

12.2 Proposals for Solutions

I hope that it was clear by now that the fight to secure freedom of expression has reached an exciting new stage. The internet, this brand new form of communication, can enable millions and billions to speak freely. While it is unrealistic to assume that access to the internet is a human right, it was a real possibility that it might be necessary to regulate it as a public internet,[19] even along the lines of public service media (PSM), or that legal understanding would consider the most important online platforms as public forums. Sándor Lénárd cites[20] the example of public services (water and electricity).[21]

Although such regulation is currently only seen in the context of net neutrality, States have been trying to take back control since the mid-2010s and regulate the conditions for the disclosure of illegal content. In addition, states have a major responsibility for the creation of these huge tech mammoths: the rudimentary regulation that provided immunity has naturally contributed to the strengthening of some players.[22] Of course, cooperation can be negatively influenced, not only by tech companies, but also by politicians and the political environment. It certainly does not help when the President of the United States of America (POTUS) accuses the world's largest social media providers of 'killing people'.[23]

12.2.1 *The Scientific Position(s)*

It is worth looking at the main solutions proposed and the overlap between them. In Judit Bayer's view, "because of the international nature of the services, the regulation should take place at the supranational level of the EU and extension of the rules to the global community should be sought."[24] In view of the conceptual inconsistencies described above, she considers it necessary to introduce a single but flexible concept, which would greatly facilitate the unification and harmonisation of legislation.[25] Daphne Keller and Paddy Leerssen argue that any content regulation and censorship laws that are created should prevent harm, protect legitimate online speech and support innovation. However, as the authors note, these objectives are

---

[19] Public Service Media and Public Service Internet Manifesto; CM/Rec(2007)16.

[20] Lénárd (2021).

[21] However, opponents of the theory argue that this would make access significantly more expensive for users. Downes (2016).

[22] Kosseff (2017), p. 9.

[23] The reasoning was that they are giving space to false or misleading information about vaccinations. Even if the point could be valid, the wording of POTUS was definitely badly chosen. Rodriguez (2021).

[24] Bayer (2019), p. 19.

[25] Ibid., pp. 20–21.

often presented in competing ways, which significantly undermines the willingness to regulate and therefore the effectiveness of regulation.[26] Jan Oster argues that the reason that censorship needs to be addressed at all is because there is legal uncertainty due to an inadequately designed framework,[27] while Kevin Park argues that this is due to a lack of precision and clarity in the use of legal concepts.[28] Kate Klonick sees the solution as a public role for private actors, i.e. letting big tech companies do the 'dirty work' of content regulation, as has been the practice so far, but making it mandatory for them to do so by law.[29] In a 2018 report, researchers at the London School of Economics and Political Science called for the creation of a new authority to monitor and evaluate the effectiveness of platform self-regulation.[30] András Koltay criticises the lack of transparency in the content decisions of tech companies, noting that they are currently "devoid of any substantive and procedural guarantees of the rule of law."[31] At the same time, Tamás Szigeti and Éva Simon also point to the new US and European copyright legislation, which sets up exception rules, stating that "in rethinking the liability regime, we warn against making the mistake of basing the regulation on commercial copyright infringements and extending the procedure."[32] At the same time, building on Niklas Luhmann's thesis, Marta Maroni adds that we cannot expect from legal regulation what it cannot deliver,[33] that no legal norm, however perfect and uniform, will be able to regulate and control the social, economic and cultural relations and technological changes of the world at that moment.

Miriam Buiten and her colleagues note, with regard to the idea of a harmonised European legal system, which is desired by many, that national liability rules are much more difficult to standardise than exceptions to liability.[34] For this reason, they would expect voluntary 'proactivity' by tech companies instead, to monitor certain uploaded content. Although they stress that this should not mean a general obligation to monitor,[35] they do not cut the Gordian Knot seen in the Glawischnig-Piesczek case. The threefold set of requirements they set out is certainly a remarkable summary:

- "liability rules in this overall framework should efficiently share the responsibility for the detection and the removal of illegal material online among the many actors involved;

[26] Keller and Leerssen (2020), p. 223.

[27] Oster (2015b), p. 367.

[28] Park (2013), pp. 946–947.

[29] Klonick (2020), p. 2448.

[30] LSETTTC (2018), pp. 36–38.

[31] Koltay (2017), p. 131.

[32] Szigeti and Simon (2016), p. 122.

[33] Maroni (2019), p. 17.

[34] Buiten et al. (2019), pp. 15–16.

[35] Ibid., p. 17.

- liability rules of providers of hosting services should be principles-based to be easily adaptable to technology and business models, which evolve quickly and often in unpredictable ways;
- the liability hard-law rules may also be complemented with co-regulation or self-regulation such as codes of conduct."[36]

Their proposal echoes the suggestion of Natali Helberger and her colleagues, who would shift the emphasis from the competitive responsibility of the era to a cooperative responsibility between actors.[37] Marc Bourreau and Anne Perrot, on the other hand, draw attention to the cost and risk involved in regulating this area, and to the fact that rules that seem simple and sound are often not well founded because they lack detail.[38] Gábor Polyák points out, almost in summary, that "the greatest challenge for the period ahead is therefore to find a new balance between the normative capacity of public authorities and that of market forces, which are self-regulating."[39]

12.2.2 Position(s) of NGOs

Theorists are not the only ones to come up with suggestions: the Global Network initiative launched in 2008, in its document *Principles on Freedom of Expression and Privacy,*[40] has compiled a set of operational principles that it can recommend to all industry players. Among these, it highlighted the need to promote accountability and transparency as fully as possible.

A few years later, the *Manila Principles*[41]—developed by NGOs—published in March 2015, attempted to establish a single set of standards for censorship and content removal legislation. Their six principles:

- Intermediaries should be shielded from liability for third-party content;[42]
- Content must not be required to be restricted without an order by a judicial authority;

[36]Ibid., p. 18.

[37]Helberger et al. (2018), pp. 1–14.

[38]Bourreau and Perrot (2020), p. 9.

[39]Polyák (2020), p. 140.

[40]https://globalnetworkinitiative.org/gni-principles/.

[41]https://manilaprinciples.org/.

[42]Of course, only if they did not contribute to the production of the content. I. b. Ibid. The same emphasises the maintenance of the general prohibition of monitoring. I. d), ibid.

- Requests for restrictions of content must be clear, be unambiguous, and follow due process;[43]
- Laws and content restriction orders and practices must comply with the tests of necessity and proportionality;
- Laws and content restriction policies and practices must respect due process;
- Transparency and accountability must be built into laws and content restriction policies and practices.

In 2018, a conference on content moderation and censorship was held in Santa Clara, California, followed by a second one in Washington DC, later that year. Participants at the conference published the *Santa Clara Principles*[44] which, unlike before, set standards for tech companies but not for states to follow. Amongst others, these are:

- Companies must publish the number of posts removed and the number of accounts permanently or temporarily suspended for violating their content policies;
- Companies must notify the reason for removal or suspension to any user whose content is removed or account is suspended;
- Companies should provide meaningful opportunities for users to appeal the removal of content or account suspension in a timely manner.

12.2.3 Policy Position(s)

We have seen that the US regulation has been called into question in the context of the three major liability models, the fate of the European DSA-DMA proposals is still unknown, and the path of Asian censorship is clearly emerging. The politicians' position is clearly in favour of regulation as soon as possible. However, these are not the only positions of the political actors...

---

[43] Although, as we have seen above, legislators and international courts have addressed the question of the justification for notifying service providers, the Manila Principles are clear on the minimum content of notifications:

1. The legal basis for the assertion that the content is unlawful.
2. The Internet identifier and description of the allegedly unlawful content.
3. The consideration provided to limitations, exceptions, and defences available to the user content provider.
4. Contact details of the issuing party or their agent, unless this is prohibited by law.
5. Evidence sufficient to document legal standing to issue the request.
6. A declaration of good faith that the information provided is accurate. Ibid., III. b).

[44] https://santaclaraprinciples.org/.

In 2011, the UN Special Rapporteur on Freedom of Expression stressed that states should never delegate censorship measures to private organisations and that no one should be held responsible for content on the internet that they did not author.[45]

In 2018, the Council of Europe's Committee of Ministers issued a recommendation[46] on the role and obligations of internet intermediaries, in which it clearly argues in favour of maintaining the existing liability rules: "States should ensure, in law and in practice, that intermediaries are not held liable for third-party content which they merely give access to or which they transmit or store."[47] They underline that the regulatory framework is multi-faceted, multi-layered and constantly evolving. Thus, as seen above, States face the complex challenge of regulating an environment in which private parties play a crucial role in the provision of services with significant public service value. The task of regulation is further complicated by the global nature of the Internet, the diversity of intermediaries and the volume and speed of Internet communications.[48]

In the same year, the European Commission's Recommendation 2018/334 on the *status quo* notes that service providers must be able to take swift decisions on unlawful online content and put in place effective and adequate safeguards to act in a prudent and proportionate manner and prevent the unintentional removal of non-unlawful content.[49]

In July 2019, the United Nations (UN) Special Rapporteur on Freedom of Expression, the Organization for Security and Cooperation in Europe (OSCE) Special Rapporteur on Freedom of the Press, the Organization of American States (OAS) Special Rapporteur on Freedom of Expression and the African Commission on Human and Peoples' Rights (ACHPR) Special Rapporteur on Freedom of Expression and Access to Information issued a jubilee statement outlining the challenges for freedom of expression in the next decade.[50] These include the practical implementation of transparency and accountability requirements as opposed to the current 'privatised' regulation[51] and increasing transparency of content aggregation by algorithms and artificial intelligence.[52]

In 2021, a study for the European Parliament identified six key directions for tackling the issue, based on a multifaceted analysis. The analysis was based on the following criteria:

---

[45]The Special Rapporteur cites the example of the Korean Communications Standards Commission, a quasi-public and quasi-private body established by the Republic of Korea to regulate online content. UNHRC (2011), p. 43.

[46]CM/Rec(2018)2.

[47]Ibid., 1.3.7.

[48]Ibid., 9.

[49]Commission Recommendation (EU) 2018/334, (3).

[50]UN – OSCE – OAS – ACHPR (2019).

[51]Ibid., 3. a.

[52]Ibid., 3. d.

- "cost and benefits;
- feasibility and effectiveness;
- sustainability;
- risks and uncertainties that may impact the policy and its objectives;
- coherence with EU objectives;
- ethical, social and regulatory impacts;
- effect on EU citizens' fundamental rights and freedoms."[53]

Based on these, the six directions identified in the document are:

1. maintaining the status quo;[54]
2. awareness-raising, and media literacy campaigns;
3. promoting self-regulation;[55]
4. establishing co-regulation mechanism and tools;
5. adopting statutory legislation;
6. Modifying online platforms' secondary liability (...)
    1. clarifying the conditions for liability exemptions under the ECD or
    2. establishing a harmonised regime of liability."[56]

In the same year, in its paper "Digital Agenda 2030: Europe's way to the digital decade",[57] the European Union expressed its ambition to pursue digital policies that enable people and businesses to create a people-centred, sustainable and more prosperous digital future where "governments, civil society, the private sector, academia and other stakeholders work together" in it.[58]

12.3 Genuine Re-buttoning of the Coat

While there is overlap in the above, it would be difficult to argue that, a few decades after the emergence and widespread adoption of the internet, the world knows exactly where it is going. Bernát Török notes, however, that the increasing irrationality of public discourse, the locking up in echo chambers or the lack of authoritative bodies that are commonly accepted and considered credible by the critical mass of society are not just products of the social media age."[59]

---

[53] Bertolini (2021), p. IX.

[54] However, see the Australian Supreme Court ruling in autumn 2021 that Australian media companies can be held liable for defamatory comments. Mao (2021); Gosztonyi and Huszár (2022).

[55] However, on the limits of self-regulation, see Bayer (2019), p. 18.

[56] Bertolini (2021), pp. 74–83.

[57] COM/2021/118 final, p. 1.

[58] Ibid., p. 18.

[59] Török (2021).

This complex framework—which combines legal, political and economic aspects—is still to be established. And although the creation of a global *Internet Magna Carta*, as proposed by Tim Berners-Lee in his 2014 TED Talk,[60] is unrealistic due to the different approaches of different governments, it is certainly food for thought. At the same time, it does not answer the main question: who should take action? What seems certain is that none of the three main players will be able to tackle the situation alone. Neither the states—although the intention, as we have seen, is increasingly evident on their part[61]—nor the tech companies, nor the civil society or users. As Paulina Wu has described it, "Although private actors alone are insufficient for successful regulation, they must be included in the regulatory process",[62] meaning that all three actors in the "platform governance triangle"[63] must be involved. Public and self-regulation should be replaced or complemented by co-regulatory solutions.[64]

And if this does not happen, the path that many countries have already embarked on will only be the beginning. It could "pave the way for a world characterised by limited cooperation, managed conflict, or bearable coexistence."[65] In its annual report on the internet in 2021, Freedom House wrote: "Global norms have shifted dramatically toward greater government intervention in the digital sphere. Of the 70 states covered by this report, a total of 48 pursued legal or administrative actions[66] against technology companies."[67] We have seen how issues of internet sovereignty are influencing the fight for freedom of expression, and the narrow and broad interpretation of censorship can be a warning of the dangers of under- and overuse. In addition, legal concepts are often, as Romain Badouard puts it in his 2020 book, *The new laws of the web,* "vague enough to encompass very different types of speech, potentially opening the way to the political instrumentalisation of online content regulation."[68] State regulation is thus becoming inevitable,[69] and, given the international nature of the internet, this will, it is feared, in many cases have collateral damage. It is also clear from the practice of the international courts that large tech companies can no longer hide behind users on the grounds that they themselves do not produce content or carry out editorial activities. At the same time,

---

[60] The presentation is available at: https://www.youtube.com/watch?v=rCplocVemjo/. Berners-Lee (2014), pp. 39–41. The issue is closely related to the issue of *digital constitutionalism*, which this book does not discuss. See Celeste (2019), pp. 76–99; De Gregorio (2021), pp. 41–70.

[61] Cf. "We need laws, not platform policies." European Parliament News (2021).

[62] Wu (2015), p. 309.

[63] Gorwa (2019).

[64] "A blanket condemnation of self-regulation for being contaminated by the seed of censorship is as mistaken as the view that welcomes self-regulation on the sole grounds that it means (or appears to mean) less governmental intervention." Tambini et al. (2008), p. 284.

[65] Bradford (2023)

[66] Fazekas (2020), pp. 907–931.

[67] FH (2021), p. 11.

[68] Badouard (2020), p. 13.

[69] Cf. "Now, however, it is entirely possible that the ultimate cyberlord is government itself." Yen (2020), p. 145.

the exponentially increasing amount of content in the new media environment can only be controlled by human moderators and artificial intelligence with a view to proactivity. It is clear that the fundamental right to freedom of expression must be respected, and any violation of the general prohibition of monitoring or monitoring will certainly lead to censorship.

It has come to the point where a real re-buttoning of the jacket is needed. As David Kaye writes, "One possibility: #DeleteFacebook. That may be compelling and relatively pain-free in developed and democratic environments",[70] but it is far from the solution in the less developed and less (or not at all) democratic countries described above. Moreover, although more and more politicians are using the phrase "breaking up Big Tech",[71] at the moment they do not seem ready to overthrow these giant corporations (yet).[72] The option may be to do nothing and let the market regulate itself, hoping that alternative models of speech regulation will challenge each other. "This was the initial model, but it is hardly discussed today, and for good reason: the companies are super-dominant and ravenous, knocking down any future competition (as their purchases of smaller competitors have shown)."[73]

There is certainly no simple and quick solution to this complex issue. As Alan Dershowitz puts it, "We should be cautious about approving short-term solutions that pose long term dangers."[74] It is clear that "Internet freedom should be a comprehensive one."[75] From the above, we can set out a few basic requirements that can help us to have a firmer hand on the regulation of the internet as a complex ecosystem, on the more thorough definition of liability issues and on the issues of unlawful content regulation, i.e. censorship. However, it is important to underline that the various documents impose obligations either on the state or on service providers, but we need solutions that address these in a holistic and integrated way.[76] These solutions must certainly comply with the following:

1. Respect for human rights and fundamental freedoms in the regulation and operation of the internet.[77] This includes access to the internet, the restriction of which is the most modern form of censorship. The internet must be accessible, available and affordable to all sections of the population without discrimination.[78]

---

[70] Kaye (2019), p. 84.

[71] Culliford (2020).

[72] On the hypothetical demise of Facebook and its ethical and legal implications, see Öhman and Aggarwal (2020).

[73] Kaye (2019), p. 84.

[74] Dershowitz (2021), p. 44.

[75] CM/Rec(2016)5, p. 5.

[76] Sanders (2021), p. 171.

[77] Cf. "The power of such intermediaries as protagonists of online expression makes it imperative to clarify their role and impact on human rights, as well as their corresponding duties and responsibilities." CM/Rec(2018)2, 7.

[78] CM/Rec(2016)5, 2.1.1.; UNESCO (2023), pp. 55–59.

2. Respecting the characteristics of the internet as a complex, constantly changing and diverse ecosystem, and to this end, developing a complex regulatory system that does not only address the immediate problems of the present. Moreover, this regulation must be designed "without destroying the massive benefits that an open and diverse global internet can bring."[79]
3. Compliance with the three-part test explained above, i.e. any intervention of a legal or judicial nature must be "A) suitable to achieve the legitimate aim pursued (*suitability*); B) the least intrusive instrument amongst those which might achieve the legitimate aim (*necessity*); and C) strictly proportionate to the legitimate aim pursued (*proportionality sensu stricto*)."[80]
4. Ensure diversity, pluralism and (ideally) impartiality of content on the internet.
5. Cooperation[81] between the actors in the "platform governance triangle",[82] which is both relevant for the creation of regulations and "the sharing on a voluntary basis of experiences, technological solutions and best practices."[83] This implies that the actors play their respective roles, i.e. that states no longer 'privatise' the task of content regulation and censorship to private companies.
6. Radically greater transparency of the parties involved,[84] including transparency of legislative intentions and processes. Lawmakers should "refrain from shutting down, throttling, or blocking the internet, and make a state pledge to refrain from imposing any unlawful restrictions on internet access and telecommunication in the future, particularly in upcoming elections and protests, and amid the COVID-19 pandemic."[85]
7. Widest possible citizen, civil and user participation in decision-making.
8. Independent regulatory authorities should ensure effective enforcement of the relevant rules.[86]
9. More frequent expression of the professional views of NGOs in court proceedings in the form of *amicus curiae* briefs.[87]
10. A real test of the effectiveness of different types of notification systems (NTDS, NAM).
11. Increasing access to data of public interest.
12. Develop media literacy in all segments of society.[88]

---

[79] Suzor (2019), p. 114; A declaration for the future of the Internet.

[80] Oster (2015a), pp. 123–124.

[81] UNESCO (2023), p. 29.

[82] "Laws and policies relating to the Internet are developed by State authorities in an inclusive and transparent process which enables the participation of all stakeholders, including the private sector, civil society, academia and the technical community." CM/Rec(2016)5, 1.4.

[83] Commission Recommendation (EU) 2018/334, (30).

[84] Puddephatt (2021), pp. 7–9.

[85] UNHRC (2021), p. 70; Kokoly (2021), pp. 67–75.

[86] Article-19 (2021), p. 19.

[87] Noorlander (2021), pp. 1–4.

[88] LSETTTC (2018), pp. 25–27.

13. The aim should be "to deter unwanted speech but they should not deter communications that are legal even socially valuable."[89]
14. Based on the ECtHR's guidelines in the Pihl case, platforms with different functions and roles, or providing different services, should be treated differently according to their role in the social debate, their legal status and their size.
15. The liability of platform providers should only be established after direct intervention in the content.
16. Precisely define the active and passive roles of service providers.[90]
17. Maintain a general ban on monitoring to ensure freedom of expression and prevent excessive content removal. "Requiring or allowing internet intermediaries to monitor and censor content produced by third parties not only has a profound *chilling effect* on the freedom of expression of internet users, but also makes them complicit in a substantial invasion of their customers' personal privacy."[91]
18. User reports of illegal (or perceived illegal) content must be sufficiently accurate and substantiated, as this will lead to actions and then decisions by online platforms, and thus determine whether they are legal or censorship-related.
19. Adequate knowledge must be assessed on the basis of the specificities of the individual case in question.
20. Notifiers must be duly informed during the procedure.
21. Precisely define the relationship between human moderation and the use of artificial intelligence.
22. Different content needs to be handled through different procedures, it is not possible to have one set of procedures for all the content that is uploaded. In defining services, it is necessary to take into account not only the current situation, but also future situations generated by technological changes.
23. Allow platforms sufficient time to make a legally sound and acceptable decision.
24. Increasing accountability for decisions made on online platforms.
25. Ensuring that users have access to effective redress after decisions are taken is essential.
26. Processes can only be regulated if adequate safeguards are given, as censorship can be induced by excessive penalties. "By increasing the of possible liabilities to the provider, high penalties provide an incentive to block or limit communications that may give rise to liabilities."[92]

But even if this were to happen, we can be sure that the legally and ethically questionable practice of censorship, i.e. content regulation, which "deprives the cultural man of one of the main sources of creative power, the prestige of

[89] Sartor (2017), p. 12.

[90] "It remains challenging to establish criteria according to which intermediaries' interventions can clearly be classified as active or passive. Plenty of interventions or activities, particularly regarding content moderation, remain in a grey area." Barata (2021).

[91] Article-19 (2013), p. 14.

[92] Sartor (2017), p. 15.

difference",[93] will never disappear. Sometimes it will recede, sometimes it will grow stronger. The struggle for freedom of expression has only taken new directions with the advent of the internet, but old fears have remained with us in new guises. As technology advances, speech will prevail, and those who seek to suppress it will also prevail. It is vital for all of us that states do not push their citizens into the digital darkness.[94]

References

A declaration for the future of the Internet, 2022. https://www.whitehouse.gov/wp-content/uploads/2022/04/Declaration-for-the-Future-for-the-Internet_Launch-Event-Signing-Version_FINAL.pdf

Article-19 (2013) Internet intermediaries: dilemma of liability. 20 Aug. https://www.article19.org/wp-content/uploads/2018/02/Intermediaries_ENGLISH.pdf

Article-19 (2021) Taming Big Tech. Protecting freedom of expression through the unbundling of services, open markets, competition, and users' empowerment. 8 Dec. https://www.article19.org/wp-content/uploads/2021/12/Taming-big-tech_FINAL_8-Dec-1.pdf

Badouard R (2020) Les nouvelles lois du web. Modération et censure (The new laws of the web. Moderation and censorship). Le Seuil, Paris

Balkin JM (2018) Free speech in the algorithmic society. The new school of big data, private regulation and the regulation of expression. Columbia Law Rev 118(7)

Ball M (2021) A framework for the metaverse. MatthewBall.vc, 29 June. https://www.matthewball.vc/all/forwardtothemetaverseprimer/

Barata J (2021) The digital services act and the reproduction of old confusions: obligations, liabilities and safeguards in content moderation. VerfBlog, 2 March. https://verfassungsblog.de/dsa-confusions/

Bayer J (2019) Between Anarchy and Censorship. Public discourse and the duties of social media. CEPS Papers in Liberty and Security in Europe, 2019(3). https://www.ceps.eu/wp-content/uploads/2019/05/LSE2019-03_Between-Anarchy-and-Censorship.pdf

Bayer J (2021) Rights and duties of online platforms. In: Bayer J, Holznagel B, Korpisaari P, Woods L (eds) Perspectives on platform regulation. Concepts and models of social media governance across the globe. Nomos Verlagsgesellschaft mbH & Co. KG, Baden-Baden

Bennett P, Naim M (2015) 21st-century censorship. Columbia Journal Rev 14(1)

Berners-Lee T (2014) We need a Magna Carta for the Internet. New Perspect Q 31(3)

Bertolini A (2021) Liability of online platforms. European Parliamentary Research Service, European Union, Brussels

Bourreau M, Perrot A (2020) Plateformes numériques: réguler avant qu'il ne soit trop tard (Digital platforms: regulate before it's too late). Notes du Conseil d'Analyse Économique 60(6)

Bradford A (2023) Digital empires. The global battle to regulate technology. Oxford University Press, Oxford

Buiten M, De Streel A, Peitz M (2019) Rethinking liability rules for online hosting platforms. CRC TR 224 Discussion Paper Series, 74

Celeste E (2019) Digital constitutionalism: a new systematic theorisation. Int Rev Law Comput Technol 33(1)

[93] Haraszti (1991), p. 25.

[94] Jain and Variath (2020).

Commission Recommendation (EU) 2018/334 of 1 March 2018 on measures to effectively tackle illegal content online, C/2018/1177, OJ L 63, 6.3.2018, pp 50–61
Communication from the Commission of the European Parliament, the Council, the European Economic and Social Committee and the Committee of the Regions: 2030 Digital Compass: the European way for the Digital Decade. COM/2021/118 final
Culliford E (2020) Where U.S. presidential candidates stand on breaking up Big Tech. Reuters, 24 Jan. https://www.reuters.com/article/us-usa-election-tech-factbox-idUSKBN1ZN16C/
De Gregorio G (2021) The rise of digital constitutionalism in the European Union. Int J Const Law 19(1)
Dershowitz A (2021) Case against the new censorship. Protecting free speech from big tech, progressives, and universities. Hot Books, New York
Downes L (2016) Why treating the Internet as a public utility is bad for consumers. The Washington Post, 7 July. https://www.washingtonpost.com/news/innovations/wp/2016/07/07/why-treating-the-internet-as-a-public-utility-is-bad-for-consumers/
European Parliament News (2021) Social media and democracy: we need laws, not platform guidelines. European Parliament News, 10 Feb. https://www.europarl.europa.eu/news/en/headlines/society/20210204STO97129/social-media-and-democracy-we-need-laws-not-platform-guidelines/
Fazekas J (2020) Médiaigazgatás (Media administration). In: Lapsánszky A (ed) Közigazgatási jog: Szakigazgatásaink elmélete és működése (Administrative law: the theory and functioning of our specialised administrations). Wolters Kluwer, Budapest
Freedom House (FH) (2021) Freedom on the Net 2021. The Global Drive to Control Big Tech. 16 Sep. https://freedomhouse.org/sites/default/files/2021-09/FOTN_2021_Complete_Booklet_09162021_FINAL_UPDATED.pdf
Friedmann D (2014) Sinking the safe harbour with the legal certainty of strict liability in sight. J Intellect Prop Law Pract 9(2)
Galewska E (2021) Zwalczanie nielegalnych treści zamieszczanych przez użytkownik w platform internetowych – kierunek regulacji Unii Europejskiej (Combating illegal content posted by the user on online platforms - the direction of European Union regulation). In: Flaga-Gieruszyńska K, Gołaczyński J (eds) Prawo nowych technologii (The law of new technologies). Wolters Kluwer, Warszawa
Gorwa R (2019) The platform governance triangle: conceptualising the informal regulation of online content. Internet Policy Rev 8(2)
Gosztonyi G, Huszár D (2022) Az anonim kommentelés aktuális jogi megítélése az Emberi Jogok Európai Bírósága és az Ausztrál Legfelsőbb Bíróság gyakorlata alapján (Current legal assessment of anonymous commenting based on the case law of the European Court of Human Rights and the Australian Supreme Court). In Medias Res 11(2)
Gurri M (2018) The revolt of the public and the crisis of authority in the new millennium. Stripe Press, San Francisco
Haraszti M (1991) A cenzúra esztétikája (The aesthetics of censorship). Magvető Kiadó, Budapest
Helberger N, Pierson J, Poell T (2018) Governing online platforms: from contested to cooperative responsibility. Inf Soc 34(1)
Hertig Randall M (2016) Freedom of expression in the Internet. Swiss Rev Int Eur Law 26(2)
Horváth K (2021) Digital Services Act. In CMS: Digital Horizons. A series of reports exploring CEE's digital future. CMS. https://cms.law/en/media/local/cms-cmno/files/publications/publications/cee-digital-horizon-report-data-centres/
Jain S, Variath AA (2020) Internet shutdowns and virtual curfews: searching for rights in digital darkness. J Hum Rights Pract 4(2)
Kaye D (2019) Speech Police. The global struggle to govern the internet. Columbia Global Reports, New York
Keller D, Leerssen P (2020) Facts and where to find them: empirical research on internet platforms and content moderation. In: Persily N, Tucker JA (eds) Social media and democracy. The state of the field, prospects for reform. Cambridge University Press, Cambridge

Klonick K (2020) The Facebook Oversight Board: creating an independent institution to adjudicate online free expression. Yale Law J 129(2418)

Koebler J, Cox J (2018) The impossible job: inside Facebook's struggle to moderate two billion people. Vice, 23 Aug. https://www.vice.com/en/article/xwk9zd/how-facebook-content-moderation-works/

Kokoly Z (2021) Audiovisual media regulation during the COVID-19 pandemic – measures undertaken by the Romanian authorities during the state of emergency. Acta Univ Sapientiae Leg Stud 10(1)

Koltay A (2017) Az internetes kapuőrök és az Emberi Jogok Európai Egyezményének 10. cikke – a sajtószabadság új alanyai (Internet gatekeepers and Article 10 of the European Convention on Human Rights – the new subjects of press freedom). Állam- és Jogtudomány 58(4)

Kosseff J (2017) Twenty years of intermediary immunity: the US experience. SCRIPTed 14(1)

Lénárd S (2021) Kié az utolsó szó? A Facebook Ellenőrző Bizottság döntésének margójára (Who has the last word? In the margins of the Facebook Oversight Board decision). Ludovika Blog, 25 May. https://www.ludovika.hu/blogok/frontierblog/2021/05/25/kie-az-utolso-szo/

Lessig L (1999) Code and other laws of cyberspace. Basic Books, New York

Lessig L (2006) Code 2.0. Basic Books, New York

LSE Truth, Trust & Technology Commission (LSETTTC) (2018) Tackling the information crisis. The London School of Economics and Political Science, London

Mao F (2021) Australia media can be sued for social media comments, court rules. BBC News, 8 Sep. https://www.bbc.com/news/world-australia-58484205/

Maroni M (2019) A Court's Gotta Do, What a Court's Gotta Do. An analysis of the European Court of Human Rights and the liability of internet intermediaries through systems theory. European University Institute Working Paper RSCAS, 20

Mayer-Schönberger V, Ramge T (2018) Reinventing capitalism in the age of big data. Basic Books, New York

Newton C (2021) Mark in the Metaverse. Facebook's CEO on why the social network is becoming 'a metaverse company'. The Verge, 22 July. https://www.theverge.com/22588022/mark-zuckerberg-facebook-ceo-metaverse-interview/

Noorlander P (2021) UNESCO Guide for Amicus Curiae interventions in freedom of expression cases. CI-2021/FEJ/G-1. UNESCO, Paris

Öhman C, Aggarwal N (2020) What if Facebook goes down? Ethical and legal considerations for the demise of big tech. Internet Policy Rev 9(3)

Organization for Security and Co-operation in Europe (OSCE) (2011) Freedom of expression on the Internet. 15 Dec. https://www.osce.org/files/f/documents/e/f/80723.pdf

Oster J (2015a) Media freedom as a fundamental right. Cambridge University Press, Cambridge

Oster J (2015b) Communication, defamation and liability of intermediaries. Leg Stud 35(2)

Park K (2013) Facebook used takedown and it was super effective! Finding a framework for protecting user rights of expression on social networking. N Y Univ Annu Surv Am Law 68(4)

Polyák G (2020) A forgalomirányító szolgáltatások médiaszabályozási kérdései (Media regulation issues for traffic management services). In: Polyák G (ed) Algoritmusok, keresők, közösségi oldalak és a jog: A forgalomirányító szolgáltatások szabályozása (Algorithms, search engines, social networking sites and the law: regulating traffic management services). HVG-ORAC Lap- és Könyvkiadó Kft, Budapest

Public Service Media and Public Service Internet Manifesto

Puddephatt A (2021) Letting the sun shine in. Transparency and accountability in the digital age. CI-2021/WTR/5. UNESCO, Paris

Recommendation CM/Rec(2007)16 of the Committee of Ministers to member states on measures to promote the public service value of the Internet

Recommendation CM/Rec(2016)5 of the Committee of Ministers to member States on Internet Freedom

Recommendation CM/Rec(2018)2 of the Committee of Ministers to member States on the roles and responsibilities of internet intermediaries

Rodriguez S (2021) Biden on Facebook: 'They're killing people' with vaccine misinformation. CNBC, 16 July. https://www.cnbc.com/2021/07/16/white-house-says-facebook-needs-to-do-more-to-fight-vaccine-misinformation.html/

Sanders B (2021) Democratic disruption in the age of social media: between marketized and structural conceptions of human rights law. Eur J Int Law 32(1)

Sartor G (2017) Providers liability: from the eCommerce Directive to the future. In-depth analysis for the Directorate-General for Internal Policies. European Parliament, Strasbourg

Solomon B (2014) Facebook buys Oculus, virtual reality gaming startup, for $2 billion. Forbes, 25 March. https://www.forbes.com/sites/briansolomon/2014/03/25/facebook-buys-oculus-virtual-reality-gaming-startup-for-2-billion/

Suzor NP (2019) Lawless. The secret rules that govern our digital lives. Cambridge University Press, Cambridge

Szigeti T, Simon É (2016) A hozzászólás szabadsága: a közvetítő szolgáltatói felelősség aktuális kérdéseiről (Freedom to comment: on current issues of intermediary service provider liability). Fundamentum 20(2-4)

Szőke GL (2021) A közösségi oldalak szabályozási problémái (Regulatory problems on social networking sites). In: Kis Kelemen B, Mohay Á (eds) A technológiai fejlődés jogi kihívásai: Kézikönyv a jogalkotás és jogalkalmazás számára (Legal challenges of technological development: a handbook for lawmakers and practitioners). Pécsi Tudományegyetem Állam- és Jogtudományi Kar, Pécs

Tambini D, Leonardi D, Marsden C (2008) Codifying cyberspace. Communications self-regulation in the age of internet convergence. Routledge, London – New York

The United Nations (UN) Special Rapporteur on Freedom of Opinion and Expression, the Organization for Security and Co-operation in Europe (OSCE) Representative on Freedom of the Media, the Organization of American States (OAS) Special Rapporteur on Freedom of Expression and the African Commission on Human and Peoples' Rights (ACHPR) Special Rapporteur on Freedom of Expression and Access to Information: Twentieth anniversary joint declaration: challenges to freedom of expression in the next decade. 2019. https://www.ohchr.org/Documents/Issues/Opinion/JointDeclaration10July2019_English.pdf

Török B (2021) Platforms and fundamental rights. Hung Conserv 1(2)

Tusikov N (2017) Chokepoints. Global private regulation on the internet. University of California Press, Oakland

UNESCO (2023) Safeguarding freedom of expression and access to information: guidelines fora multistakeholder approach in the context of regulating digital platforms. CI-FEJ/FOEO/3 Rev

UNHRC (2011) Report of the Special Rapporteur on the promotion and protection of the right to freedom of opinion and expression. UN Doc A/HRC/17/27

UNHRC (2021) Report of the Special Rapporteur on the rights to freedom of peaceful assembly and of association. UN Doc A/HRC/47/24/Add.2

West SM (2019) Data capitalism: redefining the logics of surveillance and privacy. Bus Soc 58(1)

Worldometer (2022) How many countries are there in the world? https://www.worldometers.info/geography/how-many-countries-are-there-in-the-world/

Wu P (2015) Impossible to regulate? Social media, terrorists, and the role for the U.N. Chic J Int Law 16(1)

Yen AC (2020) Revisiting the Western Frontier. IDEA – The Law Review of the Franklin Pierce Center for Intellectual Property 60(1)

List of Cases

Abrams v United States, 250 U.S. 616 (1919)
ACLU v Reno, 929 F. Supp. 824 (E.D. Pa. 1996)
Ahmet Yıldırım v Turkey App no. 3111/10 (ECtHR, 18 December 2012)
Akdeniz and Altiparmak v Turkey App no. 35278/20
Akdeniz and Altiparmak v Turkey App no. 5568/20
Akdeniz and Others v Turkey App nos 41139/15 and 41146/15 (ECtHR, 4 May 2021)
Akdeniz v Turkey App no. 20877/10 (ECtHR, 11 March 2014)
Association Ekin v France App no 39288/98 (ECtHR, 17 July 2001)
AT.40462, Amazon.com, Inc.; Amazon Services Europe SARL; Amazon EU SARL; Amazon Europe Core SARL
Axel Springer AG v Germany App no. 39954/08 (ECtHR, 7 February 2012)
Belgische Vereniging van Auteurs, Componisten en Uitgevers CVBA (SABAM) v Netlog NV (C-360/10), ECLI:EU:C:2012:85
Belpietro v Italy App no 43612/10 (ECtHR, 24 September 2013)
Blume v Twitter, Landgericht Frankfurt am Main, 2-03 O 325/22, 14 December 202
Bulgakov v Russia App no. 20159/15 (ECtHR, 23 June 2020)
Bunt v Tilley & Others [2006] EWHC 407 (QB); [2007] 1 WLR 1243; [2006] 3 All ER 336; [2006] EMLR 523
Cengiz and Others v Turkey App nos 48226/10 and 14027/11 (ECtHR, 1 December 2015)
Cubby, Inc. v Compuserve Inc., 776 F. Supp. 135 (S.D.N.Y. 1991)
Daniel v Armslist, LLC, 386 Wis. 2d 449 (Wis. 2019)
Davison v Habeeb & Others [2011] EWHC 3031 (QB)
Delfi AS v Estonia App no. 64569/09 (ECtHR, 16 June 2015)
Editorial Board of Pravoye Delo and Shtekel v Ukraine App no. 33014/05 (ECtHR, 5 May 2011)
Ein Prozent v Facebook Ireland Ltd, Oberlandesgericht Dresden, 4 U 2890/19, 16 June 2020

G. Gosztonyi, *Censorship from Plato to Social Media*, Law, Governance and Technology Series 61, https://doi.org/10.1007/978-3-031-46529-1

Elvira Dmitriyeva v Russia App nos. 60921/17 and 7202/18 (ECtHR, 30 April 2019)
Engel and Others v The Netherlands App nos 5100/71, 5101/71, 5102/71, 5354/72, 5370/72 (ECtHR, 8 June 1976)
Engels v Russia App no. 61919/16 (ECtHR, 23 June 2020)
Enigma Software Grp. U.S.A v Malwarebytes, Inc., 946 F.3d 1040, 1052 (9th Cir. 2019), cert. denied, 141 S. Ct. 13, 208 L. Ed. 2d 197 (2020)
Eva Glawischnig-Piesczek v Facebook Ireland Limited (C-18/18). ECLI:EU: C:2019:821
Fatullayev v Azerbaijan App no 40984/07 (ECtHR, 22 April 2010)
Force v Facebook, Inc., 934 F.3d 53, 64 (2d Cir. 2019), cert. denied, 140 S. Ct. 2761 (2020)
Frank Peterson v Google LLC and Others and Elsevier Inc.v Cyando AG (C-682/18 and C-683/18), ECLI:EU:C:2021:503
Google France SARL and Google Inc. v Louis Vuitton Malletier SA (C-236/08), Google France SARL v Viaticum SA and Luteciel SARL (C-237/08) and Google France SARL v Centre national de recherche en relations humaines (CNRRH) SARL and Others (C-238/08). ECLI:EU:C:2010:159
Handyside v The United Kingdom App no 5393/72 (ECtHR, 7 December 1976)
Høiness v Norway App no. 43624/14 (ECtHR, 19 March 2019)
Inquérito 4.781, Distrito Federal (26 May, 2020)
Jameel (Yousef) v Dow Jones & Co. Inc. [2005] EWCA Civ 75; [2005] QB 946; [2005] 2 WLR 1614; [2005] EMLR 353
Jankovskis v Lithuania App no. 21575/08 (ECtHR, 17 January 2017)
Kablis v Russia App nos. 48310/16 and 59663/17 (ECtHR, 30 April 2019)
Kalda v Estonia App no. 17429/10 (ECtHR, 19 January 2016)
Kaschke v Gray & Hilton (No 2) [2010] EWHC 1907 (QB)
Khadija Ismayilova v Azerbaijan App no 30778/15 (ECtHR, 27 February 2020)
Künast v Facebook, Landgericht Frankfurt am Main, 2-03 O 188/21, 8 April 2022
L'Oréal SA and Others v eBay International AG and Others (C-324/09). ECLI:EU: C:2011:474
L'Oréal SA v eBay International AG [2009] RPC 21, [2009] ETMR 53, [2009] EWHC 1094 (Ch)
Magyar Jeti Zrt. v Hungary App no. 11257/16 (ECtHR, 4 December 2018)
Magyar Tartalomszolgáltatók Egyesülete and Index.hu Zrt. v Hungary App no. 22947/13 (ECtHR, 2 February 2016)
Marshall's Locksmith Serv. Inc. v Google, LLC, 925 F.3d 1263, 1267 (D.C. Cir. 2019)
OOO Flavus and Others v Russia App nos 12468/15, 23489/15, and 19074/16 (ECtHR, 23 June 2020)
Packingham v North Carolina, 137 S. Ct. 1730, 198 L. Ed. 2d 273 (2017)
Perna v Italy App no 48898/99 (ECtHR, 6 May 2003)
Pihl v Sweden App no. 74742/14 (ECtHR, 9 March 2017)
Puls 4 TV GmbH & Co. KG v YouTube LLC and Google Austria GmbH (C-500/19)
Ramazan Demir v Turkey App no. 68550/17 (ECtHR, 9 February 2021)
Sanchez v France App no. 45581/15 (15 May 2023)

Scarlet Extended SA v Société belge des auteurs, compositeurs et éditeurs SCRL (SABAM) (C-70/10), ECLI:EU:C:2011:771
Sotiris Papasavvas v O Fileleftheros Dimosia Etaireia Ltd and Others (C-291/13) ECLI:EU:C:2014:2209
Stichting Collectieve Antennevoorziening Gouda and others v Commissariaat voor de Media. CJEU, C-288/89, 1991, I-04007
Stoll v Switzerland App no. 69698/01 (10 December 2007)
Stratton Oakmont, Inc. v Prodigy Servs., (N.Y. Sup. Ct. May 24, 1995)
Tamiz v Google Inc Google UK Ltd [2013] EWCA Civ 68
Tamiz v United Kingdom App no. 3877/14 (ECtHR, 19 September 2017)
Tobias Mc Fadden v Sony Music Entertainment Germany GmbH (C-484/14), ECLI:EU:C:2016:689
United States Telecom Ass'n v FCC 825 F.3d 674 (D.C. Cir. 2016)
UPC Telekabel Wien GmbH v Constantin Film Verleih GmbH and Wega Filmproduktionsgesellschaft mbH (C-314/12) ECLI:EU:C:2014:192
Vladimir Kharitonov v Russia App no. 10795/14 (ECtHR, 23 June 2020)
Von Hannover v Germany (No. 2) App nos. 40660/08 and 60641/08 (ECtHR, 7 February 2012)
Wikimedia Foundation Inc. v Diğerleri Başvurusu (Başvuru Numarasi: 2017/22355, Karar Tarihi: 26/12/2019)
Wingrove v the United Kingdom App no. 17419/90 (25 November 1996)
Włodzimierz Kucharczyk v Poland App no. 72966/13 (ECtHR, 17 December 2015)
Zeran v America Online, Inc., 129 F.3d 327 (4th Cir. 1997), cert. denied, 524 U.S. 937 (1998)
Zeran v Diamond Broadcasting, Inc., 19 F. Supp. 2d 1249 (W.D. Okla. 1997), 203 F.3d 714 (10th Cir. 2000)

Printed in the USA
CPSIA information can be obtained
at www.ICGtesting.com
LVHW021404020124
767820LV00005B/149

9 783031 465284